H*i*PLAM

Hispanic, Portuguese, and Latin American Monographs

Department of Hispanic, Portuguese, & Latin American Studies
University of Bristol

Powers of Utterance

a Discourse approach to works of
Lorca, Machado and Valle-Inclán

Robin Warner

H*i*PLAM
Bristol
2003

ISBN 0 86292 530 4

Printed in England on acid-free paper by
Short Run Press Ltd, Exeter EX2 7LW
2003

CONTENTS

ACKNOWLEDGEMENTS

The author is grateful to Fernando José Rollán Riesco, representing the literary estate of Antonio and Manuel Machado, for permission to quote extensively from 'El hospicio', 'A José María Palacio' and 'Los olivos'; and to Manuel Fernández-Montesinos García, who gave permission, on behalf of the Comunidad de Herederos de Federico García Lorca, to quote extensively from 'Romance de la luna, luna'. Thanks are also due to all the colleagues who provided encouragement, and to David Hook for his careful and helpful textual editing.

1. CONCEPTS AND METHODS

1.1 DISCOURSE AND LITERATURE: BASIC DEFINITIONS

Discourse studies has yet to establish a firm foothold in the area of Hispanic studies, and applications of the discipline to the study of Hispanic literature are particularly rare. For this reason it is worth offering an introduction, for the benefit of readers to whom they may be unfamiliar, to some of the basic concepts and methods involved in discourse approaches to language-use in general and literary texts in particular. The title of the present work is intended to suggest two basic features of the critical approach adopted. Firstly, it presupposes a distinctive view of language (or rather, of language-use) for which one authoritative figure in the field of discourse analysis has proposed the snappy definition 'discourse is utterances',[1] a formula that points to a shifting of emphasis away from the more traditional concern in linguistics with the grammatical and semantic properties of sentences and toward the functional and contextualized use of language in communicative situations. Secondly, it is assumed that it is valid and useful to analyze and evaluate works of literature via a theoretical framework based on this perspective. There are, of course, deeper issues involved in both these proposals that will require some unpacking; it is probably more useful, however, to begin with an overview of discourse studies.

Although the field has been established for two decades and more, it is still standard practice for general introductions to discourse studies—and especially those proposing discourse applications to other disciplines—to begin by carefully describing

[1] Deborah Schiffrin, *Approaches to Discourse* (Oxford: Blackwell, 1994), p. 39.

the theoretical parameters. The concern to establish preliminary definitions, it should be said, does not stem from pedantic motives, but from a perceived need to counterbalance the prevalence of models of language that are incompatible with a discourse perspective. This is not merely a matter of challenging some stubbornly persistent folk-linguistic misconceptions, nor even of contesting the preference, in a number of disciplines in the social sciences and humanities, for static and more-or-less decontextualized paradigms of language. The problem is that the conditions of intellectual activity in virtually any discipline make it natural to think of what is studied as a thing, or product, the 'object of study'. While it is not difficult in itself to conceive of language as a socially-conditioned process, when it comes to actual analysis it is much harder to represent a process than it is to represent a product; even conversation analysis has to turn transient interactions into permanent objects (transcriptions) in order to attend to them.[2] It is important, therefore, to make it clear from the outset that there is a need to maintain focus on the activities which led to the production—and reception[3]—of instances of discourse, as well as on the instances themselves.

The term 'discourse' is itself capable of being used in many different ways. It can be used, for instance, as a count-noun, applied to particular instances of stretches of talk (or writing) produced by real persons or fictional characters; at the opposite extreme, the term can be used in a far more general way to refer to a type, social domain or ideological function of language-use, as in 'medical discourse', or 'the discourse of colonialism'. In fact many advocates of discourse approaches to language treat as one of its strengths the capacity to cover all points on the above scale, and more; two fairly recent definitions specify, respectively, 'the theory and analysis of text and talk in virtually all disciplines of the

---

[2] See M.A.K. Halliday, *An Introduction to Functional Grammar* (London: Arnold, 1994), p. xxii.

[3] Gillian Brown, *Speakers, Listeners and Communication* (Cambridge: Cambridge University Press, 1997), pp. 43-44.

humanities and social sciences',[4] and 'the study of the use of language for communication in context [...] embracing a broad range of disciplines from sociology to anthropology and from education to psychology'.[5] It is undeniable, however, that concurrent development of lines of approach derived from different disciplines in a field that embraces such broad key terms as 'language', 'communication', 'interaction', 'society' and 'culture' has led to a potentially confusing proliferation of theoretical perspectives and analytical methods. The complaint made over a decade ago (and in a work in the subject-area of social psychology!) that it was 'perfectly possible to have two books on discourse analysis with no overlap in content at all' could certainly be repeated today.[6] Nevertheless, and especially if we exclude the concern with non-linguistic systems of signification favoured by semioticians and theorists in film, art or cultural studies, it is possible to discern a set of more-or-less shared principles and a cluster of theoretical approaches linked by a shared view of language-use as contextually situated communication. Perhaps the most central of these principles is that attention should be directed as much to social context as to the language-text itself; as one of the classic manuals of the discipline insists from the outset: 'the analysis of discourse is, necessarily, the analysis of language in use. As such it cannot be restricted to the description of linguistic forms independent of the purposes or functions which these forms are designed to serve in human affairs'.[7]

The nature of the particular contributions a discourse approach can make to literary studies is a question that will shortly be addressed. For the moment, however, it is worth devoting some attention to the obvious preliminary query as to whether the

---

[4] Teun van Dijk (ed.), *Discourse Studies: a multidisciplinary introduction. Vol. I, Discourse as Structure and Process* (London: Sage, 1997), p. xi.

[5] Alexandra Georgakopolou and Goutsos Dionysis, *Discourse Analysis: an Introduction* (Edinburgh: Edinburgh University Press, 1997), p. viii.

[6] Jonathan Potter and Margaret Wetherell, *Discourse and Social Psychology* (London: Sage, 1987), p. 6.

[7] Gillian Brown and George Yule, *Discourse Analysis* (Cambridge: Cambridge University Press, 1983), p. 1.

discipline has anything important to add to the long-running debate over how the status and nature of the literary is to be defined and how the effects it promotes are to be evaluated. Where the first question is concerned, discourse studies does not so much align itself against views of literary form and style as uniquely privileged as legitimately sidestep the issue. The concepts and methods of the discipline are geared to investigating the principles underlying naturally-occurring language, and it is merely claimed that there is no a priori reason for excluding any specialized discourse genre (such as avowedly literary, author-centred texts) from this category.[8] One practical consequence of such an approach is that the focus of discussion is often aimed at broad functional relationships, such as those of discourse production and reception, that transcend the distinction between spoken or written modes of language use. Accordingly, and unless the distinction is specifically indicated, what is said about speakers can normally be taken as applying more or less equally to writers, and use of the terms 'reader' and 'hearer' (or 'audience') should similarly not be regarded as contrastive. Such a convention, of course, makes it possible to be sparing in the use of neutral but more fussily technical paired expressions such as 'addressor' and 'addressee'.

On the other hand, discourse studies can have important things to say about some of the qualities and effects that are generally considered to distinguish literary from non-literary language, and, in particular, about the ways complex meanings are produced in carefully planned and stylized texts as opposed to spontaneous or routine uses of language. In addition, the concern of discourse studies with language in context has increasingly, in recent years, taken in the macro-contextual level of discourse as social practice. As a consequence, insights have been provided into the ways in which the production and interpretation of meaning in texts with institutionally-authorized literary status are conditioned by the

---

[8] The definition of literary texts is taken Ronald Carter and Paul Simpson, *Language, Discourse and Literature: an introductory reader in discourse stylistics* (London: Routledge, 1995), p. 7.

broader network of social relations and signifying practices within which they are embedded.

These days, moreover, the case for discourse applications to literature hardly needs to be made. Quite apart from the fact that there now exists a substantial body—in both quantitative and qualitative senses—of discourse-based literary analysis, the respected status of theories and methodologies of literary criticism carried out from similar or related perspectives also argues for the general validity of discourse approaches. The dialogic model of Bakhtin and the types of analysis inspired by his work, with its emphasis on language as utterance and the production and reception of texts and meanings as a socially-embedded process, is similar to the broad approach adopted by discourse studies if not always coinciding in details of emphasis and choice of features to examine. While the characteristic semiotic view of communication as the encoding and decoding of messages is more suited, in some ways, to the analysis of systems of signification other than natural language,[9] theorists such as Barthes, Greimas and Eco have undeniably provided very useful insights into what are essentially linguistic features of literary texts.

Typically, however, the main thrust of discourse studies approaches to literature (and the present work is no exception) has come to bear on the interpretation of—and on providing theoretical underpinning for the interpretation of—particular textual functions and effects. The underlying assumption is that there are analyzable links between form and function in literary texts and that through analysis along lines developed in different branches of discourse studies it is possible to make claims about the meanings texts communicate. Several areas of discourse applications to literature have already become well established. The pioneering work of Michael Halliday and Roger Fowler in applying to literary texts both a detailed attention to choice among systemic features of

---

[9] For a discussion of the limitations of the encoding-decoding model of verbal communication as opposed to the ostension-inference model proposed in linguistic pragmatics, see Dan Sperber and Deirdre Wilson, *Relevance: communication and cognition*, 2nd ed. (Oxford: Blackwell, 1995), pp. 3-27.

language and an overview of discourse (including literary language) as social semiotic has influenced a whole school of what, in Britain, has tended to be termed linguistic stylistics. Despite the somewhat literal-minded approach of one of its founding figures to utterances in a fictional mode,[10] Speech Act Theory, that is, the treatment of saying as doing and the attribution of a performative function to utterances in general has proved a productive approach both to poetry and to theatre and novel dialogue. The question of audiences' readiness to catch what is implied as opposed to what is said is particularly suited to types of analysis developed in linguistic pragmatics. J.P. Grice's work on the interpretation of non-explicit meanings (of the type he termed conversational implicatures),[11] adapted and extended in Relevance theory to a more comprehensive description of processes of inference, has applications that go beyond the study of implicit information conveyed in dialogue to include metaphors and verbal irony in general. Fictional conversations have proved as susceptible as real ones to analysis along lines developed on both sides of the Atlantic to study the organization of socially-situated verbal interaction, such as conversation analysis, politeness phenomena and the ethnography of communication in general; and concepts developed in the field of cognitive linguistics (and in related work by the American linguist George Lakoff) have opened up important new perspectives for the

---

[10] See 'The Logical Status of Fictional Discourse', in John Searle, *Expression and Meaning: studies in the theory of speech acts* (Cambridge: Cambridge University Press, 1979), pp. 58-75. Searle broadly supports here the view of fictional / poetic utterances as 'hollow or void' taken by J.L. Austin in his pioneering account (in the William James Lectures, 1955) of 'how to do things with words'. See J.L. Austin, *How to Do Things With Words*, 2nd ed. (Oxford: Clarendon Press, 1975), p. 22 and p. 104.

[11] Grice's seminal Harvard lectures of 1967, introducing concepts such as the Co-operative Principle underpinning human communication and strategies for the production and interpretation of implicatures are conveniently collected in J.P. Grice, *Studies in the Way of Words* (Cambridge, Mass.: Harvard University Press, 1991).

study of the discursive functions of metaphor in literary as well as in non-literary texts.[12]

The present work aims to draw on various aspects of discourse theory, such as those mentioned above, with a view to making a contribution to the understanding and appreciation of the achievement of some of the major Spanish literary figures of the last century. There can be no question, of course, of providing systematic coverage either of the literary output of any of the writers under study or of the many areas of discourse analysis that are relevant to the study of literature; in both cases the aim here is to offer what is hoped are instructive selected examples. In one sense, the canonical status of some of the texts concerned will serve in itself as a test of the efficacy of the approach adopted, since so much has been written and so many interpretations offered of some of the plays and poems of the three writers under study that any claim to have produced completely new readings would justifiably be greeted with scepticism. On the other hand, a measure of originality, it is suggested, is to be found in the particular focus of the analysis, which is not so much on meanings and effects in themselves as on the discursive processes through which they are communicated to and interpreted by readers and audiences.

Where matters of overall methodology are concerned, it is natural for practitioners of discourse stylistics to regard their approach as an improvement on impressionistic analysis of the language of literary texts, although not many would associate themselves with the dismissive view once expressed by David Robey ('the rag-bag of grammatical and metaphorical terminology on which criticism has traditionally depended').[13] It is worth stressing, however, that intuitions themselves are by no means regarded as suspect. On the contrary, discourse studies does not provide a mechanical method for unravelling meanings, and it is subjective impressions and hunches concerning the effects produced

---

[12] See G. Lakoff and M. Johnson, *Metaphors We Live By* (Chicago: University of Chicago Press, 1980), and G. Lakoff and G. Turner, *More Than Cool Reason: a field guide to poetic metaphor* (Chicago: University of Chicago Press, 1989).

[13] Ann Jefferson and David Robey, *Modern Literary Theory*, second edition (London: Batsford, 1986), p. 70.

in a literary texts that provide the starting points for analysis. The claim is merely that, when it comes to corroborating such intuitions, the use of discourse methods and concepts can convert them, in Ronald Carter's phrase, into 'harder currency'.[14] A discourse approach, that is, can result in more principled and systematic accounts of language effects.

Finally, and to counterbalance what may seem too narrow an emphasis on the linguistic constituency of texts, it seems worthwhile clarifying one broad principle informing the approach adopted here: it is based on a strongly positive and practical view both of language as the primary vehicle of meaning in social communication and of literature as valuable specialized instances of language use. Accordingly, there is a particular concern to avoid the danger of two types of reductionism that can arise when critical focus is on the language of literary texts.

One has to do with restrictions of scope. Although the present work is primarily concerned with the language of literary texts, and much of it, inevitably, consists of detailed linguistic analysis of individual passages, it is nevertheless assumed that the 'direction of fit' between linguistics and literature should be from word to world. To use literary texts merely to exemplify models of linguistic description, or to restrict critical activity to purely textual matters, identifying distinctive features that seem likely to have literary significance, but not attempting to determine what the nature of that significance is, seems unproductive to say the least. Literary texts, like texts in general, are about meanings that are constructed in an extra-textual world of social, political, psychological and historical activity, and to avoid all commentary at this level is surely to miss the point.[15] Occasionally, too, it is appropriate to raise the question of the extent to which accepted interpretations are themselves the product of culturally conditioned ways of thinking about literature (and, for that matter, about language).

---

[14] See R. Carter, 'Poetry and Conversation', in Carter and Simpson, *Language, Discourse*, pp. 58-76, at p. 60.

[15] See Jefferson and Robey, *Modern Literary Theory*, pp. 68-70, and Carter and Simpson, *Language, Discourse,* pp. 5-8, for an account of 'minimalist' approaches in linguistic stylistics.

It seems equally counterproductive to give undue weight to views of textual meaning as inherently and problematically elusive. It is undeniable that processes of signification tend to be complexly open-ended and negotiable, and the link between words and what is meant by them is by no means predictably stable. A text then, can have a number of meanings, but this does not justify concluding, and certainly not where communicative functions are concerned, that those meanings are bafflingly indeterminate or hopelessly enmeshed in aporia. The flexibility, multi-functionality and contextual sensitivity of verbal communication, especially in the hands of producers of literary texts, are, instead, qualities that should be unequivocally celebrated.

1.2 TEXT, CONTEXT AND COHERENCE

While it has to be acknowledged that within the discipline itself there is some degree of variation in usage, some preliminary definition of the way certain key concepts and terms are used in the approach adopted here is clearly desirable. Returning, for a moment, to Schiffrin's apparently straightforward formula 'discourse is utterances', we find that her accompanying explanation makes it clear that, in the first instance, the definition is intended to capture the notion that utterances, rather than sentences, are the smallest units of which discourse is comprised. It also takes into account, however, a view of utterances themselves as 'units of language production (whether spoken or written) that are inherently contextualized'.[16] Discourse is thus viewed as 'above' (larger than) other units of language, and analytical attention should primarily be directed to collections of utterances and the context within which they are used and ordered. Nevertheless, the choice of terminology for units or word-strings should probably not be too rigidly specified. The conceptual contrast between utterances, seen as instantiations of actual language use, and sentences, considered as 'abstract entities which are context independent', is a relatively clear one. In practical terms however, especially in written

[16] Schiffrin, *Approaches to Discourse*, p. 41.

language, a sentence can be regarded an utterance and an utterance can take the form of a sentence.[17] There seems to be no compelling reason, then, not to use the term 'sentence' when drawing attention to morpho-syntactical aspects of utterance-form; it seems preferable to speak of utterances, however, when the focus is on the extended patterns and sequential organization of the units that make up a piece of language.

Broadly similar practical considerations apply where choice between 'discourse' and 'text' is concerned. Both terms presuppose a certain connectedness and functional unity (indeed, text comes from Latin TEXTUS, something woven together)[18] and many commentators treat them as more or less interchangeable; others (although there is not complete unanimity as to which is which) apply one to spoken language and the other to written language; yet others consistently use only one of them.[19] The approach adopted here is to employ the terms to suggest two slightly different if complementary types of analytical perspective: thus the term 'discourse' is often preferred when attention is being drawn to extra-linguistic features that influence the production and reception of meaning, especially those reflecting the fact that language is a form of social practice; whereas the use of the term 'text' suggests that analytical focus is more on specifically linguistic organization, the meaning and use of particular expressions and constructions, in a record—typically, a written record—of a communicative event. This view of text is by no means at odds with the standard uses and central position of the term in the study of literature, and it has the further advantage of supporting the conceptual opposition of 'text' and 'context', a particularly important one for our present purposes, since a systematic concern with context is probably the trait that most distinctively characterizes discourse approaches in general.

---

[17] For a 'neutral' discussion of this issue, see John Lyons, *Language and Linguistics* (Cambridge: Cambridge University Press, 1981), pp. 163-70.

[18] See Robert Hodge and Gunter Kress, *Social Semiotics* (Cambridge: Polity, 1988), p. 7.

[19] For instance, some writers 'avoid the term discourse altogether and prefer the term *text* for all recorded instances of language use'. See David Nunan, *Introducing Discourse Analysis* (Harmondsworth: Penguin, 1993), p. 6.

Discourse analysis, as we have seen, necessarily maintains a dual focus on form—whether in terms of morpho-syntax or extended sequential patterns—and function, in the sense of the purposive use of language in social and interpersonal settings. It is precisely this attention to the complex interlocking of formal and functional aspects of discourse, I would argue, that is involved in exploring the relationship between text and context. Thus, overall, while the expression 'text' is sometimes be used here to refer to consensually prestigious pieces of writing in published or similar definitive form, such usage in no way suggests belief in the existence of autonomous linguistic artefacts; as Halliday remarks, 'Every text—that is everything that is said or written—unfolds in some context of use'.[20] In any case, the idea that a literary work necessarily has an authoritative written form is disputable. In justifying his preference for the term 'verbal art' as opposed to 'literature', Nigel Fabb points out that, of the four characteristics conventionally associated with the genre,

> Literary texts have literary form
> Literary texts require skill for their production and can be evaluated
> Literary texts are written
> Literary texts exist in authoritative versions which are preserved relatively unchanged[21]

only the first two can be regarded as universally defining ones. In oral cultures performed songs and narratives have analogous functions and a similar status to poems and literary narratives in written cultures such as our own, yet the third characteristic is absent and the fourth is by no means guaranteed, since certain aspects of the text may vary from performance to performance. Doubts as to the fixity of the purely verbal text are also raised by the fact that each instance of reception has its own context. The verbal component, that is, may have a fixed form, but the meaning cannot remain constant, since different individuals in different times

---

[20] *Introduction to Functional Grammar*, p. xiii.
[21] Nigel Fabb, *Linguistics and Literature: language in the verbal arts of the world* (Oxford: Blackwell, 1997), pp. 13-14.

and places will bring their own frameworks of interpretation to it and make it mean something new.[22] On the other hand, it is perfectly possible to view written genres from a performance perspective as verbal production for evaluation by an anticipated prospective audience rather than a real one.[23]

Matters such as cultural assumptions, interpretational frames and audience design are all, of course, aspects of the broader discursive notion of context; it would be as well, at this point, to clarify what is understood here by the term. Discourse approaches generally seek to define context as widely as possible, regarding it as involving rather more (and in more complicated ways) than the standardly-envisaged elements of setting, participant identities and immediately preceding text. Contextual information of the type often called background knowledge or knowledge of the world is also brought into play, although this sort of information should not be thought of as neutral factual data, since it includes all sorts of culturally and even ideologically constructed beliefs.[24] Again, an important part of participants' knowledge is their awareness of the social function or purpose of the speech situation, and their general familiarity with the way linguistic practices and genres interlock with social practices and institutions. When we add to these complexities the recursively shared nature of much participant information, it becomes clear that it is probably better to avoid conceiving of context in terms of external frames or environments, and to keep in mind instead the broad psychological definition proposed by Relevance theorist Diane Blakemore:

> By context we mean the beliefs and assumptions the hearer constructs for the interpretation of an utterance either on the basis of her perceptual abilities or on the assumptions she has stored in memory or on the basis of her interpretation of previous utterances.[25]

---

[22] See Dick Leith and George Myerson, *The Power of Address: explorations in rhetoric* (London: Routledge, 1989), p. 9.

[23] See William Foley, *Anthropological Linguistics: an introduction* (Oxford: Blackwell, 1997), p. 371.

[24] See Norman Fairclough, *Critical Discourse Analysis: the critical study of language* (London: Longman, 1995), pp. 42-44.

[25] Diane Blakemore, *Understanding Utterances* (Oxford: Blackwell, 1992), p. 87.

One advantage of the model proposed by Relevance theory is that it makes it clear that, where interpreting particular segments of discourse is concerned, context consists of a limited subset of the hearer's beliefs and assumptions about the world. A participant in communication potentially has access to an enormous amount of background information, any part of which, in principle, could be used in the interpretation of an utterance. Contextual information is put to use, however, in an efficiently selective way: 'hearers do not interpret utterances in just any context [...] successful communication depends on selecting the *right* assumptions—the ones that yield the intended interpretation.'[26] Hearers, that is, concentrate on those elements of context that are judged appropriate.

This notion is a very fruitful one for understanding the importance of context in the interpretation of discourse that qualifies as verbal art. The proposal put forward here is that the amount of background information—contextual assumptions in Relevance terms—that audiences select in the course of interpreting literary texts is considerably more extensive (and more complexly interlinked) than the items of knowledge accessed for interpretation of more routine pieces of communication. Audiences of verbal performances certainly tend to accord them a higher level of attentiveness than they would bring to less focused types of interaction, and expect them to contain a much higher proportion—and range—of significant linguistic (and often paralinguistic) features. This notion of greater density of signification is equally useful whether we go along with the Jakobsonian notion that what distinguishes verbal art is that it emphasizes the poetic function of communication (in the sense of drawing attention to its own form), or whether we incline more to the view that it involves an undertaking, before an audience, to conform to prominent conventions and rules of performance.[27] The requirement of enhanced attentiveness still holds even if we merely acknowledge

[26] Blakemore, *Understanding Utterances*, p. 18.
[27] See Leith and Myerson, *Power of Address*, p. 16; Foley, *Anthropological Linguistics*, pp. 363-371; Fabb, *Linguistics and Literature*, p. 16.

that verbal art routinely involves not only artistically-stylised self-expression and the creation of fictional worlds, but also irony, transposed and paradoxical language-modes, and other games played with language.[28] In everyday situations of communication, such specialized effects and types of meaning tend to appear singly rather than in combination, and are normally carefully introduced in order to alert the reader or hearer to the need for additional frames of interpretation.

Looking at these qualities of verbal art from a slightly different perspective, we could say that the coherence of a literary text is of a more complex order than is the case in more routine pieces of discourse. The notion of coherence in itself is worth examining a little more closely. One serviceable basic definition is that given by David Crystal as 'the underlying functional connectedness of a piece of language',[29] and there is general agreement that it denotes the quality that differentiates text or discourse from a random jumble of words or sentences. Discourse analysis, however, tends to emphasize two further aspects. Firstly, coherence is regarded not as an innate property of a piece of language, but an as interactive achievement, a product of the intentions and judgements of participants in communicative exchanges. Indeed, it is often seen as belonging primarily to the domain of discourse reception, something constructed by readers and hearers as they interpret texts along the lines presumably intended by writers and speakers. Secondly, successful interpretation is achieved not merely through narrow linguistic competence, but is inextricably bound up with the way people make sense of life in general. One of the central claims of discourse studies is that 'the question of how people know what is going on in a text is a special case of the question of how people know what is going on in the world at all'.[30]

---

[28] See Jürgen Habermas, *The Theory of Communicative Action*, I, translated by Thomas McCarthy (London: Heinemann, 1984), p. 331.

[29] David Crystal, *An Encyclopedic Dictionary of Language and Languages* (Harmonsworth: Penguin, 1994), p. 70.

[30] Robert de Beaugrande, *Text, Process and Discourse* (London: Longman, 1980), p. 30.

There is some variation, however, when it comes to determining the interpretative level at which coherence is constructed; some approaches focus on the connectedness of relatively small segments of discourse, especially conversational exchanges, and seek to establish functional or pragmatic rules of binary combination, governing the ways an utterance can form a coherent sequence with the preceding utterance.[31] Other approaches, geared to the concepts of sense-making at a higher level, ascribe as much importance to cognitive frames of understanding as to connections between segments of discourse,[32] or prefer notions of over-arching unity of the sort envisaged by Deborah Tannen, who defines coherence as 'an organizing structure that makes collections of words and sentences into a piece of unified discourse that has cultural significance for those who create and comprehend it'.[33]

Where literary texts are concerned, the first point to make is that, in the first definition above (which could be broadly characterized as absence of non-sequiturs), coherence is not invariably sustained. Passages of poetic or figurative language, for instance, often contain sequences of utterances that break with the functional rules found in more routine pieces of discourse. For instance, even more traditional examples of verse composition tend to contain a relatively high number of so-called rhetorical questions, with a consequent blocking of expected second-part utterances. In more recent poetry it is by no means unusual to encounter sometimes startling effects of discontinuity that seem to be aimed at recoding experience or critically questioning categories ingrained in habitual usage.[34] The following lines, for example, from a jocularly experimental poem of Rafael Alberti, seem calculated to break

[31] For a good example of this approach see Amy Tsui, 'Sequencing Rules and Coherence in Discourse', *Journal of Pragmatics*, XV (1991), 111-129.
[32] As do, for instance, Brown and Yule, *Discourse Analysis*, p. 197.
[33] Deborah Tannen, (ed.), *Coherence in Spoken and Written Discourse* (Norwood, New Jersey: Ablex, 1984), p. xiv.
[34] In one neat formulation, 'getting readers to see through and round the conventional grids of meaning'. See Roger Fowler, *Language in the News* (London: Routledge, 1991), p. 31.

down both functional connectivity and congruence of propositional content:[35]

¿Qué significa que en mi hombro se enjuaguen los dientes los angelitos
y que la luna no me parezca la más mínima expresión de un pescado?
A mi mamá le importa bastante poco que llueva.[36]

Such effects, moreover, are not limited to self-consciously 'modern' poetry (the example above is from the end of the nineteen-twenties, when avant-garde experimentalism was in fashion). The following lines, from 'Garrote vil', one of the poems of Ramón del Valle-Inclán's *La pipa de kif*, demonstrate that even relatively more traditional types of poetic expression can exploit non sequiturs very effectively to dismantle unity of mood and enhance an ironic clash of perspectives. The poem describes the crowd gathering around the garrotte being erected in a town square in the last hours before dawn on the day of an execution. The closing stanzas evoke the condemned man closeted with the priest, and end with a re-evocation of the scene outside:

Canta en la plaza el martillo,
el verdugo gana el pan,
un paño enluta el banquillo.
Como el paño es catalán,
se está volviendo amarillo
al son que canta el martillo.[37]

The sudden incongruous switch from morbid thoughts of impending death to a jibe directed against the protected Catalan textile industry is highly effective here, both creating macabre humour and establishing a certain critical perspective on national life and the mentality of the crowd.

---

[35] Following the view that coherence is a product of 'relations between discourse segments which depend on their propositional content' (Blakemore, *Understanding Utterances*, p. 85.)

[36] 'Harry Langdon hace por primera vez el amor a una niña', in Rafael Alberti, *Poesías completas* (Buenos Aires: Losada, 1961), p. 325.

[37] Ramón del Valle-Inclán, *Obras completas*, I (Madrid: Plenitud, 1954), p. 1160.

If Valle-Inclán's verse expression is not markedly experimental, the later plays and novels—those written in the decade following the composition of *La pipa de kif* in 1919—embody important innovations in both language and theatrical or narrative techniques. From a performance point of view, for instance, the stage-directions of the plays are often regarded as problematical in that they sometimes specify effects of décor, action or characterization beyond the technical resources of the theatre of Valle's day; it is worth noting, however, that, even readers of the printed texts can also find them a little disconcerting in terms of relevance to the action and even in narrower terms of textual coherence. The following examples are part of the opening descriptions (of a bedroom, in both cases) of the sixth scene of *Las galas del difunto*, and the fifth of *Los cuernos de Don Friolera* respectively:

> El tálamo de hierro fundido y boliches de cristal translúcido, perfila bajo la luz el costado donde roncaba el difunto. En la pila del agua bendita, un angelito toca el clarinete—alones azules, faldellín movido al viento, las rosadas pantorrillas en un cruce del bolero—.
>
> Tras de la puerta, la capa y la gorra colgadas con la guitarra, fingen un bulto viviente. Por el ventano abierto penetra, con el claro de la luna, el ventalle silencioso y nocturno de un huerto de luceros. Y la brisa y la luna parecen conducir un diálogo entre el vestiglo de la puerta y el pelele, que abre la cruz de los brazos sobre la copa negra de una higuera.[38]

Quite apart from their lexical richness and allusiveness, the problems for full comprehension of passages such as these go beyond the fact that what should be guidelines for the creation of certain static visual effects on the stage become animated micro-scenes in themselves, full of suggestive connotations. A further rather unsettling perception is that there seems to be no functional correlation between these word-scenes and the episodes of dialogue and action that follow. The staged episodes, in both cases, involve characters who seem completely oblivious, through their crass materialism or vulgar sentimentality, to either nuances of

---

[38] Ramón del Valle-Inclán, *Martes de carnaval*, ed. Ricardo Senabre (Madrid: Espasa-Calpe, 1990), p. 87 and p. 155.

mood or paradoxical subtleties of situation. Such techniques of dissociation, we suggest, challenge readers to subsume apparently non-functional details in a higher, aesthetically more satisfying level of theatrical meaning. Valle himself was probably thinking of such effects when, in a letter of 1922 to Cipriano Rivas Cherif, Margarita Xirgu's artistic director, he mentioned his preference for a 'sucesión de lugares para sugerir una superior unidad de ambiente; volumen en el tiempo; y tono lírico del motivo total sobre el tono del héroe'.[39]

Even with everyday discourse hearers tend to be reluctant to dismiss a sequence of utterances as incoherent, and often show considerable ingenuity in constructing a context, or attributing some plan to the speaker, that enables sense to be made of them.[40] Where verbal art is concerned (as we have seen with the examples above) writers often exploit, for particular effects, their audience's assumption that contiguous utterances will form a coherent text; equally, readers and hearers tend to know in advance that they are expected to have an elastic definition of local coherence and put greater effort into identifying sense-making links and frames. Indeed, the appeal of verbal art resides, in the view of many theorists, precisely in an emergent perception of complex coherence, in audiences coming to see how many different kinds of meaning converge in a particular utterance. To link the understanding of meaning with a sense of co-participation in creating it can thus be seen as the crux of the aesthetic response:

---

[39] Reproduced in John Lyon, *The Theatre of Valle-Inclán* (Cambridge: Cambridge University Press, 1983), p. 207.

[40] For a useful account of the processes of inference required for addressees to 'construct a reasonable plan to attribute to the text producer in producing the text' see Georgia M. Green, *Pragmatics and Natural Language Understanding* (Hillsdale, New Jersey: Lawrence Erlbaum, 1989), pp. 101-06. Some striking examples of the mental agility required to recognize the appropriateness of everyday utterances involving indeterminate or indirect meanings, interpreting them via 'the crucial relationship between what we say and the context in which it is most relevant' are discussed in Peter Grundy, *Doing Pragmatics* (London: Arnold, 1995), pp. 5-12.

> Perceiving meaning through the coherence of discourse constraints, as well as perceiving oneself as coherent in interaction constituted by the discourse, creates an emotional experience of insight (understanding the text) and connectedness (to other participants, to the language, to the world).[41]

Such heightened experiences of meaning, however, do not mean that we cannot approach literary discourse as we do discourse in general, as language in use, as 'instances of real communication in real social contexts'.[42] While it is true that literary texts tend to be regarded by their readers as privileged discourse events requiring a high level of attentiveness, with a concomitant quantitative difference in the range of knowledge and interpretive skills called on, their meanings are produced and understood in ways that are not qualitatively distinct from what happens in the case of non-literary texts. Many basic underlying features of communication, that is, are common to both modes, and attention to them can uncover meanings and patterns not normally revealed by analysis and commentary of the type more traditionally associated with 'literary criticism'.

One feature of communication in general that can be usefully highlighted when it comes to evaluating written literary discourse is the interactive dimension. Literary texts can be regarded as scripts for creating communicative events (or, alternatively, as records or transcripts of the utterances that constituted them).[43] Indeed, where poetry and theatre texts are concerned, most readers readily recognize that they are in some way required to compensate imaginatively for not participating directly in the situation of

---

[41] Deborah Tannen, *Talking Voices: repetition, dialogue and imagery in conversational discourse* (Cambridge: Cambridge University Press, 1989), p. 13. (Tannen summarizes here formulations on aesthetic theory of John Dewey and A.L. Becker.)

[42] Michael McCarthy and Ronald Carter, *Language as Discourse: perspectives for language teaching* (Harlow: Longman, 1994), p. 135.

[43] For discussion of the convenience of distinguishing between transcripts as the 'the record of the words actually uttered in performance' and script as 'the words the performer has in front of him or her', see Leith and Myerscough, *The Power of Address*, pp. 8-9.

utterance of which the text is a script or record. Narrative fiction may at first seem a different case until we consider such features as the 'voice' of the narrator and the underlying similarities between stage and fictional dialogue. What this means in practice is that the internal linguistic organization of a text is importantly influenced by its ultimately extra-linguistic functions as a communicative event. The language of a poem, novel or play, for instance, can profitably be approached, in much the same way as news reports or advertisements, whether on television or in newspapers, as an act—or series of acts—of communication, specifically designed for hearers and readers who belong to the same culture and broadly share the various types of knowledge possessed by the writer or speaker.

This is not to claim there is no difference between speech and written or printed text; an important part of the recursively-shared knowledge involved in the latter as opposed to face-to-face interaction consists precisely of mutual awareness of its distinctive features. For instance, the fact that in written language production and reception take place at different times and in different places rules out communicative aids such as gesture and intonation as well as feedback and repair work between participants; this loss is more than compensated for, however, by the greatly enhanced opportunity to devote care and reflection to linguistic choices and their interpretation.

1.3 TEXT AND PERFORMANCE

(i) Foregrounding, Utterance Function and Gricean Implicature in a Poem of Neruda

At this point perhaps the most effective way of taking further discussion of the theoretical issues raised is to consider a specific example in some detail. The following lines are the opening of Pablo Neruda's well-known poem 'Explico algunas cosas':[44]

---

44 'Explico algunas cosas' appears in 'España en el corazón', the fourth section of the collection *Tercera residencia.* See Pablo Neruda, *Obras completas*, I (Buenos Aires: Losada, 1967), pp. 275-77.

Preguntaréis: ¿y dónde están las lilas?
¿Y la metafísica cubierta de amapolas?
¿Y la lluvia que a menudo golpeaba
sus palabras, llenándolas
de agujeros y pájaros?
Os voy a contar todo lo que me pasa.

While Neruda is not one of the three writers to whom this study is substantially devoted, the expressive strategies of this poem do provide some exceptionally clear examples of the sorts of effect on which discourse theory can shed useful light. Accordingly—and although it is recognized that one of the pitfalls of discourse stylistics can be too exhaustive an attention to linguistic detail—it is worth looking fairly closely at some passages of the poem in conjunction with a brief indication of areas of theory which are relevant to their analysis.

Perhaps the most basic principle of linguistic communication, manifestations of which range from the production of sound sequences with potential for meaning to the production of meanings that are completely different from what is actually said, is the functional contrast between repetition and variation, the normal and the deviant, the expected and the unexpected. As we have already noted, this principle is particularly marked in poetic texts whose language is often stylized in ways that do not merely differ in certain ways from the organization of everyday discourse, but seem more a deliberate strategy of defamiliarization. Readers' perceptions are unsettled by the use of linguistic devices—such as metaphor, unusual collocations, breaking syntactic rules—that serve to interrogate habitual encodings of experience.[45] Thus a very productive way of analysing poetry is to concentrate on instances of deviation from normal linguistic usage, since they have the effect of foregrounding in the reader's attention the features or passages of text concerned. Although it is often an unusual formal feature, such

45 For a useful overview of the important role of habitualization and defamiliarization in modern aesthetic strategies—in the visual arts as well as writing—see Roger Fowler, *Linguistic Criticism* (Oxford: Oxford University Press, 1986), pp. 40-43.

as an odd combination of words, that first attracts our attention, it is worth noting that our interpretation of such foregrounding depends basically on our knowledge of the ways utterances are used to represent patterns of experience and build mental pictures of reality.

Where the opening lines of 'Explico algunas cosas' are concerned (and even after consulting our mental encyclopaedia of standardized and basic cognitive metaphors) we recognize that it is not normal for a noun referring to an abstract entity such as 'metafísica' to be qualified as 'cubierta de amapolas'. A similarly intriguing incongruity of the elements making up a process-type in what Halliday terms 'the grammar of experience' into which we construe the variety and flow of real-world events,[46] is created by the expression 'llenándolas [palabras] de agujeros y pájaros'. Rather than venturing in any depth into the complex relationship between cognitive processes and linguistic representation, it is probably sufficient for present purposes to remain with the relatively straightforward notion of expressions whose contents are not in accord with what we consider normal options of combination. Instances of this sort of foregrounding are accepted by readers as part of the stylized density of poetic language, with its rich rewards for the greater interpretive effort invested. We should also note, however, that telling effects of significant deviation can equally be achieved by the contrastive introduction of everyday language. The final line quoted above, 'os voy a contar todo lo que me pasa', is a very good example of just such a move. My intuitive starting-point, in fact, is that the poem as a whole systematically exploits the potential tension between these two discourse polarities, the poetic and the prosaic. To consider how this is achieved, and with what objectives, it is necessary to devote some attention to the relationship constituted in the poem between the speaker and his audience.

'Explico algunas cosas' strikingly illustrates a useful strategy available to the producer of written texts: the creation and maintenance of the fiction of a unified speech situation through the projection of a voice that addresses the reader or readers in the 'here

---

[46] *Introduction to Functional Grammar*, p. 108.

and now'. The device is not distinctively literary—writers of personal letters as well as producers of posters and advertisements regularly make use of it—but in literary texts it can be used to particularly good effect. This is especially so in poetry, where there are many advantages to be gained in encouraging the reader to recreate imaginatively the conditions of an actual recital and, as it were, inwardly attend to the cadences and rhythms of the poet's voice. The markedly interactive 'en directo' style of this particular poem is apparent from the very first words: with 'preguntaréis ¿y dónde están las lilas [...]?' the poet directly addresses his readers and predicts their response to his poem. The predicted response is itself vividly evoked through prefacing the question with 'y', creating the effect of an interlocutor's immediate reaction to a just-heard piece of discourse. But what matters, of course, is not so much whether such a communicative relationship is set up, as what particular use is made of it. In particular, it is worth looking at the exploitation of what could be called the situation of performance.

The first point to note is the element of pragmatic ambiguity as to the force of the opening verb, 'preguntaréis'. In Spanish, the future tense of verbs is generally used to convey, depending on context, either a supposition or a strong undertaking as to the performance of the action concerned. The speaker, that is, can be taken to be displaying either a markedly weak or a markedly strong commitment to what is said. We might note that while speakers often undertake to carry out future actions themselves (promising), a strong commitment to the future actions of addressees is rather less usual, since it constitutes a prediction, and thus lays claim to the exceptional powers or knowledge necessary for its valid utterance. In the absence of further contextual information, it would be difficult, in fact, to interpret 'preguntaréis' along these lines, were it not for our awareness that that one of the roles traditionally claimed by poets is that of visionary or prophet.

Whether the poem's opening is prediction or conjecture—or, indeed, whether the ambivalence is meant to be left unresolved—we need to look more closely at the presumption that the interrogators are familiar with the salient characteristics of the poet's work to date and will therefore notice that the present poem does not conform to them. A situation that allows for precisely this sort of prediction of other participants' expressions of surprise or puzzlement is that of the announcement or acknowledgment of the non-fulfilment of obligations as a way of leading up to the provision of a pretext or justification. At the start of this poem, then, we have a verbal performer about to give just such an explanation to his habitual audience.

The point of this line of analysis is that it is precisely by configuring the situation of address in this way that Neruda, as well as starting to uncover the significance of the poem's title,[47] is able to pinpoint the interactive function of the line 'os voy a contar todo lo que me pasa', itself an important key to patterns of meaning that will emerge in the poem. The discursive structure of the poem's opening lines thus consists, unmistakably, of an undertaking, on the part of a poet, to provide an explanation, for what he anticipates will strike his readers as a surprising departure from his previous style and themes. Since 'os voy a contar todo lo que me pasa' clearly functions to introduce some sort of justification, excuse or apology, there is a strong hint that the changes in question are not so much the result of a personal evolution in artistic practice as a reaction to external events.

What the poet in fact goes on to provide is not an apology or even, superficially, an explanation. He first evokes scenes of the pleasantly convivial and peaceful conditions of existence in his apartment in a popular suburb of Madrid,

> [...] mi barrio de Argüelles con su estátua
> como un tintero pálido entre las merluzas:
> el aceite llegaba a las cucharas,
> un profundo latido
> de pies y manos llenaba las calles,
> metros, litros, esencia
> aguda de la vida […].

---

[47] Neruda seems to have carefully considered the title, since the change to 'Explico algunas cosas' from the original 'Es así' is the only substantial textual amendment of the version that appeared in *El Mono Azul*, XXII (1937).

and then switches to descriptions of the damage inflicted on the besieged city and the loss of life among its civilian population during the Spanish Civil War, denunciations of Franco's forces and their supporters, and warnings that their depredations will only strengthen the people's will to resist. With a typical use of performer's licence, the identity of the poem's addressees changes as he acts out his anger:

> pero de cada hueco de España
> sale España.
> pero de cada niño muerto sale un fusil con ojos,
> pero de cada crimen nacen balas
> que os hallarán un día el sitio
> del corazón.

This indirectness of the poet's response to the original question is strikingly confirmed at the end of the poem, where the poet again predicts a puzzled query from his readers as to why his poetry doesn't speak 'del sueño, de las hojas, / de los grandes volcanes de su país natal'; again, in formulating his answer, he avoids picking up the questioners' obvious cues, insistently urging them instead to come and see the destruction and loss of life for themselves:

> Venid a ver la sangre por las calles,
> venid a ver
> la sangre por las calles,
> venid a ver la sangre
> por las calles.

Where the functional interpretation of utterance-sequences is concerned, it is still instructive to go back to some observations first made over thirty years ago by the sociolinguist William Labov, in an essay which, although concerned with street-corner exchanges rather than literary texts, established the methodological progression from intuition to underlying principles which has been the characteristic strength of linguistic stylistics. For Labov, the interpretation of replies that are superficially unrelated to preceding questions depends on shared knowledge, in the form of a proposition known to both participants, that connects the reply with the question.[48] We might say that the proposition known to both poet and readers is that the visual images evoked in the poem are examples of sources of poetic inspiration; it is in this sense that the landscape, flora and fauna of his own country have been supplanted by the ruined and bloodied streets of a foreign city. This interpretation assumes, however, that the question-response sequence is precisely what it seems. As Labov perceived (effectively combining his own insights into functions of utterances in sequence with some contemporaneous observations of John Searle on indirectness in speech acts regarded in isolation):[49]

> There are no simple one-to-one relations between actions and utterances […]. Sequencing rules do not operate between utterances but between the notions performed with those utterances.[50]

One such sequencing rule that is of particular interest here is that for hearing a question as a request for action rather than for information. Labov proposes that this interpretation depends on it being recursively known that the requested action will serve a desirable purpose, that the speaker has the right to request it and that the hearer has both the ability and the obligation to perform it.[51]

---

[48] 'A statement follows a question: the question is a request for information; but in what way does the statement form an answer to that request? In answering A's request for information Q-S_1 with a superficially unrelated statement S_2, B is in fact asserting there is a proposition known to both A and B that connects this with S_1'. See W. Labov, 'Rules for Ritual Insults', in D. Sudnow (ed.), *Studies in Social Interaction* (New York: Free Press, 1972), pp. 120-69, at p. 138. (Cited in Carter and Simpson, *Language, Discourse*, p. 62.)

[49] See Searle, *Expression and Meaning*, pp. 31-64.

[50] W. Labov, 'The Study of Language in its Social Context', in P.P. Giglioli (ed.), *Language and Social Context* (Harmondsworth: Penguin, 1982), pp. 283-316, at p. 301.

[51] 'If A requests B to perform an action X at a time T, A's utterance will be heard as a valid command only if the following pre-conditions hold: B believes that A believes (= it is an A-B event that)

1. X should be done for a purpose Y
2. B has the ability to do X
3. B has the obligation to do X
4. A has the right to tell B to do X' ('The Study of Language', p. 302).

We have here a sound basis for interpreting the query, at the start of Neruda's poem, as to the whereabouts of the lilacs and other things, as conveying a protest about their removal and a call for their restitution. However, a common strategy for putting off requests is to call into question the assumptions in which it is grounded—as Labov remarks, 'if any of the pre-conditions are not shared knowledge the request is obviously not valid'.[52] When Neruda responds with a superficially unrelated statement he is making just such a move. Answering—or rather not answering—interrogation of his writing by talking about some personal experiences and asking the questioners to come and see the situation for themselves amounts to challenging his questioner's competence to judge obligations and accusing them of parochial short-sightedness both in their aesthetic standards and in their collective allegiances. In particular, by 'telling things as they are' and characterizing his current way of writing as something forced on him by events, he is denying not only the obligation but also the *ability* to accede to the request by reverting to his previous way of writing. A narrow concern with verbal expression for its own sake, he is implying, would be literally impossible amid the shocking reality in which he and others find themselves. To borrow the words of a writer more recently concerned with the violence and suffering engendered by civil conflict, Neruda is asserting here the responsibility of poets 'to say what happens, to be not concerned with Poetry.'[53]

This implied line of argument is backed up in a number of ways. For instance, rather than indirectly reporting the words or thoughts of his readers, Neruda quotes them directly. This is not simply a device to evoke the situation of surprised reaction more vividly, but creates a further effect: the transposed deixis of direct quotation results in the figure of the poet himself being presented in a third person perspective, 'sus palabras'. This distanced viewpoint, which aptly conjures up the poet as he used to be, switches strikingly to personal experience with the first two words, 'os voy' of the

---

[52] *The Study of Language*, p. 303.

[53] The Nobel Lecture, 1995, in Seamus Heaney, *Opened Ground, Poems 1966-1996* (London: Faber and Faber, 1998), pp. 447-67 (at p. 451).

'punch-line' of the poem's opening passage. The description of the poetry written to date, moreover, suggests it is based on meta-poetic fabrication of verbal correlatives for inner cognitive states, again bluntly contrasted with straightforward narration of events in transparent language. The undertaking to 'contar lo que me pasa' itself implies disapproval of poetic artifice deployed for purely aesthetic ends, an attitude which is exemplified in the uncomplicated, natural style of much of the poem. The nostalgic evocation of the poet's home in pre-war Argüelles:

> Mi casa era llamada
> La casa de las flores, porque por todas partes
> estallaban geranios: era una bella casa
> con perros y chiquillos.

is a revealing case in point, not only for the prosaic language in which the description is couched, but also for the punctilious explanation of the house's name, satisfying, as in an ordinary conversation, the curiosity mention of the name might have aroused.

What Neruda is doing in this poem is apparently breaking the rules of engagement of literary discourse, in that he purports to reject many of the special conventions and generic framing devices by which the verbal performer undertakes to be constrained if he is to produce good examples of his art. By exploiting the performance situation in this way the poet is effectively dramatizing an ideological debate between two fundamentally opposed views or evaluations of the role of writers and the function of creative writing. It hardly needs saying that, as direct addressees, readers are put in the position of having to choose between supporting artistic detachment and cognitive-expressive individualism, or accepting that priority must be given to the obligations of social communication in the public sphere. Furthermore, in overtly shifting the parameters of artistic choice and the creation of meaning away from purely verbal expressive options and toward the configuration of the situation of utterance, Neruda is also holding up a model of the approach he is advocating. His consistent deployment of basic, widely-understood metaphors of binary opposition, such as house/street, sky/ground, human/animal and flowers/weapons, is a further clear example of this tendency.

There is more to the poem's 'message' than this, however; we need to take some account of the social situation of performance. The text should be read, that is, not as an abstract given but as emerging in the contextualized 'here and now' of its original audience, creatively indexing a broader discourse of social relations and cultural issues. Indeed, since the poem specifically raises the issue of fitting word to world, the audience is encouraged to reflect precisely on such relations. At this level of contextualization, however, it becomes clear that Neruda's proposal that language should be matched to reality is not as straightforward as it might seem.

To give readers to understand that 'artistic' lyrical poetry can no longer be written because of the urgency and emotional impact of public events is just as much a poetic conceit as, say, the traditional claim that the power of love and the beauty of the beloved have struck the poet dumb. In both instances the discursive realization of the poem contradicts its central assertion, just as in both, the allegation of expressive constraints is meant to be taken as a metaphor for a set of attitudes and values. The readers explicitly addressed in 'Explico algunas cosas' are characterized as detached and distant from the events described, and, in a broad sense, the poem can be interpreted as an appeal, to the Hispanophone world at large, and to Neruda's Chilean countrymen in particular, for sympathy with and support for the beleaguered Spanish Republic. On the other hand, the poem embodies a number of attitudes and ideological positions that suggest it is designed for Peninsular audiences and supports a particular set of policies. In insisting that expression should be geared to reality Neruda is defining his poetic activity in terms of civic responsibilities rather than personal concerns, emphasizing that the role of the poet is to give voice to collective experience rather than express private feeling. One important duty of this 'oficio de poeta' is that of promoting solidarity and collective morale. The motif of renouncing individualistic pretensions—such as 'artistic freedom'—in the service of a greater cause is very much in line with Popular Front policy objectives in the first year of the Spanish Civil War. Government propaganda constantly stressed the imperative need for all sectors of society—industrial workers, peasants, militia, wives and mothers, artists and intellectuals—to accept sacrifice and discipline in pursuit of the all-important objective of winning the war. It is worth adding that such a call confirmed the centralizing, stabilizing and relatively authoritarian tendencies of the governing coalition as opposed to the more libertarian or radically revolutionary outlook of certain sectors and groupings in anti-Franco Spain. Moreover, stirring appeals for disciplined solidarity and heroic resistance predicated on broad human values had the useful effect of blurring ideological differences between the various political organizations, as well as deflecting attention from the way the Communist Party (which Neruda himself supported) had, in effect, renounced its traditional revolutionary aims.[54] To draw attention to such matters is by no means to suggest that 'Explico algunas cosas' should be categorized as mere political propaganda. What is very evident, however, and precisely because of the poem's conscious engagement with a particular historical set of circumstances, is that writing, even in so apparently personal a genre as poetry, is a socially-constituted activity, and that artistic paradigms and even more detailed questions of style and form can have important social dimensions.

Before leaving this poem, it is worth looking at a particularly clear example it provides of a fundamental area of pragmatics theory with many useful applications to the analysis of literary language. The feature in question is that of implied (or, from the hearer's point of view, inferred) meanings, that is, 'the mechanisms whereby a speaker can mean more than, or something quite different from what he actually says'.[55] Perhaps the most striking instance of deprecation of poetic artifice in 'Explico algunas cosas'

---

[54] Although his membership of the party was not officially acknowledged until after the Spanish Civil War, Neruda had been close to the Communists through personal contacts from the mid-thirties onward.

[55] Stephen Levinson, *Pragmatics* (Cambridge: Cambridge University Press, 1983), p. 27.

is the final detail of the description (or rather, in line with our remarks on indirect speech acts above, the denunciation) of aerial bombardment of civilian targets:

> y la sangre de los niños
> corría simplemente como sangre de niños.

The analogy—or rather non-analogy—presented in these lines constitutes a clear example of a type of superficially uninformative utterance—'patent tautologies like *Women are women* and *War is war*'—specifically mentioned by the linguistic philosopher H.P. Grice in his seminal lectures on conversational implicature.[56] The basis of Grice's theory is his proposal that, in conversing, people generally follow a behavioural dictum he termed the Cooperative Principle:

> Make your conversational contribution such as is required, at the stage at which it occurs, by the accepted purpose or direction of the talk exchange in which you are engaged.[57]

Although I have followed hallowed practice, where expositions of this theory are concerned, by reproducing the wording of the Cooperative Principle itself, it seems preferable here to depart from the tradition of following up by quoting in full the four categories of its application that Grice terms maxims (of quality, quantity, relation and manner) and simply give instead Levinson's helpful résumé: '[participants in conversation] should speak sincerely, relevantly and clearly, while providing sufficient information'.[58] The point, of course, is that speakers do not always follow these guidelines. When a speaker conspicuously infringes one or more of the maxims, the hearer assumes that, contrary to appearances, the principle of cooperation is nevertheless being adhered to at some deeper level, and seeks to construct inferences that justify this assumption.

---

[56] See Grice, *Studies in the Way of Words*, p. 33.
[57] *Studies in the Way of Words*, p. 26.
[58] *Pragmatics*, p. 102.

Grice characterizes tautologies as utterances which, at the level of what is said, are totally non-informative, and thus, by blatantly failing to meet the requirement to give sufficient information, seem to infringe the maxim of quantity. It is this flouting (as Grice terms it) of the maxim that encourages the hearer to look for meanings that can be inferred:

> They are, of course, informative at the level of what is implicated, and the hearer's identification of their informative content at this level is dependent on his ability to explain the speaker's selection of this particular patent tautology.[59]

In the case of Neruda's tautologous likening of the blood of children to the blood of children, it is not, in general terms, difficult for the reader of the poem to identify the informative content, although it is worth pointing out that it is often more useful to think in terms of a range of stronger or weaker implicatures than to deduce a single specific inference from the utterance in question. There would seem to be two strands of meaning suggested by the poet in offering this apparently void piece of information. One of them is that the shocking impact of what has been witnessed is such as to defy the capacities of language, or the writer's powers of invention. Giving a new twist to poets' traditional rhetorical disclaimers of ability to match expression to inspiration, Neruda is suggesting he is *unable* to find an apt simile. The other implication is that a comparison would be morally or aesthetically wrong—he *chooses* not to provide a correlative, either as a pointed refusal to allow figurative language to cushion the impact of the atrocious, or because the only adequate analogy is to repeat the original wording. Whether we interpret the implied meaning along one or another or both of these lines, our attention is inevitably drawn not only to the overwhelming impact of reality, but equally to questions of the use of language and the abilities and duties of writers in relation to that reality—precisely, of course, the issues that are placed firmly in focus in the poem as a whole.

---

[59] *Studies in the Way of Words*, p. 33.

(ii) Dialogue, Speech Acts, and Irony in the Theatre of Valle-Inclán

Dialogue in the theatre has many things in common with dialogue in works of prose fiction. The main difference is one of immediacy and consequent greater density of communicative effects; a live theatre audience is not engaged in interpreting a script or record for reconstructing a speech event separated in time and place, but is party to a performance of that script, with intonation, gestures, movements and a setting as well as spoken words. The spectator thus has a dual participant role, on one level picking up clues as if overhearing a real-life conversation, and on another interpreting a complexly designed and mediated piece of communication. Matters to do with the discourse structure of performed dialogue, such as the relationship between different types of participant (author, actors, characters and audience), the functioning of generic communicative conventions and the importance of contextual knowledge are thoroughly interdependent, and for that reason it is more effective to consider them through concrete examples. Accordingly, the analysis here will be tied to examples chosen from the later theatre of Ramón del Valle-Inclán, including some consideration of a short piece that has received relatively little critical attention, the 'esperpentillo' *¿Para cuándo son las reclamaciones diplomáticas*? Examination of dialogue in Valle's theatre from a discourse perspective also provides an opportunity to shed some light on the way irony and humour, aesthetic effects and socio-cultural criticism are combined in his 'esperpento' mode.

Theatre dialogue constitutes, in a number of ways, a complex model of communication. In the first instance, it involves the collaborative acceptance by the audience of special conventions and norms. One very basic convention is that whatever is said on stage is spoken action, requiring modifications in the audience's mental picture of the development of events and the relationship between characters. Another is that the hesitations, repetitions and pieces of simultaneous talk that are characteristic of ordinary conversations are normally dispensed with, as well as most of the routine signals from the speaker as to how to take the message and those from the hearer indicating it has been received and understood.[60] Both of these conventions are related to a broader, aesthetic objective: dialogue in verbal art differs from day-to-day communication precisely in that each utterance is carefully designed to carry a greater weight of significance, and the use of language in general has a density and meaningfulness (and will bear a degree of attention) that is rarely expected from or accorded to speech in everyday life.

The communication of such larger meanings in the theatre often depends, in fact, on the conventionally embedded nature of dialogue. As one manual puts it, 'los actores simulan que intercambian información entre si, cuando, de hecho, repiten un texto que conocen de memoria, y en realidad es el público a quien se dirigen'.[61] The canonical structure of a single communicative event is one in which one person addresses and gives information to another, but what distinguishes actual conversation, whether in the theatre or in everyday life, is that the participants continually exchange roles.[62] Even if this level of performed utterances is considered in isolation things can be quite complex, since characters often quote or report the words of others, or enact verbal formulas and rituals, and it is not uncommon for pieces of theatre to be embedded in the performed action. The underlying level of discourse in the theatre, however, is that of communication between author and audience, although this is principally constituted by what characters say to and about each other. The model of production and reception of meaning might be represented thus:

---

[60] For the way the density of such signals characterizes face-to-face interaction in real life, see Brown, *Speakers, Listeners and Communication*, p. 30. When such features do appear in stage dialogue, they are marked, signalling uncertainty of opinion, or as to how an interactive task is to be carried out—see Mick Short, *Exploring the Language of Poems, Plays and Prose* (London: Longman, 1996), pp. 170-171.

[61] Rafael Portillo y Jesús Casado, *Abecedario del teatro* (Madrid: Centro de Documentación Teatral, 1988), pp. 57-58.

[62] See Mick Short, 'Discourse Analysis and the Analysis of Drama', in Carter and Simpson, *Language, Discourse,* pp. 139-170 (at p. 142).

AUTHOR → [Character A → Character B] → AUDIENCE

What adds extra complexity to this model, however, is the question of contextual knowledge. Discourse is normally planned and interpreted on the basis of what has been previously said, a shared immediate environment, and assumptions as to mutual knowledge of extra-linguistic states of affairs. To interpret what authors communicate to them through stage dialogue, however, audiences have to derive non-explicit meanings from exchanges that are also expected to sustain an illusion of being geared to their own, idiosyncratic contexts.

It is worth making clear that, in spite of such complexities, it is perfectly viable and useful to analyze performed dialogue using concepts developed to account for features of real-life conversations. Although we are dealing with fabricated exchanges between fictional characters, and are expected to regard as spontaneous speech what is really a script constructed by writers and delivered by performers, the principal conventions we have for interpretation are precisely those we apply to ordinary language use. This does not mean, however, that we have to describe complicated processes in terms of relatively straightforward ones. As Stephen Levinson has pointed out, real-life situations often involve participant roles—such as planned overhearing—of a complexity equal to that of the model of communication found in fictional dialogue.[63] Indeed, such dialogue can only make sense to us in relation to the conventions of interaction in the wider world of human affairs in which fictional productions are themselves embedded. In the particular case of a theatre audience, 'the norms, values and modes of conduct which regulate how "real" people organize their linguistic behaviour form the basis for interpreting the speech and action of the fictional characters in the world of a

---

[63] Stephen Levinson, 'Putting Linguistics on a Proper Footing' in P. Drew and A. Wootton (eds), *Erving Goffman: exploring the interaction order* (Cambridge: Polity, 1988), pp. 161-227 (at p. 193).

play'.[64] Indeed, it is familiarity with the basic norms of communicative interaction that guides writers' composition of dialogue (and, for that matter, critics' and analysts' interpretation of it) just as much as with the production and interpretation of everyday talk.[65]

Valle's theatre after 1918 provides particularly appropriate examples for analysis of theatre dialogue, particularly since imaginatively envisaging what characters would say to each other in a given situation seems to have been his preferred compositional method. It is also worth noting, in this respect, that dramatic or fictional dialogue in his later works is closely tied to its situational context and less geared than was the normal practice of his time to providing audiences and readers with explicit guidance as to matters of plot and character. Valle's dialogue thus plausibly reproduces one of the most characteristic features of real-life exchanges and relies on audiences having a good measure of the sense-making abilities of real-life overhearers. Indeed, this handling of dialogue is the most marked manifestation of the aim, in his writing in general, to achieve density of meaning by exploiting the inferencing powers of his audiences and readers, rather than through overt authorial provision of information. As Estrella Montolío notes, Valle possesses 'la virtud de sugerir intencionada y deliberadamente significados que no aparecen explícitamente' and, in this way, 'nos invita a colaborar muy activamente en el proceso de negociación del auténtico significado textual'.[66]

Before describing this tendency in a little more detail, however, it should be acknowledged that making strong claims for the central importance of dialogue in Valle's theatre is not in itself uncontentious. Many commentators have tended to see his writing

---

[64] Paul Simpson, 'Odd Talk', in J. Culpepper, M. Short and P. Verdonk (eds), *Exploring the Language of Drama* (London: Routledge, 1998), pp. 34-53 (at p. 41).

[65] See E. Hess-Lüttich, 'How Does the Writer of a Dramatic Text Interact With His Audience?' in R.D. Sell (ed.), *Literary Pragmatics* (London: Routledge, 1990), pp. 225-51.

[66] Estrella Montolío Durán, *Gramática de la caracterización en Valle-Inclán*, (Barcelona: PPU, 1992), pp. 197-98.

for the theatre as primarily concerned with large themes and broad effects, such as the evocation of collective perspectives and values, whether in terms of an unchanging ethos or in accordance with an aesthetic of distortion geared to social and historical critique. Another frequent approach has been to concentrate on features of style and register, drawing attention to the language of the plays in its own right, as an exotic brew of prosodic effects, lexical range and variety, tonal contrasts, inter-textual reminiscences and poetic metaphor and imagery.[67] All of these qualities are indeed present in Valle's theatre, but to commend them too insistently courts the risk of suggesting that on-stage exchanges merely serve an aesthetic programme or provide a showcase for stylistic effects, rather than mapping a dynamic process of interaction between individually-motivated characters. In particular, there is a tendency to point approvingly to frequent instances of de-individualized speech—proverbs and 'sentencias', ritual or choral passages, puppet-like sequences or parodies of well-known models—without making it clear that the effectiveness of such passages depends on contrasting them with more mainstream dialogic modes. Good fictional dialogue—and especially in the theatre—should give the impression of an open-ended process of tactical exchanges involving both tension and collaboration between manipulators of discourse; it is precisely this quality that dialogue in Valle's plays, especially the later ones, has in abundance.

It is undeniable that Valle made a number of comments to journalists and others along the lines that the creation of overall aesthetic and emotional effects should take precedence over narrative and dialogue construction. He also, on occasion, claimed that the genius of the Spanish language and theatrical culture in general was for confrontational language, such as strong assertions,

---

[67] Some names and works concerned are discussed, as well as some of Valle's own comments on his creative methods and preferences, in Robin Warner, 'Words of Power: dialogue and dominance in Valle-Inclán's *Divinas palabras*', *Modern Language Review*, LXXXVII (1993), 343-53; and Robin Warner, 'Co-operative Contests: dialogue modes in the late novels of Ramón de Valle-Inclán', in D. Cruikshank (ed.), *A Lifetime's Reading: Hispanic essays for Patrick Gallagher*, (Dublin: University College Dublin Press, 1999), pp. 203-13.

exclamations, curses and insults rather than more subtle dialogic cut-and-thrust, or envisaged the way forward for the Spanish theatre as through 'escenarios y gritos'.[68] On the other hand, due weight should also be given to a number of statements made by Valle to the opposite effect, such as that dialogue was the basis of good theatre—'el alma, [...] la médula vital del verdadero teatro',[69] and that his favourite technique was to write 'en forma escénica, dialogada', that is, creating episodes of contextually situated dialogue.[70] The relaxed, ironic humour of the following exchanges (from the third scene of *Los cuernos de Don Friolera*, a play whose language is often characterized as exaggeratedly formulaic) is based on a complex interplay of apparent speech strategies and characters' actual motives and objectives. A group of 'contrabandistas' are apparently teasing Pachequín over his gossiped-about relationship with Friolera's wife, but, ever alert to the possibility of an advantageous deal, are really congratulating him on having acquired an influential ally. The lame Pachequín, however, loyally protects his paramour's reputation with a neat allusion to the imperfect state of his own lower limbs (and hence, he implies, his unattractiveness to the opposite sex.

> PACHEQUÍN. Aprendo la doctrina.
> EL NIÑO. Cultivando la Tenienta.
> CURRO. ¡No es mala mujer!
> EL PENEQUE. Cartagenera y esposa de militar, pues dicho se está que buen pico, buen garbo y buena pierna.
> PACHEQUÍN. En ese respecto, un servidor se declara incompetente.

The audience needs to be alert to the scope of such innuendo, since corrupt dealings between the military and the unofficial import agents are always referred to through indirect allusions, and this conversation is the first time the topic has been broached in the play

---

[68] 'Formas totales y definitivas: la sentencia, la imprecación, el denuesto, el grito [...] concretemos la fórmula que tiene por delante el el dramaturgo español: escenarios y gritos'. See Dru Dougherty, *Un Valle-Inclán olvidado: entrevistas y conferencias* (Madrid: Fundamentos, 1983), p. 186.
[69] Dougherty, *Un Valle-Inclán olvidado*, p. 168.
[70] Dougherty, *Un Valle-Inclán olvidado*, p. 190.

(if we discount Friolera's comment '¿y si cerrase los ojos para ese contrabando?', uttered when he first learns of the gossip about his wife).

The counterpart of the prevalence of such indirect strategies is that the traditional functions of dialogue are correspondingly less in evidence. Those listed by Ángel Loureiro as absent from *Luces de Bohemia*

> En el teatro tradicional el diálogo sirve para informar sobre lo sucedido fuera de escena o antes de que la obra haya comenzado, para caracterizar a los personajes, explicar motivaciones o acontecimientos, producir enfrentamientos dramáticos o avanzar la acción.[71]

are to a large extent eschewed in Valle's later plays as a whole. It would be more accurate to say, however, that Valle, rather than dispensing with these functions altogether, was more concerned not realize them in too obvious a way. On several occasions he expresses his determination to avoid he what called 'contar' or 'relatos', whether in theatre dialogue or in narrative fiction (a generic distinction to which, in any case, he attached no particular importance in his later years).[72] While this tendency is an integral part of a broader policy of authorial non-interventionism,[73] it also

---

[71] 'A vueltas con el esperpento', in A. Loureiro (ed.), *Estelas, laberintos, nuevas sendas: Unamuno, Valle-Inclán, García Lorca* (Barcelona: Anthropos, 1991), pp. 205-29. Nevertheless, Loureiro's assertion that 'en *Luces de Bohemia* predomina un diálogo en que los personajes hablan pero no se entienden' (made about a play in which a working-class Catalan anarchist and an uneducated young gypsy prostitute alike understand Max's allusions—jocular or serious—perfectly well) is typical of many commentators' tendency to incautious over-generalizing where Valle's handling of dialogue is concerned.

[72] Valle describes the later novels as 'ficciones casi de teatro porque todo está expresado por medio del diálogo' (Dougherty, *Un Valle-Inclán olvidado*, p. 178); conversely, the third edition of the play *Cara de Plata*, bears the subtitle 'Novela satírica'. See Ramón del Valle-Inclán, *Cara de Plata*, ed. Antonio Risco (Madrid: Espasa-Calpe, 1992), p. 31.

[73] See, especially, 'Autocrítica del esperpento', in Dougherty, *Un Valle-Inclán olvidado*, pp. 189-192, at p. 191: 'quiero que mis personajes se presenten siempre solos y sean en todo momento ellos, sin el comentario, sin la explicación del autor'.

reflects, at the more technical level of scene construction, a marked distaste for passages of dialogue too obviously set up for purposes such as bringing the audience up to date with what has 'happened' off-stage and providing them with the information they need to understand character relationships correctly.

The traditional dramatic convention of over-explicitness, which 'allows characters to say to each other things they already "know" and even things that are strictly irrelevant, in order to transmit economically to the audience essential information',[74] has tended to fall out of favour in more recent writing for the theatre; as Short notes, the characters in the opening scene of Shaw's *Arms and the Man*, for instance, talk in ways that seem to us unnatural precisely because the informative function is predominant.[75] Items of information about important concerns and circumstances in their lives are allowed to intrude into a conversation between a mother and daughter, who we would expect to be well aware of them already. In pragmatic terms, such provision of over-explicit information violates the Gricean maxim of quantity (do not make your contribution more informative than required) and possibly that of relevance as well. If hearers, that is, fail to react appropriately (by looking for implicatures) when speakers blatantly draw attention to uncontroversial shared knowledge, the exchanges can only seem somewhat contrived and implausible.

In Valle-Inclán's later plays dialogue rarely supplies information in this overt way (one minor exception is the structural device of a narrative link between scenes; in *Luces de Bohemia*, for example, the closing remarks of one episode often serve to predict the setting of the subsequent one, as with '¡hay que visitar las redacciones!' at the end of the fifth scene). The audience is often placed in a position in some ways analogous to that of overhearers of real-life conversations, and is obliged to deduce many aspects of the circumstances, relationships, preoccupations and motives of the characters from the unspoken assumptions behind what they say to

---

[74] M. Coulthard, 'Forensic Discourse Analysis', in M. Coulthard (ed.), *Advances in Spoken Discourse Analysis* (London: Routledge, 1992), pp. 242-58 (at p. 249).
[75] *Exploring the Language*, p. 185.

each other. Moreover, as in real life, the possibility of deliberate or unconscious misrepresentation cannot be ruled out. It is possible Valle had in mind the cooperative (in the Gricean sense) and thoroughly contextualized quality of the sort of stage dialogue he preferred when he insisted, in 1928, that, in opposition to the artificiality of 'este mundillo de bastidores', genuine theatre is 'diálogo y vida'.[76]

Grice's theory of conversational implicatures is one of a number of areas in discourse studies that offer productive approaches to theatre dialogue. While we have already considered the functional accounts of utterance sequences in conversational interactions, a related view of utterances performing actions of some sort that has attracted considerable interest among critical commentators on the theatre has been touched on only briefly. Speech act theory, as developed in directions mapped out by the linguistic philosophers J.L. Austin and J.R. Searle, concentrates not so much on interactive moves and strategies in conversational exchanges as on the way that, when we produce utterances, we perform, directly or indirectly, actions of one sort or another, such as issuing commands, requests and proposals, making threats, promises or predictions, asserting, disclosing, thanking, commending, deploring and so on.

Two related aspects of this model of language use have been of particular interest both to linguists and to commentators on theatrical texts. One has to do with the way speech acts are usually performed not explicitly but through utterances that have the form of one class of act but are meant to have the force of another. That is to say, using Searle's terminology, when 'the primary illocutionary point differs from the literal illocutionary point'.[77] The other area of interest is in the particular conditions necessary for the successful performance (and interpretation) of different sorts of speech act. Since the first would regard all utterances as acts, and thus allows performed dialogue to be regarded as a series of interrelated linguistic events constitutive of dramatic action, and the second has to do with evaluating sincerity, authenticity and

[76] Dougherty, *Un Valle-Inclán olvidado*, p. 69.
[77] *Expression and Meaning*, p. 34.

legitimacy in terms of psychological states, interpersonal relations and social-institutional roles, it is easy to understand the high hopes placed in speech act theory as a methodological break-through in theatre studies. In particular, the theory seemed to provide a convenient link between textual detail and the broader thematic trends with which critical interpretation of drama is inevitably concerned.

Unsurprisingly, some very strong claims have been made for the theory's explanatory power. One influential critic has characterized it as the key to 'a mode of praxis which sets in opposition the different personal, social and ethical forces of the dramatic world', and another, with a particular interest in its applications to Hispanic drama, enthuses that 'speech act principles have such broad applicability that it can be scary to experience their explanatory power'.[78] The attitude adopted here to the concept of actions done with words is that it is useful but should be used with care. In particular, the linguistic-pragmatics approach developed by Austin and Searle seems, in practice, to be somewhat limited in scope, centred on individualistic, intention-based notions of meaning rather than embedded social and cultural processes, and on the production and reception of individual utterances rather than on on-going interactive exchanges. On the one hand there is a certain danger of reductionism (characterizing passages of dialogue in terms of taxonomies of illocutionary acts and limiting contextual constraints on utterances to the application of constitutive rules of one sort or another). On the other, the risk is one of encouraging somewhat over-generalized assertions about the relationship between language and life. For example, the judgement on *A secreto agravio, secreto venganza* that 'Calderón makes it blindingly apparent that what words do isn't the creation of the *individual* who speaks them'

[78] The first quotation is from Keir Elam's influential *The Semiotics of Theatre and Drama* (1980), cited in Sandy Petrey, *Speech Acts and Literary Theory* (London: Routledge, 1990), p. 87; the second is from Petrey himself, p. 101. Petrey summarizes the debate in the 1980s among North American literary critics as to the performative dimension of language, and provides a useful review of the essays collected in the volume on speech acts in Hispanic drama edited by Elias Rivers (see n. 80).

might well strike us as begging more questions than it answers.[79] Similarly, simply to count the explicit directives in Bernarda's language at different stages of *La casa de Bernarda Alba,* treating their frequency as a straightforward indicator of changes in her outlook, is to assume that utterances such as the furiously vengeful '¡matadla!' in the episode of the apprehended infanticide occupy the same functional category as the politely insincere 'espérate mujer' at the end of the visit of her neighbour Prudencia.[80]

The humorous hedge around the claim, in the same collection, that 'except for making love, killing and dying, the story of *La Celestina* is a story of speech acts'[81] seems, on closer examination, little more than an acknowledgment of the fact the work is in dialogue form, and, not uncommonly for its period, displays a certain reflexive concern with its own rhetoric. The analysis goes on to take a rather narrowly theoretical view (centred on the conditions for performing commissives) of Melibea's initial rejection of Calisto's overtures, postulating the transformation of a promise, 'igual galardón te daré yo, si perseveras' into a threat, 'la paga será tan fiera cual merece tu loco atrevimiento'.[82] It is just as plausible, however, to regard the exchanges as a recognizable conversational routine, a set of moves in a piece of verbal fencing often encountered in both theatrical and real life dialogues of this sort. The following two examples show the principal female character in Valle-Inclán's *Divinas palabras* using exactly the same strategy of a preliminary move (or feint) that consists of misleadingly (that is, ambiguously) hinting at acceptance of her interlocutor's arguments, then following this up by a forceful repudiation of them:

---

[79] Petrey, *Speech Acts*, p. 93.

[80] See Janis Ozimek-Maier, 'Power Plays in La casa de Bernarda Alba', in Elias Rivers (ed.), *Things Done With Words: speech acts in Hispanic drama* (Newark, Delaware: Juan de la Cuesta, 1984), pp. 73-84 (at p. 83).

[81] Inés Azar, 'Self, Responsibility, Discourse: an introduction to speech act theory', in Rivers, *Things Done with Words,* pp. 1-13 (at p. 6).

[82] See Azar, 'Self, Responsibility, Discourse', pp. 7-8. The passage from *La Celestina* is quoted by Azar from the text edited by Dorothy S. Severin (Madrid: Alianza, 1978), I, pp. 46-47.

EL CIEGO DE GONDAR. Y verás tu provecho si te pones en un acuerdo conmigo.
MARI-GAILA. De acuerdo ya estamos, salvo que tú llames acuerdo al dormir juntos, y eso de mi no lo esperes.

SÉPTIMO MIAU. Usted no querrá mi muerte.
MARI-GAILA. Ni la de usted ni la de nadie. ¡Demonio fuera! ¡No me pase usted el brazo!
SÉPTIMO MIAU. ¿Tiene usted cosquillas?
MARI-GAILA. Sí, las tengo. ¡Estése quieto![83]

The fact that Mari-Gaila is by no means as virtuously-inclined as the young Melibea, and, indeed, where the second passage is concerned, is on the point of agreeing to sexual intimacy, by no means invalidates the comparison. The eventual acceptance of Calisto as a lover is prefigured, as it were, by the use of a manoeuvre often encountered in flirtatious exchanges.

An analysis of a brief piece of dialogue along speech-act lines may give some idea of the advantages and drawbacks of the concept: the following extract is the closing words of *¿Para cuándo son las reclamaciones diplomáticas?* One of the characters tactfully leaves the room as the other, his employer, answers the telephone:

DON HERCULANO. ¿Estás sola? ¿Te veré esta noche? ¿Por qué me martirizas, cielito lindo?[84]

Since this is a telephone conversation the audience has only one side of the talk-exchange to go on, and, there is no explicit information as to the identity of the person on the other end of the line. Nevertheless, no one will have difficulty in working out that, of the series of questions produced by Don Herculano, only the first qualifies as a genuine request for information. In terms of illocutionary point or force, the utterances which follow it count

---

[83] Ramón del Valle-Inclán, *Divinas palabras*, ed. L. Iglesias Feijoo (Madrid: Espasa-Calpe, 1991), pp. 216-17 and p. 259.

[84] *¿Para cuándo son las reclamaciones diplomáticas?*, in Ramón del Valle-Inclán, *Martes de Carnaval,* 4th edition (Madrid: Espasa-Calpe, 1977), pp. 231-43.

respectively as a request and a complaint. The audience will also probably notice that interrogatives of any sort, let alone those functioning as requests, are uncharacteristic of Don Herculano's speech (indeed the only previous occasions of use have been to demand specialized information from his subordinate). The conditions for successful utterance of questions that are relevant here include the presumption that Don Herculano does not know and has good reasons for wanting to know whether his interlocutor is alone or not and whether it will be possible to visit her that night. In addition, we might note that '¿por qué me …' followed by a transitive verb in the second person counts as one of the forms that, in Searle's view, 'become conventionally established as standard idiomatic forms for indirect speech acts',[85] in this instance a complaint or protest at unfriendly behaviour.

Speech act theory proper, however can only take us only so far in interpreting these utterances, and accounting for the humorous disparity of their effect.[86] One reason for this is that the theory encourages too exclusive a focus on the intentionality of utterances, while, in fact, readers or spectators of fictional dialogue are expected to scrutinize the linguistic behaviour of characters not only for intentional meanings but also for unintended ones. Indeed, such a dual mode of interpretation is applied by Graciela Reyes in her analysis of another well-known promise in *La Celestina* (Melibea's 'más haré por tu doliente, si menester fuere, en pago de lo sufrido') precisely to demonstrate the limitations of approaches that take account only of consciously intended inferences. The fascination of the episode—its literary merit, as it were—stems from a disturbing ambiguity as to whether the girl is aware of the extent of commitment the wording of her promise suggests. Her words 'nos

---

[85] *Expression and Meaning*, p. 49.

[86] It is interesting to note that attempts by theorists such as Ferrara to expand the scope of 'classical' speech act theory to cover substantial utterance sequences end up regarding their meaning as determined by far broader, socio-cultural constraints, such as 'sus relaciones con otros dominios de la acción sometida a reglas'. See A. Ferrara, 'Condiciones de adecuación para secuencias enteras de actos de habla', in María-Teresa Julio and Ricardo Muñoz (eds), *Textos clásicos de pragmática* (Madrid: Arco, 1998), pp. 41-65 (at p. 65).

parecen imprudentes porque traicionan [...] un interés por Calisto que parece estar fuera de su propio control y del que quizás ella no tenga conciencia', and as a consequence of this ambiguity a number of tragically ironic effects are set in train.[87]

In any case, as early as the mid-eighties it was becoming apparent that 'there are some compelling reasons to think that Speech Act Theory may slowly be superseded by much more complex, multifaceted approaches to the functions that utterances perform'.[88] In analyzing stage dialogue, in particular, we also need to take account of other categories of actions done through words of the sort recognized in conversation analysis and interactional sociolinguistics. At one level we need to take due account of such actions as turn-taking, interrupting, pausing, reformulating, initiating new topics, signalling attentiveness and so on; and at another we need to recognize more complex strategies such as being polite by mitigating acts of imposition (or going ahead and openly performing them anyway) and higher-level language events such as telling a joke, describing an experience, reciting a formula, and so on, none of which can easily be categorized as speech acts in terms of single utterances and the intention behind them. Secondly, it is important to bear in mind that the functional meaning of an utterance is often not pre-given, but is acquired or negotiated in context. This is particularly the case with indirect speech acts, since 'illocutionary force is conveyed as an inference the addressee is expected to make from the literal sense of the expression and the mutually assumed context in which it is uttered'.[89] Thus Don Herculano's '¿Estás sola?' in the piece of dialogue we began by considering is clearly a pre-sequence to asking something the response to which would be compromising if overheard, and '¿Por qué me martirizas, cielito lindo?', to be relevant, must be his reaction to an evasive reply to his '¿te veré esta noche?'. Whatever the particular speech-act configuration of each utterance, in fact, the

[87] Graciela Reyes, *La pragmática lingüística* (Barcelona: Montesinos, 1990), pp. 57-61.
[88] Levinson, *Pragmatics*, p. 278.
[89] Green, *Pragmatics*, p. 110.

piece of dialogue as a whole is readily identifiable as a set of ritualized moves appropriate to an illicit liaison, expressed with a wheedling sentimentality likely to reinforce the audience's scornful attitude to a character already known to be a moral hypocrite.

Another clear example of the need to locate speech acts within the constraints of other discourse functions is provided by the following exchange between a mother and her young daughter from the third act of Valle-Inclán's *Cara de Plata*:

> LA SACRISTANA. ¿Quieres tú echar un trago Ginera?
> LA BIGARDONA. Luego los mozos me sienten el aliento.[90]

The humour here derives not simply from the unexpected revelation (through a prediction) of the girl's plans for the evening, but equally from the discrepancy (to which she herself is oblivious) between her rustic, free-and-easy sexual mores and her politely decorous gesture of refusal. Her reply, that is, by virtue of giving a reason, can be identified as having the dual function of declining an offer and simultaneously apologizing for doing so.

Speech act theory, then, and in particular the concept of the illocutionary force of utterances, can be a useful and flexible means of explaining how we interpret what we hear and read, especially if it is combined with other discourse theories that treat language use as agency. One point to bear in mind is that a speech act typically has more than one function. The concept should envisage not only that a speaker 'is doing something with words', but also that a speaker 'is doing more than one thing at once with words'.[91] This notion is particularly important where imaginatively scripted speech is concerned, and mappings of multiple functions on to a single form are the essence of good theatre dialogue. The whole question, in fact, of the various discourse approaches that might be taken to dialogue—turn management, politeness strategies and forms of address, ideational patterns, speech acts, and so forth—can all be subsumed in broader notions of the importance of context and

---

[90] Ramón del Valle-Inclán, *Cara de plata*, ed. A. Risco (Madrid: Espasa-Calpe, 1992), p. 187.

[91] Schiffrin, *Approaches to Discourse*, p. 91.

inference in the determination of function. Whether we attend a theatre performance or read the text of a play, an important part of our activity consists of forming judgements about its characters. From their actions and words we both infer the meanings they intend and infer things that they might not even intend us to realize. Both in the theatre and in real life we use informed observation of people's (or characters') behaviour both to help us to work out what they are suggesting (as opposed to what they actually say) and to draw our own conclusions as to their motives and preoccupations. It is worth investigating in more detail the principles that guide audiences in making such judgements by considering their operation in a concrete example, the short play of Valle-Inclán already touched on.

The one-act (or rather, one-scene) piece *¿Para cuándo son las reclamaciones diplomáticas?* offers a particularly useful opportunity for analysing Valle's mature dramatic techniques. While the work has not attracted a great deal of critical attention, it is invariably accorded the status of an 'esperpentillo', that is, an example in miniature of the plays that systematically exploit an aesthetic of the grotesque.[92] The short piece introduces a number of topics and treatments found in Valle's full-scale 'esperpentos' and thus presents some central features of the genre in a conveniently well-defined form. The setting and development of the situation is reminiscent of the seventh scene of *Luces de Bohemia*, in which a group of 'modernista' writers attempt to get the editor of a newspaper to intervene on behalf of the imprisoned Max Estrella, and which turns into a satirical treatment of the cynical bombast of leading Spanish politicians and their journalistic cronies ('el Congreso es una gran redacción y cada redacción un pequeño congreso' a character proudly remarks).[93] Newspaper editors' cringingly power-sensitive readiness to compromise their duty to inform is similarly exposed in the sixth scene of *La hija del capitán*,

[92] Rodolfo Cardona's earlier account of this play as an 'esperpentillo olvidado' is strongly endorsed in Manuel Aznar, 'Esperpento e historia en *¿Para cuándo son las reclamaciones diplomáticas?*', in Manuel Aznar and Juan Rodríguez (eds), *Valle-Inclán y su obra* (Barcelona: Associació d'Idees, 1995), pp. 565-78.
[93] *Luces de Bohemia*, p. 102.

and the admiration of conservative Spain for Germany, evident in the polarization of opinion between 'aliadófilos' and 'germanófilos' during the First World War, is shown to continue unabated both in *¿Para cuándo...?* and *Los cuernos de Don Friolera* (in one episode of the latter play the Spanish military's strong approval of duelling is backed up by the observation that it is a custom retained in 'Alemania, pueblo de una superior cultura') [94].

Published in a literary weekly in 1922,[95] *¿Para cuándo...?* is set in the office of a provincial newspaper 'El abanderado de las Hurdes'. Although the work does not seem to offer much scope for complexity of discourse structure (the action consists simply of a discussion between two characters, the paper's proprietor, Don Herculano Cacodoro, and its editor, Don Serenín, on fleshing out an idea the former has for an article), it is worth noting, nevertheless, that there is some variation in levels of communication and participant roles. The main categories are:

> Basic-level dialogue: characters exchange information, offer their own views and experiences and attempt to get the other to do or believe certain things.
> Meta-commentary: (a) one character comments on the form or meaning of the other's utterance; (b) both characters comment on what third parties have said or written, and on projected utterances (the wording of the projected article).
> Absent addressee: a character talks on the telephone to an interlocutor who cannot be seen or heard.
> Meta-theatrical language: the author, through the 'acotaciones', communicates information about the characters and their world to directors, performers, and other interested parties, such as readers of the play's text.

The brief telephone conversation has already been considered, and we will shortly return to the question of the 'acotaciones'. Where meta-commentary is concerned, however, it is probably worth making it clear at once that this is not a case of giving a pretentious label to the feedback mechanisms that are a regular feature of most

[94] *Martes de Carnaval* (1990), p. 203.
[95] *España*, 329, 15 julio 1922. See Aznar Soler, *Esperpento*, p. 573, note 1.

conversations. The following exchanges are by no means an isolated example of the complexly allusive—and subversive—effects Valle can achieve through this device:

> DON HERCULANO. Yo soy un político de la derecha, un pensador de la derecha, un patriota de la derecha.
> DON SERENÍN. Como que la izquierda sólo hace falta en el toreo.
> DON HERCULANO. No sea usted chabacano.
> DON SERENÍN. Lo he dicho sin querer. Vengo del teatro.[96]

The precise nature of Don Herculano's brainwave itself does not emerge until half-way through the scene: Don Herculano has noticed a certain similarity between the technique used in the recent murder of the German democratic politician, Walter Rathenau, and the method employed by the assassins of Eduardo Dato in Spain the previous year. (In this respect, those familiar with *Los Cuernos de Don Friolera* will recall that in the seventh scene the smuggler Curro Cadenas cynically adduces, as evidence of the spread of progressive ideas in Spain, the fact that 'por de pronto, ya le han dado mulé a Dato'.)[97] Consequently, the newspaper's owner argues, the technologically and culturally advanced Germans can be said to have paid Spain the compliment of imitating her techniques, a form of flattery, or 'homenaje', the proposed article will patriotically acknowledge:

> Reconozco que han desplegado una técnica muy perfeccionada los canallas que asesinaron al pobre Don Eduardo. Alemania noblemente acaba de reconocerlo en el asesinato de Rathenau. La actitud alemana adoptando para el asesinato de sus grandes hombres la técnica hurdana, nos fuerza a un acto de agradecimiento.[98]

This sort of absurdly para-logical argument as to the state of the nation is frequently heard in Valle's later plays. What is interesting is that is it is as often heard from ironically critical commentators as from blimpish right-wingers. If we disregard the occasional

[96] *Para cuándo...?*, p. 239.
[97] *Martes de Carnaval* (1990), p. 179.
[98] *¿Para cuándo...?*, pp. 233-34.

attitude-revealing formulation such as 'canallas' and 'el pobre Don Eduardo', the cynically egregious assertions of Don Herculano and his crony are not fundamentally dissimilar in nature to the ironic banter of Don Gay and Max Estrella in the second scene of *Luces de Bohemia*:

> DON GAY. Si España alcanzase un más alto concepto religioso, se salvaba.
> MAX. ¡Recémosle un Réquiem! Aquí los puritanos de conducta son los demagogos de la extrema izquierda.[99]

The point is, of course, that the audience is fully aware that while Don Gay and Max do not intend their remarks to be taken entirely seriously, but are rather engaging in the fanciful exaggeration characteristic of witty conversations, Don Herculano believes his assertions to be plausible. The question of his seriousness, or sincerity, however, is not completely straightforward. The main objective is to produce patriotic rhetoric that will convince his newspaper's readers; thus the question of whether he believes his own arguments or not is, in an important sense, irrelevant. Both his claim that Rathenau had been a traitor to his country's ideals and 'simpatizante con las ideas bolcheviques' and his application to Dato's assassins of a distorted version of the ideas of Concepción Arenal, a well-known—if no longer living—campaigner for penal reform,

> [...] abominemos el delito, pero reconozcamos el mérito de nuestros delincuentes, cuyas inteligencias, encaminadas desde la niñez por santos principios, hubieran, acaso, dado días de gloria a la Patria.[100]

could derive equally from crass ignorance or informed cynicism. Even when it is clear that Don Herculano knows the truth, he does not scruple to misrepresent it:

---

[99] Ramón del Valle-Inclán, *Luces de Bohemia*, ed. A. Zamora Alonso (Madrid: Espasa-Calpe, 1993), p. 62.
[100] *¿Para cuándo...?*, p. 239.

DON HERCULANO. ¿Doña Concepción Arenal de dónde era?
DON SERENÍN. De La Coruña.
DON HERCULANO. Pregunto si era de la derecha.
DON SERENÍN. Lo dudo.
DON HERCULANO. Diga usted que lo era.[101]

Whether the audience is meant to doubt Don Herculano's perspicacity as much as his sincerity—and often, in the 'esperpentos', characters are presented as hapless puppets manipulated by their own ideological attitudes and beliefs—it is clear that the basis for scepticism is to be found in contextual knowledge, both of the specific dramatic situation (the relationship between the characters, the purpose of their discussion, and so forth) and of issues and events in the 'real world' outside the theatre. The contextual frame, in this sense, is that of European politics in the turbulent aftermath of the First World War, viewed from the perspective of a relatively backward country—a perspective neatly established by locating the newspaper in Las Hurdes, one of Spain's most impoverished regions, and consistently using this term, or the adjective 'hurdano' rather than 'España' or 'español' (as in Don Herculano's claim that the Kaiser once referred to him as 'el primer hurdano').

The main reason however, for raising here the issue of what attitude the play's audience is meant to adopt to what the characters say and the assumptions behind their words, is that it offers a convenient starting-point for investigating the intuition that, in this piece as with the later theatre in general, Valle's most consistent strategy is to exploit the contradictions and tensions inherent in various types of verbal and dramatic irony. In theatrical dialogue as a whole ironic effects tend to produce in the audience a sense of complicity with the author, and a heightened awareness of the play and its characters as invented artefacts. It is the systematic creation of such 'distanced' awareness through strikingly ironic effects, I would argue, that is central to the aesthetic of the 'esperpento'.

Verbal irony can be thought of in simplified terms as meaning the opposite of what is literally said, while dramatic irony could be

---

[101] *¿Para cuándo...?*, p. 240.

broadly defined as an effect produced when the audience knows something a character does not. Neither of these definitions, however, captures the scope of the uncertainty and tension between different contexts and points of view that is typically involved. The approach adopted here is to regard irony not as a rhetorical figure or a matter of sentence semantics, but as a term covering various kinds of communication in which the speaker conveys a thought or utterance that is attributed to someone else, and at the same time conveys a distanced or sceptical attitude toward it.[102] Such a view of irony in verbal art is broadly in line with the approach to irony, based originally on the distinction between use and mention, developed in the mid-eighties by Sperber and Wilson as part of Relevance theory.[103] Although this account has recently been slightly modified,[104] the main lines continue to be valid. In the convenient summing up of Torres Sánchez, what is involved is an echoing of words or thoughts:

> Ironizar sería producir un enunciado utilizándolo no como 'uso' (para hablar de la realidad), sino como 'mención' (para hablar de él), y significar la distancia que se toma al respecto. [...] Todas las ironías se interpretan como menciones que tienen un carácter de eco: eco más o menos lejano, de pensamiento o de palabras, reales o imaginararios, atribuidos o no a individuos determinados.[105]

Where verbal art is concerned, of course, there are obvious aesthetic reasons for limiting the incidence of verbatim repetitions of immediately-preceding utterances. Ironic echoing in fictional and theatre dialogue, therefore, more often takes the form of a sly challenge to the assumptions behind what has just been said, as in the mocking response of a character in the second act of *Divinas*

---

[102] See Fabb, *Linguistics and Literature*, p. 263.
[103] See D. Sperber and D. Wilson, 'Irony and the Use-Mention Distinction' in Steven Davis (ed.), *Pragmatics: A Reader* (Oxford: Oxford University Press: 1991), pp. 550-563.
[104] See Sperber and Wilson, *Relevance*, pp. 237-43.
[105] M.A. Torres Sánchez, *Aproximación pragmática a la ironía verbal* (Cádiz: Universidad de Cádiz, 1999), p. 75.

palabras to the protestations of a supposed pilgrim that his only sustenance is the stone he carries to use as a pillow:

> EL PEREGRINO. Tres días llevo sin tocar sustento.
> EL CIEGO DE GONDAR. ¿Indigestado?[106]

A similar strategy lies behind Max Estrella's tongue-in-cheek exaggeration of the crassly sentimental view the Minister has just expressed of the benefits of a penurious bohemian life-style in the eighth scene of *Luces de Bohemia*:

> El MINISTRO. ¡Cómo te envidio el humor!
> MAX. El mundo es mío, todo me sonríe, soy un hombre sin penas.[107]

In fictional and performance discourse, however, and while it is important for dialogue to reveal the contrasting viewpoints and objectives that make for situational tension, irony goes beyond the echoic challenges in paired utterances of the type just considered. Indeed, in the theatre, the dissociated attitude of scepticism, amusement or disapproval manifested as irony is typically encountered in situations where the contextual information possessed by one character is less than that possessed by other characters, or the audience. Dramatic irony is thus an instance of a sceptical attitude not so much on the part of one character toward the opinions of another (or toward those of a certain type of person, or conventional wisdom), but on the part of an author toward the utterances of one of his creations, inviting the audience to see that character's thoughts as stemming from a cognitively defective point of view. In terms of Gricean implicatures, we could say that irony arises when the author flouts a maxim, as it were, by putting in the mouth of a character words that fail to match the cognitive or normative expectations of readers or spectators. Thus dramatic irony is not essentially dissimilar to verbal irony, since what is involved in both cases is the critical subsuming of one context of

---

[106] *Divinas palabras*, p. 222.
[107] *Luces de Bohemia*, p. 115.

utterance—the fictional or staged speech-situation—in another whose participants have superior knowledge.

Stage directions, as Valle uses them, represent a particularly direct form of ironic commentary. Their distinctive quality—and this is one of the reasons, no doubt, why they are so frequently cited in critical interpretations of the plays—is that they deliberately invite the readers of the text to share the author's more comprehensive point of view, and regard the subordinate frame of the characters and their concerns in a relatively detached and sceptical way. For readers of the text of the play (and, to a considerable extent, it could be argued, for audiences at a performance of it) an effect of this sort is achieved by the appearance of Don Herculano's office in *¿Para cuándo...?* even before a character has opened his mouth:

> Paredes patrióticas listadas de azafrán y pimentón. Estantería con ramplonas encuadernaciones catalanas. Retratos de celebridades: políticos, cupletistas y toreros. Los pocos que saben firmar han dejado su autógrafo. El de Don Antonio Maura tiene una cruz.[108]

While the joke about literacy (and subsequent detailed descriptions of ornaments and furnishings) seem to be geared to textual reading rather than the practicalities of stage 'decoración', the main point of the description is the overall impression given of ostentatiously patriotic bad taste. A similar overlay of literary detail on a basic impression can be found in the description that follows of the peremptory summons of the newspaper's editor:

> Don Herculano toca el timbre: tres llamadas y un repique. El toque de botasillas para Don Serenín.

Whatever fancifully evocative wording the author chooses to use (the allusion is to the cavalry signal to saddle horses), an underlying point is made, by the action itself, that the editor is at Don Herculano's beck and call. A similar insight into Don Herculano's character is later provided by the gesture (again imaginatively

[108] *¿Para cuándo...?*, p. 235.

worded) of pausing to look at himself in the mirror and give his moustache a twirl before presenting his momentous idea.

The inclusion in Valle's stage directions of material for the benefit of textual readers clearly encourages an ironic sharing with the author of a distanced or dissociated attitude to the content of the representation. Such distancing can be seen, however as a special instance of the way dramatic irony is created by contextualized dialogue. When what is said creates consciousness of superior knowledge, irony is produced, whether it is a relatively simple case of awareness that one character knows more than another, or whether it involves awareness of privileged access, as a spectator, to the sum of all the characters' information and to the overall communicative designs of the author. It is this consciousness of epistemic discrepancy that we call dramatic irony, blocking empathetic absorption in or identification with characters and action, and replacing such responses with an awareness of and complicity in the author's plans.

In this way the audience's attention is inevitably drawn to the doubled structure of performance discourse; to see the ironic point of a situation is to become reflexively aware of attending, as spectators, to a constructed fiction that reflects an overall authorial design. The creation of this sort of ironic awareness—and self-awareness—which constitutes one of the strengths of the dialogue in *¿Para cuándo...?* depends, of course, on encouraging the audience right from the start to take an evaluative and potentially sceptical view of the talk on stage. It is worth briefly considering the means through which such a critical orientation is brought about in the opening exchanges of the play.

The effect produced when the expressed plans and intentions of a character are remembered by the audience and judged against the actual outcome is sometimes classed as dramatic irony.[109] There is a good case, however, for seeing the ironic effect as simultaneous rather than delayed. When characters on stage confidently predict the outcomes of their proposed actions, spectators are usually inclined to look for clues as to their powers of judgement or

[109] See Leith, *The Power of Address*, p. 76.

possession of the attributes necessary to achieve their objectives, and are quick to draw their own conclusions when such qualities appear to be lacking. Thus, even without the inferences to be drawn from the décor of Don Herculano's office, there are aspects of the opening exchanges that will predispose an audience to take a sceptical view of the characters and their words. Don Serenín's exaggerated praise of his employer's intellectual capacities, for instance, certainly suggests his own insincerity. In addition, however, Don Herculano's immodest acceptance of such obvious flattery can only raise our doubts as to his powers of discernment and shrewdness of judgement well before he reveals his 'great idea':

DON HERCULANO. ¡Tengo una idea, Don Serenín!
DON SERENÍN. ¡Es usted indefatigable!
DON HERCULANO. ¡Una gran idea!
DON SERENÍN. ¡Lo son todas las de usted!
DON HERCULANO. ¡Ésta es colosal![110]

This self-professed great communicator, in his enthusiasm for his plan (or because he is completely unfamiliar with the concept of self-deprecation) mistakes the meaning of a conventional metaphor for authorial modesty (much as Colonel Pancho Lamela in *Los cuernos de Don Friolera* is puzzled by the absence of actual blood dripping from the protagonist's hands) and to his subordinate's 'haría falta una pluma mejor cortada' responds 'espere usted a que le exponga mi idea'. After such an opening, few in the audience will take Don Herculano's arguments entirely seriously (a very different matter, of course, to doubting that he intends them to be taken seriously).

A further reason his proposals attract the audience's critical scrutiny is precisely because it is clear no genuine evaluation is permitted in the performed situation; Don Serenín is an economic dependent with no choice but to offer unfailingly favourable comments. One of the basic contradictory effects, in fact, is that Don Serenín's adulatory responses could easily be taken, in a less

[110] *¿Para cuándo...?*, pp. 235-36.

coercive context, as sarcastically ironic. The audience realizes that the expressions understood by Don Herculano as sincere praise could well be interpreted, especially by someone with a realistic estimation of the cogency of the arguments concerned, as inappropriate hyperbole designed to convey the opposite meaning.

This sort of effect—and it makes little difference if we suspect some of the newspaper editor's comments are made tongue-in-cheek—consistently comes down to a question of ambivalence in standards of evaluation. With Don Herculano's claim to have been singled out for praise by the German Emperor, for instance:

> DON HERCULANO. ¡Me llama el primer hurdano!
> DON SERENÍN. ¡Ese puesto se lo reconocen a usted en todas partes![111]

the audience's interpretation of Don Serenín's response in an ironic light derives not only from mistrust of boastfulness in general but also from the realization that not everyone would necessarily be in agreement with the underlying assumption that being 'el primer hurdano' is something to boast about. A similar evaluative ambivalence can be detected in 'rhetorical' questions such as '¿dónde tienen las izquierdas un Vázquez de Mella?',[112] since the presupposition of charismatic qualities possessed by the politician concerned might well strike many members of the contemporary audience as ludicrously ill-founded.

Much of the irony, in fact, derives precisely from the fact that Don Herculano's mode of discourse is argumentational, both in that it is aimed at convincing Don Serenín that the idea for an article is an excellent one, and in that it contains specific examples of the rhetorical strategies that are to be employed in the piece. By and large, one of the ways discourse makes sense to addressees is when it reveals a consistent set of beliefs and objectives on the part of the speaker. Such coherence, however, by no means depends on the discourse being successfully persuasive. Indeed, when speakers

---

[111] *¿Para cuándo...?*, p. 237.
[112] *¿Para cuándo...?*, p. 241.

pursue self-interested goals by appeal to generalized reasons, or by putting forward a line of reasoning that is unsound, we usually understand perfectly well what they are getting at, but maintain a sceptical attitude, often manifested in ironic amusement. Don Herculano, aided and abetted by his editor, frequently demonstrates an ignorance of the standards of evaluation and cultural norms by virtue of which reasons count as valid. His ludicrous attempt to disprove what (in accordance with his own muddled categories) he takes to be a counter-position to arguments in favour of German technological and cultural superiority is a good case in point: 'En la actualidad su técnica no tiene rival. Hablan algunos de que sus mujeres son chatas. ¡Tonterías! ¡Hay chatas que dan el ole!'[113]

The ironic effect of failed argumentation is perhaps more complex than it seems in that, just as the audience can never be quite sure of the real opinions of the obsequious Don Serenín, so it is not always clear whether Don Herculano genuinely holds an idiosyncratic and internally contradictory set of beliefs or whether, as a cynical press baron with political ambitions, he cares little for matters of truth or consistency, but is simply concerned with presenting facts and arguments in ways favourable to his interests and with some sort of veneer—however thin—of plausibility. For all the humorous exaggeration of the piece, there is a certain element of serious criticism in the ironical disjunction between the audience's familiarity with definitions and explanations that represent a reasonable account of the world and its ways, and the absurd word-spinning of Don Herculano and his fawning crony. Patriotism, in the Spain of the early nineteen-twenties, is shown to be the first choice rather than the last resort of the scoundrel, but there is also, perhaps, a warning here that the detachment of language from reality is not just a symptom of a degenerate political system, but can also be a means of perpetuating it.

---

[113] *¿Para cuándo...?*, p. 238.

2. POETRY AS UTTERANCE: ANTONIO MACHADO

2.1 A CONDEMNED BUILDING: UTTERANCES AND ADJECTIVES IN 'EL HOSPICIO'

But observe
the oppressive weight
of the squat edifice![1]

Following the method indicated in the introductory chapter, this analysis of what is widely recognized as one of Antonio Machado's most successful poems builds on intuitions as to the function of certain features of its linguistic form to raise more generalized issues of interpretation. As with the analysis of Neruda's 'Explico algunas cosas', the emphasis will be on poetry as interactive discourse and on the means by which the poet establishes a situation of address and sustains a communicative relationship with the reader. When Machado asserts, in 'Retrato', that his poetry is a conversation 'con el hombre que siempre va conmigo',[2] he is not simply alluding to his constant alertness to what has been called 'that most intimate, congenial and attentive listener whom we carry beneath our skins'.[3] He is also insisting on his inherently dialogic concept of poetic language as utterances produced in accord with a contract of communication and oriented to a 'tú' (whether such an

---

[1] From William Carlos Williams, 'The Jasmine Lightness of the Moon', in George Lakoff and Mark Turner, *More than Cool Reason: a field guide to poetic metaphor* (Chicago: University of Chicago Press, 1989), pp. 140-41.

[2] Antonio Machado, *Campos de Castilla*, edited by Geoffrey Ribbans (Madrid: Cátedra, 1989), p. 100.

[3] R.H. Smith, quoted in R.A. York, *The Poem as Utterance* (London: Methuen, 1986), p. 7.

interlocutor is envisaged as an inward listener or the reader). It is the intuitive experience of most readers of Machado's work that such a relationship is strongly established. Indeed, especially when compared to his contemporary Juan Ramón Jiménez, who often gives the impression of permitting the reader to share his experiences vicariously, Machado seems to be inviting or even actively engaging in some sort of dialogue. One of the claims, of course, of the approach adopted here is that the means by which such a rapprochement is achieved can be identified and analyzed rather than left as a matter of impressionistic judgement.

'El hospicio', one of the poems to appear in the first (1912) edition of *Campos de Castilla*, provides an exceptionally clear example of the fusion of factual observation with evaluative—aesthetic and moral—response that characterizes the collection as a whole. The first intuition to be tracked down is that without the aid of second person expressions (or even of any form of self-reference) the poet firmly establishes a situation of address and a context of dialogic interaction. This effect is achieved, I would argue, right at the start: 'Es el hospicio, el viejo hospicio provinciano [...]'. As a number of commentators have pointed out, Machado has a tendency to begin poems with (in the words of one of the first to recognize the importance of this device) 'a simple statement based on the verb "to be"';[4] and indeed a number of the poems of *Campos de Castilla* start in this way. Some examples are shown below:

> Es la tierra de Soria árida y fría ('Campos de Soria')
> Mi infancia son recuerdos de un patio de Sevilla ('Retrato')
> El acusado es pálido y lampiño ('Un criminal')
> Es una tarde mustia y desabrida ('Un loco')
> Fue un tiempo de mentira, de infamia ('Una España joven')

Of these initial lines, however, only the last two are at all comparable in linguistic structure to the opening of 'El hospicio'. The real point at issue here, in fact, is not so much the use of the

---

[4] Arthur Terry, *Antonio Machado: Campos de Castilla* (London: Tamesis, 1973), p. 31.

verb 'ser' in itself as its use in combination with ellipsis of the grammatical subject.

Spanish is, of course, one of the so-called 'pro-drop' languages, and ellipsis of the subject pronoun before a verb is normal when the speaker believes the intended referent of the 'missing' pronoun can be straightforwardly deduced by addressees from the context. Indeed, with existential processes encoding weather conditions (as in 'es una tarde mustia', a Spanish reader would no more feel it necessary to speculate as to the identity of the subject than would an English reader of 'it's a damp afternoon' wonder what 'it' referred to. With 'fue un tiempo de mentira' and 'es el hospicio', however, we are dealing with genuine instances of zero anaphora, a device normally used only when the referent is assumed to be straightforwardly recoverable, either because it has recently been mentioned, or because it is something salient in the perceptual environment. As Talmy Givón makes clear, the device is normally used only when there is no danger of ambiguity: 'it is only in the least ambitious processing tasks that one can safely resort to zeros [...] because their lexical identity is already activated'.[5] In both these opening lines, however, there is potential disturbance of communication. The poet, puzzlingly, speaks as if the referent in both cases is topical, that is, as if his readers have just been informed or for some other reason are perfectly well aware what epoch is being characterized and which interesting building is being commented on.

In fact, the effect of treating the problematic reference as straightforwardly assignable is not to weaken the communicative link, but to strengthen it, since the reader is by this means situated as a participant in an already initiated dialogue. To understand how the interactive relationship is cemented in this way, it is worth considering some comments of Roger Fowler on ellipsis in fictional dialogue:

---

[5] Talmy Givón, *Functionalism and Grammar* (Amsterdam: Benjamin, 1995), p. 386.

> Ellipsis is a very cohesive device in dialogue, a guarantee that the speakers are concentrating together on a single topic and on the background knowledge relevant to the topic. [...] Ellipsis suggests intimacy, intensity.[6]

Use of ellipsis then, in general, signals close communicative involvement of the speaker with the hearer, and the particular effect achieved in the opening line of 'El hospicio' is to invite us, as readers, to put ourselves in the position of a companion of the poet in a first-hand situation of utterance. It is as if he were replying to a question, of ours, 'aquel edificio, ¿qué es?', or as if he had just drawn attention to something, '¿ves aquel edificio?'. Similarly, at the start of 'Una España joven', it is as if we are in the middle of a retrospective discussion of the shameful events of 1898 and the poet sums up the general opinion: 'fue un tiempo de mentira, de infamia'.

It is worth pointing out that in using opening strategies of this sort the poet is not simply drawing us in as interlocutors. He is also presuming there is a common point in time and space, a 'here and now, in this place', which he and the reader share, and that there is a common present and future for both. This shared perspective is important, since it allows for judgement and proposals for change rather than mere passive description of what is. We will return to this point, but for the moment, and concentrating now on 'El hospicio', it is better to remain with our intuition that there is an implicit or explicit question to be answered as to the function or nature of a building in view.[7] Our attention has been drawn to some quality or feature that is noteworthy or warrants an explanation. The rest of the poem will be a response to this questioning or expression of curiosity, and the reader is drawn in not merely as a conversational interactant, but as a confidant. Approval or

---

[6] Fowler, *Linguistic Criticism*, p. 63.

[7] It is not easy to determine the precise function and status of a Spanish 'hospicio provinciano' in the first decade of the last century; it seems to have been more or less equivalent to a poor-house, taking in those too old or infirm to maintain themselves. Given the process of rural depopulation, on which Machado comments on more than one occasion, it is possible that a fair proportion might be old people without younger relatives to look after them.

understanding is being sought for comments that will clearly include evaluative judgements rather than being limited to non-committal description.

In the first two stanzas of the poem the moment of recognition, the initial identification of the building, is immediately expanded into a more comprehensive definition. This in turn gives way to further descriptive details, before reaching an exclamatory resting point, inviting the reader to share the poet's strong emotional response to the scene as a whole:

> Es el hospicio, el viejo hospicio provinciano,
> el caserón ruinoso de ennegrecidas tejas
> en donde los vencejos anidan en verano
> y graznan en las noches de invierno las cornejas.
>
> Con su frontón al Norte, entre dos torreones
> de antigua fortaleza, el sórdido edificio
> de grietados muros y sucios paredones,
> es un rincón de sombre eterna. ¡El viejo hospicio![8]

Exclamations of this type, consisting of the naming 'entre admiraciones' of an object or feature of the landscape, frequently make an appearance at key moments in Machado's descriptive poems (and will, indeed, be encountered again in the present one). It is thus worth briefly considering the very relevant comments the poet made, a number of years later, on the use of such interjections in José Moreno Villa's *Colección*.

In Machado's view, one effect of this device is to present material so treated as 'signos de una idea, de una visión mental, que el poeta recomienda a nuestra contemplación admirativa'.[9] Just as importantly, however, especially when the expression concerned is an observed object or landscape, the intention is to draw attention to the characteristic dual polarity of lyrical poetry: the co-presence of the observed object and the poet's emotional response to it, creating a continual tension or oscillation between the alternative

---

[8] Antonio Machado, *Campos de Castilla*, p. 106.

[9] Antonio Machado, *Obras: poesía y prosa*, edited by Aurora de Albornoz and Guillermo de Torre (Buenos Aires: Losada, 1973), p. 908.

perspectives or modes of experience represented by the exclamations '¡maravillosa vista!' and '¡ojos maravillosos!':

> [...] encontramos, como casi siempre en Moreno Villa, su parte interjectiva entre signos de admiración. [...] Surge el asombro del poeta al choque de las cosas—vivas o no—que se le presentan como objectos líricos—de emoción; no de conocimiento—; pero como tales objetos, que estaban allí, donde el poeta los descubre.[10]

The contrast alluded to here between cognition and affective response is probably more a matter of broad principle than of sharply distinguished types of poetic description. In 'El hospicio', even before the ominously universalized 'sombra eterna' and the emotion-filled exclamation is reached, readers will have sensed that the descriptive details can only superficially be interpreted as merely factual evocations of perceptual data. In terms of illocutionary force (that is, the overall discursive action the speaker performs by using the words he does) Machado is not so much asserting that the building shows evidence of structural deterioration as denouncing a state of affairs that is morally, socially, or in some other way seriously wrong. My intuition is that what persuades the reader to interpret this series of descriptive utterances as judgemental in force—the linguistic elements, that is, that function most clearly as contextualization cues,[11] enabling the reader to infer the nature of the indirect speech acts concerned—is the careful choice, combination and positioning of adjectives. The sixteen lines of the poem as a whole contain well over thirty adjectival

---

[10] *Obras*, p. 915.

[11] The concept of contextualization cues—verbal and non-verbal signals functioning to relate what is said to the particular contextual knowledge that enables addressees to make inferences as to, for instance, the illocutionary force of utterances—has been developed in the work of John Gumperz. For a convenient summary, see John Gumperz, 'Contextualization and Understanding', in A. Duranti and C. Goodwin (eds), *Rethinking Context* (Cambridge: Cambridge University Press, 1992), pp. 229-51; for applications to performance discourse, see R. Warner, 'Making Things Clear: contextualization cues and coherence in parallel versions of a popular song', *Bulletin of Hispanic Studies*, LXXV (1998), 109-122.

expressions, and, of these, just two are quantifiers ('dos' and 'algunos'), and only five are qualifiers (prepositional phrases following the noun). The vast majority are thus modifiers that denote a quality or attribute of the noun.

Before analysing in greater detail the use of adjectives in 'El hospicio', it is perhaps worth devoting a little attention to clarifying why an approach based on a view of poetry as contextualized discourse should be concerned with a linguistic category usually considered in terms of sentence-based grammar. Firstly, from a pragmatics perspective, it is worth noting that adjectives often encode marked information. When an object is referred to by a qualified noun, that is, there is a presumption that it differs from the stereotype in a significant way, since marked, prolix or unusual forms 'signal that the described situation is itself unusual or unexpected or has special properties'.[12] This effect can be complicated in Spanish, of course, by the question of adjective position, but the principle remains basically valid. Introducing the nominal group 'el viejo hospicio provinciano' as a reformulation of an expression ('el hospicio') that is devoid of adjectives certainly prods the reader into taking notice.

From the broad viewpoint of language-use as culturally determined, moreover, it is also worth noting that adjectival and adverbial expressions play a particularly important communicative role as carriers of shared values that make subjective self-expression comprehensible and convincing to others. As Jürgen Habermas observes, evaluative expressions have a dual, descriptive-prescriptive content:

> For example, in characterizing an object or situation as splendid, ample, elevating, auspicious, dangerous, forbidding, dreadful, and so forth, we are trying to express a predilection and at the same time justify it, in the sense of making it plausible by appeal to general standards of evaluation that are widespread, at least in our own culture.[13]

---

[12] S. Levinson, *Presumptive Meanings* (Cambridge, Mass.: MIT Press, 2000), p. 6.

[13] Habermas, *The Theory of Communicative Action*, I, p. 92.

Thus the communicative effectiveness of such subjective characterizations depends on addressees, in the framework of a common cultural heritage, recognizing in them their own desires and feelings. Habermas does concede that in innovative poetic language such consensual standards are often placed in abeyance. In Machado's case, however, we should remember that one of the central features of *Campos de Castilla* is precisely the way it is not geared to privatistic expression of more or less hermetic orders of experience, but is consistently and intentionally grounded in widely-shared knowledge, values and communicative conventions.

Machado himself, moreover, was very aware of the poetic and communicative consequences of different modes of adjective use. His claim, in a verse aphorism, that nouns and adjectives were 'accidentes del verbo' (verbs being the class of word said to be most appropriate for conveying experience as temporal flux) is often quoted, together with his remark, in the same notes of 1914 on the use of images in poetry, that 'la poesía clásica en eterno presente, es decir, fuera del tiempo, es esencialmente sustantiva y adjetiva'.[14] It would be a mistake however—and the heavy incidence of adjectives and relative shortage of verbs of 'El hospicio' certainly seems to confirm such a judgement—to assume that an inferior status is assigned to modifiers in Machado's 'gramática lírica'. Machado's observations, on more than one occasion, on the essential difference between what he terms the Homeric type of adjective (for example, 'nave hueca') and expressions that give us 'la sensación viva de un objeto único o el temblor momentáneo de un alma singular' are instructive in this respect.[15] If 'lo inmediato psíquico' is an essential ingredient of successful poetry, so too is coherence. In what is one of his less-celebrated but nevertheless highly effective examples of maritime metaphor, Machado trenchantly points out that communication on the basis of a linguistically-mediated shared world should take precedence over subjective aesthetic prescriptions:

---

[14] *Obras*, pp. 786-87.
[15] *Obras*, p. 784.

¿Está la nave homérica fuera del tiempo y el espacio? Como queráis. Sólo importa a mi propósito hacer constar que todo navegante la reconocerá por suya.

At the same time he refuses to concede that the need to use the referring function of language as a common denominator in a shared world is a serious restraint on expressive capabilities:

El verso helénico, siempre definidor, nada tiene que ver [...] con lo académico o neoclásico. El diamante es frío, pero es obra del fuego.[16]

We have moved somewhat away from stylistic analysis into broader aesthetic areas, but, as it happens, the notion that adjectives can have an important communicative or intersubjective role is strongly supported in the more formally linguistic approach of functional grammar. For M.A.K. Halliday, for instance, there is an interpersonal function associated with one of the two main categories of descriptive adjectives in the nominal group, that of epithets as opposed to classifiers.[17] One convenient way of illustrating the difference between the two types is to return to the opening description of Machado's poem: 'el viejo hospicio provinciano'. In this nominal group, the second of the two adjectives, 'provinciano', functions as classifier, that is, it indicates a particular subclass of the thing in question. The adjective 'viejo', on the other hand, functions as an epithet, in that it indicates some quality attributed to this particular 'hospicio'. Significantly, for the importance of adjectives in invoking a communicative framework of shared values, Halliday notes that the quality indicated by an epithet 'may be an objective property of the thing itself, or the

[16] *Obras*, p. 787. See also *Obras*, p. 909, where Symbolism is criticised its tendency to 'prescindir del adjetivo definidor, del adjetivo homérico'.

[17] Both these terms are used here in the sense in which they are employed in Halliday's functional grammar rather than in other linguistic disciplines. 'Epithet', it should be noticed in particular, is not used here in the sense—as defined in Crystal, *An Encyclopedic Dictionary of Language and Languages*, p. 124—of a characterizing term regularly associated with a noun. For this function I have preferred to use the terms 'standard' or 'conventional' epithet. See Halliday, *An Introduction to Functional Grammar*, pp. 184-86.

speaker's subjective attitude toward it', adding that epithets used with this second function 'represent an interpersonal element in the meaning of the nominal group'.[18] The classifier 'provinciano' is superficially one of rank, but, in 'El hospicio', it also has the contrastive function of making it absolutely clear that the building is not a private one, but has an official, institutional status and function. The epithet 'viejo' immediately hints at a reason for the building not being immediately recognized, suggesting as it does that the ravages of time may have disguised its appearance. There is, of course, already a hint of criticism here; decrepitude is not, we might suspect, an appropriate quality in an institution of care for whose maintenance official entities are responsible.

It is not clear, of course, whether 'viejo' here is meant to be interpreted as experiential or attitudinal in function (where the hint of criticism is concerned, it makes little difference), but the careful characterization of the building should in itself alert the reader—the companion to whom the nature of the building is being explained—to an overall evaluative intention in the use of adjectives. More than once in the course of the poem Machado produces a nominal group that puts one in mind of Halliday's example of a cluster of attitudinal epithets, 'a horrible ugly great lump'.[19] In English, as a rule, epithets precede classifiers, and attitudinal epithets tend to precede experiential ones. In Spanish, however, the question of adjective sequence is further complicated by whether the adjective is pre-posed or post-posed in relation to the noun. The unmarked position for a classifying adjective in Spanish is after the noun (as with 'provinciano' here) but it cannot be assumed that post-posed adjectives are necessarily classifiers, or that pre-posed adjectives always function as epithets. Writers and speakers of Spanish often make use of the option of departing, for stylistic or other reasons, from the standard sequencing of nominal groups, and it is an option of which Machado certainly avails himself in the poem under consideration.

---

[18] Halliday, *An Introduction to Functional Grammar*, p. 185.
[19] Halliday, *An Introduction to Functional Grammar*, p. 184.

The various attempts to establish rules for the position of adjectives in Spanish using a purely sentence-based, morphosyntactical perspective have tended to encounter problems, especially when it comes to accounting for recalcitrant examples of actual usage. In a pioneering essay written almost two decades ago, Flora Klein-Andreu summarized these difficulties and proposed an explanation that takes account of pragmatic constraints. In her model, which involves linking semantic choices to a specific context, hearers and readers derive inferences as to particular contextual meaning from the relationship between attribute and entity (that is, between adjective and noun) in terms of the 'inherentness' or otherwise of the quality described. Starting from default assumptions that post-positioning is associated with a notion of contrast, whereas pre-positioning is non-distinctive, she observes that

> The contrastive [post] positioning can be used to suggest inferences other than distinction of referents—namely emphasis on the characterization. Noncontrastive [pre-] positioning can suggest inferences other than non-distinction—notably opinion.[20]

If we apply these insights to the use of adjectives in 'El hospicio', it becomes possible, for instance to account for the powerful impact of the expression 'un rincón de sombre eterna'. It is precisely through the residual suggestion that there is a class of shadow that is eternal that emphasis is placed on the characterization (using Klein-Andreu's terminology). A very similar effect is achieved in the phrase 'el caserón ruinoso'. On the other hand, while the pre-posing of the adjective in nominal groups such as 'el sórdido

[20] Flora Klein-Andreu, 'Grammar in Style: Spanish adjective placement', in F. Klein-Andreu (ed.), *Perspectives in Syntax* (New York: Academic Press, 1983), pp. 143-79. Klein-Andreu's conclusions are endorsed in Leo Hickey, *Curso de pragmalingüística* (Madrid: Coloquio, 1987), pp. 182 ff. Presupposition constraints on adjective position are also considered in Estrella Montolío's study of Valle-Inclán's literary style (although pre-positioning of one of a pair of adjectives is seen merely as a device 'de carácter artificioso'). See E. Montolío Durán, *Gramática de la caracterización en Valle-Inclán* (Barcelona: PPU, 1992), pp. 28 ff.

edificio' clearly reflects an evaluative (attititudinal) function, other expressions, such as 'ennegrecidas tejas' and 'grietadas muros', which are apparently examples of experiential (that is, 'objective') rather than attitudinal epithets, nevertheless acquire an evaluative quality through association with the underlying metaphorical significance of notions of darkness and decrepitude. It is also worth noting that a greater weight of emphasis is placed on the epithets by the fact that these phrases are worded as nominalizations of the type Halliday terms grammatical metaphor.[21] A more congruent realization would have been a verbal process of the type 'los muros están grietados', evoking the destructive work of time in a straightforward but less suggestive way.[22] Such nuances, it goes without saying, make an important contribution to the effects Machado is able to create in the poem.

The position of an adjective relative to the noun it qualifies cannot, of course, be considered in isolation; the effect achieved is also determined by other elements which may be present (or markedly absent) in the nominal group, such as the definite or indefinite article, indexicals, quantifiers, and additional adjectives or adjectival phrases. Nominal groups themselves, moreover, are embedded in broader syntactical structures. Thus in order to interpret the meaning of adjectives, especially in literary language, an alert reader must take into account a whole panoply of textual variables as well as the pragmatics of descriptions, that is, the

---

[21] See Halliday, *An Introduction to Functional Grammar*, pp. 342-67.

[22] Another point worth mentioning is that the adjective 'antiguo' is one of those ('viejo' and 'triste' are others that appear here) for which, in a sentence-based perspective, a so-called 'change-of-meaning' hypothesis has been proposed to account for the apparent semantic contrast of the post- or pre-positions. In such an approach, 'antigua fortaleza' would be equivalent to the English 'former fortress'. Klein Andreu rejects this model, explaining that while 'antiguo' keeps a basic meaning equivalent to 'of the past', or 'of old', it should be glossed in terms of the 'time of validity' of the assertion. In a naturally-occurring expression such as 'la antigua física de Newton' (mentioned in contrast to Einstein's theories) what is at issue is not that the Newtonian system is no longer regarded as physics, but that it is regarded as out of date. Thus the reader of Machado's poem is expected to infer that the epoch of warfare is now over, and the twin towers are a conspicuous anachronism.

already-mentioned consensus among members of the language community as to the appropriate use of descriptive and evaluative expressions. The final two quatrains of Machado's poem provide a good illustration of the dense connotations epithets can acquire:

> Mientras el sol de enero su débil luz envía,
> Su triste luz velada sobre los campos yermos,
> A un ventanuco asoman, al declinar el día,
> Algunos rostros pálidos, atónitos y enfermos,
>
> A contemplar los montes azules de la sierra;
> o, de los cielos blancos, como sobre una fosa,
> caer la blanca nieve sobre la fría tierra,
> ¡sobre la tierra fría la nieve silenciosa!

In the descriptive details 'los campos yermos' and 'los montes azules' emphasis on the characterization is created by post-posing adjectives that, in context, cannot be interpreted as classifiers. The light falls on all the fields, not on the barren sort exclusively, and it is not a special class of blue-tinged mountains that is picked out, as opposed to others of a different hue. The post-positioning of the adjectives 'yermos' and 'azules' thus strongly emphasizes the unproductiveness of the land and the aloof remoteness of the mountains (the cause of their chromatic distinctiveness for Sorian observers). On the other hand, the pre-posed epithets 'débil', and 'triste' are ambiguously poised between experiential and attitudinal in their function. 'Débil' has a possible metaphorical interpretation as a position (at the opposite end to 'fuerte') on the scale of light intensity, but is retrospectively pulled toward a subjective, evaluative meaning through parallelism ('débil luz…triste luz'), with the more clearly attitudinal term 'triste'.

Interpretation of the significance of positioning becomes more complex, of course, when the nominal group comprises more than one adjectival expression. For instance, the choice of word-order in the phrase 'su triste luz velada' may simply reflect the fact that 'triste' is an inherently more attitudinal epithet than 'velado'. Nevertheless, the post-posing of the latter hints at a classifying function, tentatively suggesting that, in this locality, solar occlusion is so routine a condition that it can be regarded as a sub-category of winter daylight in general. Again, where the first sign of human occupation of the building is concerned, 'asoman / algunos rostros pálidos, atónitos y enfermos', it should go without saying that the powerful effect of the description is in large part due to the post-positioning of all three epithets to give them accumulative force (qualifying, moreover, a reductive meronym, 'rostro', rather than a holonymic term for human individuals).

It is in combination with the prosodic and syntactic organization of the passage as a whole, however, that the full impact of this trio of adjectives is realized. Where syntax is concerned, the first thing to note is that the nominal group in which the adjectives occur constitutes the subject of the main clause of the long and complex sentence with which the poem concludes. The sentence is of the type termed periodic or anticipatory,[23] a structure that, in itself, has the effect of drawing our attention to 'delayed' (or right-shifted) elements. What contributes even more to the overall effect, however, is the fact that the main clause, when we finally get to it, not only starts with the verb, but also has a parenthetical adverbial expression 'al declinar el día' interposed between the verb and its subject. We thus have a syntactical structure expressly designed to intensify the anticipatory effect and strongly highlight the heavily-adjectivized noun-phrase that is the subject of the main clause.

From the prosodic point of view, there is an equally effective coordination of resources to give expressive weight to the string of adjectives. The fact that the nominal group takes up precisely one line of verse means that (as well as the final epithet 'enfermos') the word in initial position, 'algunos', is picked out in relief, thus inviting the reader to interpret it as specially meaningful in some way (perhaps suggesting 'few', 'sporadic', 'unorganized' rather than simply 'not all'). The fact that the verse measure concerned, moreover, is the Spanish alexandrine, a fourteen-syllable line with a

---

[23] In the sense of 'holding up the onset of one or more of the major constituents of the main clause'; see Mick Short, *Exploring the Language of Poems, Plays and Prose* (London: Longman, 1996), pp. 340-41.

marked mid-point caesura, has the effect of giving the final two adjectives, 'atónitos y enfermos', a semi-autonomous status as the constituents of the second hemistich, consolidating even further their claims on the reader's attention. In addition, and despite the risk of taking an analytical step too far, some mention should be made of the connections and analogies set up by rhyme. It is worth pointing out, for example, that in the rhyme-underpinned syntactical parallelism of 'campos yermos' and 'rostros pálidos, atónitos y enfermos', the increase of one post-posed epithet to three has the schematic structure of a basic motif being developed further. This expansion, moreover, is along lines of meaning that are very much in accordance with the main thematic thrust of the poem as a whole.

It should by now be clear that any consideration of the effects achieved by choice and positioning of adjectives in poetry (and certainly in this particular poem) cannot be limited to nuances of meaning within nominal groups, but has to take account of other features of the syntactical and prosodic framework in which the groups themselves are embedded. Only a sample of such effects has been considered, since it would be pedantic to analyze every adjective in the poem, especially since readers should now be in a position to appreciate for themselves what can be achieved through adjective-sequencing. The progressively heavier involvement of adjectives in instances of repetition and parallelism as the poem develops does include one effect, however, that merits some further discussion, since it touches on and can serve to introduce the important question of the use of figurative language in general.

An interesting type of foregrounding is achieved by the superficially surprising inclusion, in the last stanza of a poem in which adjectives are patently chosen with particular care, of a conventional epithet: 'la blanca nieve'. Whiteness is, of course, an inherent quality of snow, and we are clearly dealing with a canonical example of the type of epithet characterized by Machado in a commentary on Symbolism as 'adjetivo definidor'.[24] This is described as an adjective that designates 'lo permanente en objetos varios' and thus has a defining function, in contrast to 'imagenes

[24] *Obras*, p. 909 ff.

estremecidas por una emotividad singular', in which case 'el adjetivo califica'. Both types of adjective—or rather both types of meaning achieved through the use of adjectives—are required for successful poetry ('de ambas intenciones en su empleo necesita la poesía'). It is worth looking again at the last three lines of the poem to allow us to keep in mind the textual environment in which the traditional defining epithet (as we have seen, Machado also refers to it as 'Homeric') is deployed:

> o, de los cielos blancos, como sobre una fosa,
> caer la blanca nieve sobre la fría tierra,
> ¡sobre la tierra fría la nieve silenciosa!

The effects aimed at through choice and positioning of adjectives in these final lines seem rather different than hitherto in the poem. Whereas up to this point we have been dealing with what is principally a description of a building and its natural setting (although, admittedly, there is an evaluative subtext in the decrepitude of the edifice, the passivity of its human inmates, the barrenness of the fields and the feebleness of the light), there is now a perceptible modulation from the careful depiction of perceptual details to an emphasis on the broader psychological and social resonances created by descriptions of the natural environment, especially when they are evoked, as here, through rhythmic and semantic parallelism. What is particularly worth noting is that the effect of this ringing-the-changes on a small set of noun-epithet combinations is to emphasize depictions that model the basic domains of human perception and experience, of the type Lakoff and Johnson term 'experiential gestalt'.[25] At this point it seems better to move the focus of analysis from combinations of individual lexical items—nouns and adjectives—to higher-level concepts such as metaphors and symbols. Similarly, and while continuing to use features of 'El hospicio' as illustration, the focus will be broadened to include other texts.

---

[25] G. Lakoff and M. Johnson, *Metaphors We Live By* (Chicago: University of Chicago Press, 1980), p. 117.

2. 2 THE POWER OF METAPHOR

A convenient point to start the analysis is with some perceptive remarks by the Irish critic Frank O'Connor on a technique of descriptive writing that seems to be put to use by Machado in the final section of 'El hospicio':

> There is a deliberate repetition of certain key words, sometimes with a slight alternation of form [...] which produces a peculiar effect that is not the result of precise observation but of a deliberately produced hypnosis.[26]

This way of writing has, for the Irish critic, to do with creating a hidden structure of metaphor aimed at bringing out inner meaning, the mysterious effect of which he likens to the dissociated metaphor of dreams.[27] One example he particularly notes is that of silently falling snow, 'death's symbol'. The passage he has in mind is not, of course, 'El hospicio' (although the final stanza of Machado's poem could certainly be used to support his observation that 'whenever the emotion overflows, it is represented by inversion and repetition')[28] but an approximately contemporaneous piece of writing that has become one of the most celebrated in modern English literature. The closing paragraph of James Joyce's *The Dead* is, for O'Connor, the culminating articulation of the metaphorical hints, throughout the story, around the theme of current individuals and institutions lacking 'those qualities of humanity, of hospitality [...] that belonged to an older day', the feeling that 'all love and beauty and grace are with the dead'.[29]

> It was falling in every part of the dark central plains, on the treeless hills, falling softly on the Bog of Allen, and further westward, softly falling into the dark, mutinous Shannon waters. It was falling too on every part of the lonely churchyard, on the hill where Michael Furey lay buried. It lay

---

[26] Frank O'Connor, *The Mirror and the Roadway: a study of the modern novel* (London: Hamish Hamilton, 1957), p. 296.
[27] O'Connor, *The Mirror and the Roadway,* p. 301.
[28] *The Mirror and the Roadway*, p. 303.
[29] *The Mirror and the Roadway*, p. 300.

> thickly drifted on the crooked crosses and headstones [...] the snow falling faintly, like the descent of their last end, upon all the living and the dead.[30]

While there is a certain broad thematic similarity, it should go without saying there is no question here of suggesting any direct influence or even any common literary antecedent for the linking of the snow motif by both writers to notions of the past, the dead and buried. It is rather that the metaphor itself is one that is deeply ingrained in Western culture as a way of understanding processes of life and death in terms of shared history and the succession of generations as well as the nature of individual human existence. It is fair to say that, even without the explicit association with graves and burial, any reader would be able, from his or her everyday experience and general cultural knowledge, to map attributes of snow on to attributes of death. The silence, stillness, cold and pallor of snow are the qualities of a dead body, while the obliteration of sounds, shapes (especially paths) and colours in the human or natural world suggests a generalized absence of vital activity.

It is worth briefly mentioning two further examples from early twentieth-century Spanish literature since there is a clear assumption, in both cases, that the underlying metaphor is widely and readily interpretable: Alberti's *Fermín Galán* and Unamuno's *San Manuel Bueno, mártir*. In Alberti's play, designed to evoke the style of popular 'estampas', the persistent snow of a Jaca winter night provides an ominous backdrop to the hero's fatal decision to rebel (*'Sigue nevando. Silencio'* are the final words of the episode in question).[31] Unamuno uses the same motif to characterize the passage of time and aging as a process of progressive loss, evinced in the occlusion of memories and of the sense of life as dynamic wholeness:

> Y al escribir esto ahora, aquí en mi vieja casa materna, a mis más de cincuenta años, cuando empiezan a blanquear con mi cabeza mis

[30] James Joyce, *Dubliners* (London: Cape, 1967), pp. 255-56.

[31] See Rafael Alberti, *Fermín Galán*, in R. Alberti, *El poeta en la calle* (Madrid: Aguilar, 1978), pp. 631-746, at p. 681.

recuerdos, está nevando, nevando sobre el lago, nevando sobre la montaña, nevando sobre las memorias de mi padre, el forastero, de mi madre, de mi hermano Lázaro, de mi pueblo [...].'[32]

It should be stressed that the scope of the snow-symbolism in all the examples considered here is by no means limited to personal-existential concerns, but also includes intuitions of congealment and debilitating loss of dynamism in the broader sphere of national life, and, indeed, the reflections just quoted from Joyce's 'The Dead' are prompted by the report that 'snow was general over all Ireland'; the chilling of the soul clearly comes across as not so much subjective as intersubjective experience, the reaction of a concerned individual to the perception of a dangerous depletion of vital energies in society as a whole. As with Joyce's story, 'El hospicio', while situated in the local and the particular, in a well-defined here and now, resonates with broader socio-historical connotations. This effect is in large measure due to Machado's exploitation of the relations between a set of basic conceptual metaphors, that is, metaphors that serve as cognitive models for construing basic domains of human experience.

At this point a brief excursus into the function of metaphor in discourse may be helpful. While there are useful accounts of metaphor from the perspectives of speech act theory, Gricean implicature and Relevance theory,[33] these approaches typically deal with everyday instances of the use of figurative language in general and concentrate on accounting for the ways implied meanings are deduced from the expressions actually used. A more productive approach, perhaps, is that adopted in cognitive and anthropological linguistics, assigning to metaphor a central role in the perceptual and cognitive processes of individuals and communities. As a standard work on cognitive linguistics puts it, 'our conceptualization of models of abstract categories is grounded in

---

[32] Miguel de Unamuno, *San Manuel Bueno, mártir* (Madrid: Espasa-Calpe, 1933), p. 112.

[33] For an overview of these and other approaches to metaphor, see Andrés de Azevedo, *El lugar de la metáfora* (Montevideo: Universidad de Montevideo, 1998), pp. 99-124.

our experience with people, everyday objects, actions and events'.[34] Such cognitive models are embedded in our linguistic culture, and our access to them is through the language we use, with its store of words and idiomatic expressions whose interpretations depend on conceptual metaphors for experience.[35] Where poetry and other stylized modes of writing are concerned, we should note that metaphors, as part of the common conceptual apparatus shared by members of a culture, transcend the individual sensibility and specialized language-use of the poet. However innovative and unique a particular expression, the conceptual metaphor underlying it is often a commonly-used one; as Lakoff and Turner succinctly observe, 'metaphor isn't just for poets; it's in ordinary language'.[36]

Poets often attempt to present new modes of metaphorical thought, destabilizing routinized metaphors by employing them in unusual ways; but an equally effective technique is not to transform common metaphors, but to combine them, extend them and crystallize them in strong images. Such effects of combination are a major source of the power of poetry precisely, perhaps, because they link the expression of particular experiences to more universal issues. It is worth looking in a little more detail at the metaphorical coherence of this type created in 'El hospicio'.

Using the categories proposed by Lakoff and Turner,[37] the basic cognitive models exploited in the Machado's poem can be identified as TIME IS A CHANGER (with related notions of a lifetime as a diurnal or seasonal cycle) together with LIFE IS LIGHT and LIFE IS HEAT, models that are manifested negatively in the poem as absence or fatally diminished presence. These motifs could be subsumed as a composite, general metaphor of life as a waxing and waning cycle of life and heat. Within this broad cognitive framework the reader will interpret the series of allusions to darkness and to cold as reinforcing each other in suggesting death or dying. We perceive the dark surface of the stone, blackened over

[34] F. Ungerer and H.J. Schmid, *An Introduction to Cognitive Linguistics* (London: Longman, 1996), pp. 121-22.
[35] See Lakoff and Turner, *More Than Cool Reason*, p. 51.
[36] *More Than Cool Reason*, p. 52.
[37] *More Than Cool Reason*, pp. 76 ff.

the centuries, as related to shadow, while also registering the half-contrastive, half-analogous relationship of these motifs to the pallid featurelessness of blank faces, barren fields and whited-out skies. Similarly, the description, early in the poem, of the birds that inhabit the stonework of the building, sets up in the reader's mind a whole series of contrasts and parallels. Allusions to night and day, winter and summer are designed to remind us of time passing through repeated cycles, and just as the harsh croaking of the ravens gives way to the silence of snow, so, as the poem progresses, the busy activity of the swifts' nest-building congeals into stasis.

It is not difficult to discern further links and analogies of this type in this poem, and only the most straightforwardly recognizable have been singled out for mention. The analysis has probably sufficed, however, to give some idea of the way basic metaphors in combination can acquire a special communicative power in poetry. Their force derives not merely from the way they awaken in us the perceptions in which they are grounded, but also from the way they set new resonances in motion and 'lead us to form new coherences in what we know and experience'.[38]

The culturally-shared basis of metaphorical cognition is itself especially important, underlying as it does the more generalized and socially-oriented meanings and functions of poetry, its power 'to instruct us in what to notice, how to understand, and how to conduct our lives'.[39] It is for this reason that the cognitive function of metaphor should not be regarded as a matter of neutral representation. Just as the use and interpretation of adjectival expressions has to do with consensual standards of evaluation, so metaphorical expressions (in which adjectives, in any case, often play an important role) have an evaluative function. One example of judgmental bias supplied by Lakoff and Turner is particularly relevant not only to 'El hospicio', but to a number of poems in

---

[38] *More Than Cool Reason*, p. 89.

[39] *More Than Cool Reason*, p.160. The topic under discussion here is, in fact, proverbs, but, as the authors point out, the basic mechanisms of metaphor 'appear in high relief in proverbs but suffuse all our poetry'.

Campos de Castilla that criticize, through negative-value metaphors, a stasis or closure in national life :

> When we speak of life as a 'dead end' we are viewing an unchanging state in a negative light as a lack of progress, rather than, for instance, viewing life in terms of the security and stability that could result from stasis.[40]

While, on one hand, expressions such as 'la España que se muere' and 'la España que bosteza' ('Desde mi rincón') are typical examples of metaphorical expression explicitly geared to critical commentary on Spanish national life, it is also interesting to note that Machado's expression in more intimate and lyrical passages does not exclude the resonances normally associated with the civic dimension of his poetic personality. Turning to another example of the snow metaphor, it is instructive to consider what is evoked by the description, in 'Campos de Soria', of an old woman looking out, from her humble country dwelling, while her husband sits and broods on the death of their son, who had perished after losing his way in a blizzard up in the mountains:

> En torno al fuego hay un lugar vacío,
> y en la frente del viejo, de hosco ceño
> como un tachón sombrío
> —tal el golpe de un hacha sobre un leño—.
> La vieja mira al campo, cual si oyera
> pasos sobre la nieve. Nadie pasa.
> Desierta la vecina carretera,
> desierto el campo en torno de la casa.[41]

Beyond pointing to Machado's characteristically skillful linking of syntactic and thematic parallelism to prosodic features, there is no intention here of analyzing in detail the effects achieved (the axe-blow motif, in particular, has complicated intertextual resonances). It is worth insisting, however, that the way a passage of this sort works—not just as an aesthetically pleasing and evocative description of a particular scene, but as a correlative for a complex

---

[40] Lakoff and Turner, *More Than Cool Reason*, p. 65.

[41] *Campos de Castilla*, p. 135.

range of associations across several registers of experience—has to do with skillful exploitation of the basic schemas of absence/presence, stasis/movement and action/contemplation, as well as of the contrastive metaphors of fire and snow. The direction of the conceptual cross-mapping involved in such metaphors is typically from the particular, the individual, the concrete and the local to the general, the social, the national, the metaphysical. There is a presumption, that is, that lower-order descriptions are some sort of answer to higher-order questions. This tendency is explained by Lakoff and Turner in terms of primary principles, themselves metaphoric in nature, that underpin other forms of metaphoric understanding. One such principle is GENERIC IS SPECIFIC, the operation of which is very evident in, but is by no means limited to proverbs. Another is 'The Great Chain', a hierarchical scale of forms of being and their properties, from inanimate objects upward, which allows us 'to understand human nature in terms of animal, instinctual and biological nature' and, in turn, to understand yet higher categories such as society and the cosmos in terms of forms just below them, such as human character attributes.[42]

There is more involved in such mapping than exemplarity of description and evaluation. One particularly important feature of the Great Chain is that the higher the level of the target domain, the greater is the degree of conscious agency and, therefore, of scope for control and responsibility. Thus writing containing lower-level metaphors is typically concerned not just with standards of evaluation but also with norms of conduct and the exercise of rational control, as befits higher-order beings. Metaphors often function as exhortations to assume responsibility for making necessary changes, rather than accepting the status quo. We have returned here, in the company of conceptual metaphors, to the insight of Jürgen Habermas previously discussed: that the language—the descriptive terminology—of subjective experience remains tied to an evaluative rationality and thus partakes of the project of consensual social action:

---

[42] See Lakoff and Turner, *More Than Cool Reason*, p. 186 and p. 204.

> Actors are behaving rationally so long as they use predicates such as 'spicy', 'attractive', strange', 'terrible', 'disgusting', and so forth in such a way that other members of their life-world can recognize in these descriptions their own reactions to similar situations'.[43]

More specifically, we have here an explanation of the interpretative mechanisms by which the 'squat edifice' of the lines which serve as an epigraph to this chapter can be understood as a critically evaluative description not merely of a particular church building but of institutionalized Christianity, just as Machado's depressing picture of a particular 'hospicio provinciano' suggests to us a critical view of national institutions in general, and the bereavement of the old couple in 'Campos de Soria' is linked to matters such as the economic decline of the region's agriculture and the absence (through emigration) of the active 'middle' generation, as well as to a sense of the course of Spain's historical development having reached a past-fixated impasse.

Conceptual metaphors offer one of the solutions to the problem of achieving lyrical resonance and authenticity without treating the poet's life as a supply of simple moral exempla. The particular strength of many poems in *Campos de Castilla* is that they are not exclusively 'personal' or 'public' in orientation, but absorb and address a number of positions and by so doing stress the communicative link between the poet and his audience. 'A un olmo viejo', for instance, without flatly revealing its biographical origins, certainly reads as though it might be directly about the poet himself, and it is easy to understand why it has been so consistently ascribed to Machado's state of mind during the last stages of his wife's illness. On the other hand, the poem consistently moves from detailed observation of a natural object on a given occasion to broader reflection on alternative scenarios and typical instances of natural processes and human activity, consistently presenting individual closure as the beginning of further cycles. The poem's closing lines, switching to more explicit expression of feelings and a more personal register (first person self-references appear for the

---

[43] Habermas, *The Theory of Communicative Action*, I, pp. 16-17.

first time) acquire, at the same time, a more universal resonance through insistence on basic metaphorical mappings of experience:

> [...] olmo, quiero anotar en mi cartera
> la gracia de tu rama verdecida.
> Mi corazón espera
> también, hacia la luz y hacia la vida
> otro milagro de la primavera.[44]

This sort of closing modulation, involving both an intensification of emotional involvement and a broadening of thematic horizons, is one that is found in a number of poems of *Campos de Castilla.* From a communicative point of view, we should note that these tendencies reinforce each other, since the invitation to greater empathy created by the disclosure of subjective feelings is backed up by the universalized, readily comprehensible character of the terms in which such feelings are expressed.[45]

The final lines of 'A un olmo seco' should thus probably not be interpreted narrowly in terms of tenuous hope for miraculous recovery of a terminally ill individual; rather they have to do with an intuition that pessimistic resignation is not necessarily the only adequate response to life's great questions. On the other hand, we cannot altogether discount the possibility that readers are intentionally being given a glimpse of the man behind the artist. The explicit revelation of the poet's own emotional involvement, 'mi corazón espera también [...] otro milagro', is patently superfluous (dull indeed would be any reader who has not already realized that the poet has a large emotional investment in the scene he is describing). In Gricean terms, the provision of unnecessary information, as happens here, will generate an implicature of some

---

[44] *Campos de Castilla*, p. 172.

[45] Geoffrey Ribbans similarly argues that in interpreting such passages (he is thinking particularly of 'A un olmo seco' and the poem addressed to Palacio) 'al reconocer plenamente la validez del sentimiento no le importa al lector interesado que desconozca las circunstancias'. See G. Ribbans, 'Antonio Machado, ¿poeta provinciano o poeta universal?', in A. Vilanova y A. Sotelo Vázquez (eds), *La crisis española de fin de siglo y la generación del '98* (Barcelona: Universidad de Barcelona, 1999), pp. 241-253, at p. 252.

sort. For most readers, this will probably be along the lines that the speaker is rejecting possible interpretations of his reaction to the elm's incongruous new leaves as despairingly ironic, and is insisting that he genuinely and wholeheartedly—'mi corazón [...] también'—wishes to be identified with the tree's gesture of defiance in the face of the inevitable.

Nevertheless, while it is possible Machado wishes to suggest that his perception of the circumstantial starting point of the poem is itself deeply influenced by his state of mind with respect to his personal life, we cannot avoid noting that the 'gracia' of the stricken elm's 'rama verdecida' is a basic and traditional metaphor for renewal and new life, and is one that is broadly applicable to many areas of personal experience in which hope, despite the depressing conclusions of observation and reflection, is never altogether extinguished. Neither is it coincidental that the conceptual image of turning positively toward light and life and away from purely personal preoccupations appears in Machado's prose writings before the composition of 'A un olmo viejo' as a crystallization of his belief in the combined aesthetic and civic duty of the new generation of writers and intellectual citizens to renounce undue concern with private experience as well as with traditional conceptions of patriotic duty.[46] In fact Machado was to use the same motif in its entirety a few years later (in the prologue to the second edition of *Soledades. Galerías. Otros poemas*) as a basic metaphor for the hope of generalized artistic and social regeneration which the events of 1918 in Russia seemed to hold out:

> Cierto que la Guerra no ha creado ideas nuevas—no pueden las ideas brotar de los puños—; pero, ¿quién duda de que el árbol humano comienza a renovarse por el raíz, y de que una nueva oleada de vida camina hacia la luz, hacia la conciencia?[47]

---

[46] See Machado's reflections on Juan Ramón Jiménez's *Arias tristes* and Unamuno's *Vida de Don Quijote y Sancho,* as well as his commemorative address 'Nuestro patriotismo y la marcha de Cádiz' (*Obras*, p. 839, p. 843 and p. 846).
[47] *Obras*, p. 53.

The closing lines of 'A un olmo seco' provide a good example, in fact, of the high value Machado placed on poetic elements—whether conventional epithets or 'imágenes genéricas y familiares'[48]—that are universally understood, as well as those that convey private, intuitive experience. While couching the argument in terms of intuition versus logical concepts, Machado insists that the importance of such elements resides precisely in their communicative effectiveness. Any attempt to exclude the conceptual misses the whole point of poetry (indeed of all artistic expression) as, above all, an act of communication:

> Se ignoraba, o se aparentaba ignorar, que un poema es [...] antes que nada un objeto propuesto a la contemplación del prójimo, y que no sería tal objeto, que carecería en absoluto de *existencia*, si no estuviese construído sobre el esquema del pensar genérico, si careciese de lógica, si no respondiese, de algún modo, a la común estructura espiritual del múltiple sujeto que ha de contemplarlo.[49]

In other words, what have been regarded here as conceptual metaphors and generic-level images are, in Machado's view, as important for successful poetry as innovative and highly personal forms of expression. Indeed, it is through the combination of the two modes in 'la palabra integral' that the densely structured order of communication that is successful poetry emerges: 'con la palabra se hace música, pintura, y mil cosas más; pero sobre todo, se habla'.[50]

2.3 FRIENDLY INTERROGATION: 'A JOSÉ MARÍA PALACIO'

> A preguntas sin respuesta
> ¿quién te podrá responder?[51]

The consideration of metaphors as solutions to the problem of reconciling the twin requirements of authenticity and

---

[48] *Obras*, p. 893.
[49] *Obras*, p. 909.
[50] *Obras*, p. 893.
[51] *Campos de Castilla*, p. 215.

comprehensibility in poetic expression leads us naturally to a consideration of 'A José María Palacio',[52] another highly personal poem that successfully lends a broad resonance to the expression of private aspects of experience. The poem opens with the first of a number of questions:

> Palacio, buen amigo,
> ¿está la primavera
> vistiendo ya la ramas de los chopos
> del río y los caminos?

The most salient discursive feature of the poem, the fact that it is an epistle, or poetic letter, merits some attention in itself. In broad terms, one can only agree with Claudio Guillén's view, in his perceptive detailed study of 'A José María Palacio', that the epistolary format itself makes a crucial contribution to the poem's effectiveness in conveying nuances of meaning to do with the subjective experience of time and the status of memories.[53] Despite conceptual and terminological differences that reflect a familiarity with the Jakobsonian stylistics fashionable in 1971, Guillén's analysis comes close, at times, to a discourse-pragmatics approach. Not only is there a marked interest in the relationship between linguistic form and utterance function, but the poem's meaning overall is seen as dependent on 'a basic connection between the latent or tacit parts of the *significans* and the words actually uttered or written.'[54] The present analysis is thus intended to complement Guillén's insights, by considering the role of shared contextual knowledge in generating non-explicit, that is, inferred meanings (and carefully distinguishing such meanings and their production from generalized concepts of silence and absence), as well as

---

[52] *Campos de Castilla*, pp. 187-88.

[53] Claudio Guillén, *Literature as System: essays toward the theory of literary history* (Princeton: Princeton University Press, 1971), pp. 235-271.

[54] *Literature as System*, p. 266. Guillén even notes that the verbs in the poem tend to be of the process types Halliday was to term existentials and relationals, rather than encodings of a more direct transitivity: 'Machado focuses his attention on being, becoming, non-being; his verbs designate not an action but the absence or presence of something' (p. 238).

looking more closely at the functional interrelationship of the poem's principal utterance types and analysing some aspects of the dialogic effects created in the poem.

In addition to the direct mode of address associated with the epistolary genre, we should note a further determinant of the speech situation: the addressee is a close friend of the poet. Thus, in terms of participant status, readers are in a position not altogether dissimilar to that of audiences of performance or fictional dialogue, in that they are fully ratified auditors of a discourse nominally designed for a direct addressee.[55] The fact, however, that the direct addressee is a real-life person rather than a fictional character tends to reinforce the impression of privileged overhearing of private communication rather than the operation of the 'dual focus' of literary or performance discourse, in which an author's communication with his audience is mediated through what actors or characters say to and about each other. A further important consideration is the fact that in letters—as in published texts—the context of utterance is separated by time and space from the context of reception. We have seen elsewhere that Machado is adept at creating and sustaining the impression of a unified speech situation, as if he were directly addressing the reader in the present moment. Here, however, this effect appears not so much in the guise of a convention or device of literary texts but rather as a characteristic feature of the personal letter genre. Writers of letters often couch their remarks in such a way as to give the impression of maintaining a dialogue with their correspondents in the present moment, while simultaneously, in giving and asking for news and so forth, they tacitly acknowledge spatial and temporal dissociation. This speech situation, which could be described as semi unified, is exploited by Machado to create a number of important effects that could not be achieved in discourse grounded in a currently shared setting.

As with many of Machado's most memorable compositions, the syntactical framework of 'A José María Palacio' makes an

[55] For a discussion of some the complexities of public audience design in discourse, see Allan Bell, *The Language of News Media* (Oxford: Blackwell, 1993), pp. 92-96.

important contribution to the poem's overall impact and thus provides a convenient starting point for analysis. The structure consists of a series of questions and future-tense suppositions—five of each—mixed with occasional instances of Machado's characteristic exclamatory naming of landscape features. The earlier part of the poem provides a convenient example, in sequence, of each of these three types of utterance:

> ¿Tienen los viejos olmos
> algunas hojas nuevas?
> Aún las acacias estarán desnudas
> y nevadas los montes de las sierras.
> ¡Oh mole del Moncayo blanca y rosa,
> allá, en el cielo de Aragón, tan bella!

It is worth devoting a little preliminary attention to the function and nature of questions in general and Machado's use of them, especially since they are well represented in *Campos de Castilla;* indeed, the range of effects achieved through exclamations and questions is one of the characteristic strengths of the work as a whole (the artfully ironic query with which this piece of analysis begins is a good example). Each of what are usually considered the three main functional classes of question is well represented in the work; they can be conveniently illustrated here by lines from 'Proverbios y cantares':

> POLAR (expecting a reply of yes or no) as in '¿Dices que nada se pierde?' (*XLII*).
> WH (initiated in Spanish by terms such as 'qué', 'quién', 'dónde', that seek a response from an open range of replies) as in '¿Dónde está la utilidad / de nuestras utilidades?' (*XXVII*)
> ALTERNATIVE (expecting as the reply one of two or more options offered in the question) as in '¿Es hambre? ¿Sueño? ¿Hastío?' (*L*).

Even considered in isolation, sufficient deeper nuances of meaning are detectable in all of these examples to suggest that categorizing questions in terms of the type of answer they prospect by no means exhausts the range of discursive functions that can be realized. The complexity interrogative utterances can take on in literary texts is a reflection, in turn, of the multiplicity of uses to which they can be put in non-literary, everyday discourse. This poly-functional property of questions has been neatly summarized from a pragmatics perspective by Stephen Levinson:

> Interrogatives can be used with the illocutionary forces of 'real' questions, 'exam' questions, rhetorical questions, requests, offers, suggestions, threats and for many other functions, without overriding some 'literal force'.[56]

Especially when dealing with stylized written texts, the notion of 'rhetorical question' (in the sense of no direct reply being expected) is too generalized to be of much help in analyzing the variety of functions involved. In the case of 'A José María Palacio', however, it is at least possible to narrow the focus to one question-type, since all five sentences enclosed by 'signos de interrogación' prospect a negative or affirmative response. It may be useful to begin by summarizing the ways Machado uses polar questions in *Campos de Castilla* in general, and then go on to consider what their particular functions are in the poem addressed to Palacio.

One type of utterance to which the term 'rhetorical' could usefully be restricted is the sort of polar interrogation that is used to assert a proposition with especially convincing force. For example, when in 'Pascua de Resurrección' Machado envisages the destined maternal role of local 'doncellitas' there is nothing whatever of supposition or estimation in spite of the future tense. Indeed, the overall effect is one of enthusiastic acclamation of a certainty.[57]

> ¿No beberán un día en vuestros senos
> los que mañana labrarán la tierra?[58]

---

[56] *Pragmatics*, pp. 274-75.

[57] In English, as well as in Spanish, negative polar questions standardly function as an exclamation. See Eirian C. Davies, 'Questions: a significance-generating device for building in context', in E. Steiner and R. Veltman (eds), *Pragmatics, Discourse and Text: some systemically-inspired approaches* (London: Pinter, 1998), pp. 29-45, at p. 28.

[58] *Campos de Castilla*, p. 131.

While this last example draws its assertive force from the tendency of negatively-phrased questions to involve a bias toward an expected affirmative response, a corresponding capacity of positively-phrased questions to carry a negative bias is clearly illustrated by the much-quoted interrogations addressed to Azorín as to the prospects in Spain of a newly-emerged sense of national purpose:

> ¿Y ha de helarse en la España que se muere?
> ¿Ha de ahogarse en la España que bosteza?[59]

These two utterances are unmistakeably intended as a warning and a call to arms; the expected answer, that is to say, is an outraged, unequivocal negative. The epistemic bias of positive polar questions, however, tends to be finely graded by context rather than crudely determined *a priori*. In the poem of 1911 which begins '¿eres tú, Guadarrama, viejo amigo [...]?', for instance, Machado's aim is clearly not to cast doubt on the identity of the mountain-range that has come into view, but to affirm strongly the impact of sudden recognition of the once-familiar. The questions, in 'Llanto de las virtudes y coplas por la muerte de Don Guido', listing the eponymous aristocrat's trivial and materialistic preoccupations and enquiring whether they were all he had to take to the next world, are similarly and satirically intended to elicit (from the reader) an affirmative answer:

> ¿Tu amor a los alamares
> y a las sedas y a los oros
> y a la sangre de los toros
> y al humo de los altares?[60]

In any case, the effect is not always to enhance assertive force; Machado frequently uses polar questions for an altogether different purpose, creating an effect that is frequently encountered in *Soledades. Galerías. Otros poemas* and is equally persistent in

---

[59] *Campos de Castilla*, p. 244.
[60] *Campos de Castilla*, p. 207.

Campos de Castilla. 'Poema de un día' provides a number of examples, of which the following lines are typical:

¿Todo es
soledad de soledades,
vanidad de vanidades,
que dijo el Eclesiastes?[61]

This sort of query, rather than forcefully endorsing or rejecting a proposition, is designed to emphasize the poet's uncertainty and doubt, the impossibility of arriving at full understanding or coming to definitive conclusions, especially, as here, where existential enigmas are concerned. In terms of the speaker's epistemic bias, the expected answer would seem to be neither yes nor no, but rather 'don't know'. Even negative phrasing is not invariably a reliable guide to actual force in context; indeed, the following example,

¿No ves, Leonor, los álamos del río
con sus ramajes yertos?[62]

superficially an exclamatory drawing of attention to a natural scene, seems ultimately aimed at pathos, confirming that the poet's heart is indeed 'vagando en sueños' and giving the impression of wishful thinking, of an intentional evocation of memories as opposed to reality. In the poem Machado addresses to his friend Palacio we find further examples of carefully prepared effects. Rather than the 'rhetorical' function of conveying an attitude to the proposition expressed, whether of support, opposition or doubt, the questions in 'A José María Palacio' have more in the way of 'literal force', aimed as they are at eliciting information, and very narrowly defined information at that; it is precisely through their informational focus, in fact, that further contextual functions are realized.

In the essay already mentioned, Claudio Guillén shows an awareness of something unusual about the purpose of the queries in

---

[61] *Campos de Castilla*, p. 195.
[62] *Campos de Castilla*, p. 180.

this poem. His explanation, 'doubtless the blackberry bushes, the daisies, the plum trees, will bloom sooner or later. But when, exactly, and in what combinations and with what effects?'[63] may well be correct as a general observation, or as a surmise as to the thoughts that provided the initial inspiration of the poem, but seems to overlook the precise point of Machado's questioning, the particular sort of information he actually solicits. On one hand, the poet does not explicitly ask 'when exactly?' (or any other WH-type question); on the other, he is clearly prepared to make his own unaided guesses as to combinations and effects. The enquiries, in fact, are all aimed at ascertaining whether or not the states of affairs he describes are currently the case (with a clear presumption that any negative answer would merely signify *not yet* the case). To analyze these queries further, however, we need to look beyond the passages that have the specific syntactical form of questions. The two types of utterance that predominate in the poem—suppositions and interrogations—are, in fact, in close relationship, and could even be regarded as having the same basic discursive function. To justify this point, however, it is necessary to substitute for the notion of questions that of 'elicitations', that is, utterances that, irrespective of their form, are designed to elicit a verbal response.[64]

We have already seen that utterances formally marked as questions (by word order, intonation or punctuation) cannot be regard as solely or even principally designed to elicit information. From a functional viewpoint, on the other hand, there is a corresponding problem of definition: as we have seen, in conversational interaction for example, utterances which do not have an interrogative form are frequently responded to as if they were questions.[65] The notion of elicitation, then, defined as any utterance which prospects an obligatory verbal response, is a useful one, particularly in that it avoids confusion with the use of

---

[63] Guillén, *Literature as System,* p. 245.

[64] Amy Tsui, 'A Functional Description of Questions', in M. Coulthard (ed.), *Advances in Spoken Discourse Analysis* (London: Routledge, 1992), pp. 89-110, at p. 101.

[65] See Labov, *The Study of Language* (some principles of which we applied to questions in Neruda's 'Explico algunas cosas').

interrogatory forms for other purposes, such as requesting the performance of an action.[66] The concept is particularly useful for analyzing 'A José María Palacio', since the statements of supposition which, in the poem, alternate with questions, clearly function as a type of elicitation, asking the addressee to confirm the speaker's assumptions. The functional criteria involved in combinations of interrogative and declarative utterances are summarized by Labov in the following terms: 'if A talks about a B event it is heard as a request for confirmation; if A talks about an AB event, a "shared knowledge" is being drawn on'.[67] Where Machado's poem is concerned, the question of which event-status is more applicable is a crucial one. It is worth noting that both the questions and the suppositions comprise very detailed specifications of natural phenomena and states-of-affairs; a further textual example of the linking of the two types of utterance should give an idea of the quantity and specificity of information involved:[68]

> ¿hay zarzas florecidas
> entre las grises peñas,
> y blancas margaritas
> entre la fina hierba?
> Por esos campanarios
> ya habrán ido llegando las cigüeñas.

Given the epistolary genre's dual communicative focus—one context of discourse, that is, is embedded in another, and, in important respects, the utterances are shaped for the wider readership as much as for the nominated addressee—and that the use of elicitations, moreover, strongly presupposes that the speaker believes the hearer to be in possession of the information required, the poem seemingly courts one of the most insidious hazards for the composer of literary texts. The danger is that of creating a surfeit of

[66] See Tsui, 'A Functional Description of Questions', p. 109.
[67] Quoted in Carter and Simpson, *Language, Discourse*, p. 63.
[68] Tsui ('A Functional Description of Questions', pp. 105-6) gives some similarly detailed declarative utterances that have an elicit-confirm function, such as (in the process of asking for directions) 'the white building where they have the Psychology Department'.

details, a conspicuous over-explicitness that can have an effect on readers similar to that produced in theatre audiences by abuse of the dramatic convention that, for the purpose of transmitting essential information economically to the audience, characters may tell one another things it would be reasonable to suppose they already know. Yet the only point in the poem where the reader might detect such unconvincing over-explicitness is in the remark—important for the general reader's understanding of the poem, but something Palacio himself would undoubtedly be well aware of—that Spring arrives relatively late in the Soria region:

> […] en la estepa
> del alto Duero, Primavera tarda,
> ¡pero es tan bella y dulce cuando llega!

Machado, however, is careful to delay providing this information until the interrogations have already been set in train, so that his declaration strikes us not so much as an assertion as a request for confirmation of shared beliefs and opinions, quite possibly stemming from need for reassurance rather than from purely informational requirements. Certainly, the insistence with which the poet goes on to ask pointedly about physical manifestations of growth and change puts us in mind (although the season is the opposite one) of what Roger Fowler, discussing Keats's 'Ode to Autumn', terms 'overlexicalization', the extensive and repetitive use of sets of terms for related concepts, that has the effect of foregrounding particular lexical systems and the ideas they symbolize. Such cumulative vocabulary patterns indicate point of view, or 'an unusual preoccupation with part of the culture's, or the writer's experience'.[69] Readers of Machado's poem might well similarly conclude that the poet has something insistently on his mind.

In giving details, from the start, of the appearance of local flora and fauna, the poet is doubtless drawing on shared knowledge, but at the same time he is implicitly acknowledging that his current

[69] Fowler, *Linguistic Criticism*, p. 155.

location is elsewhere, a place where the arrival of Spring follows a different schedule, and that he is less well informed than his friend because his perceptual data derive from memories as opposed to up-to-date, 'on the spot' observation. To some extent, then, Machado, in Labov's terms, is talking about B events, and we should interpret his detailed descriptions as requests for confirmation. A pattern is thus set: the features of the landscape mentioned in the course of the poem are indeed likely to be already known to Palacio. The poet's elicitations, however, whether in the form of questions or declarative suppositions, do not, for that reason, strike readers as artificially designed to provide information for their benefit rather than for the poem's nominated addressee. They come across instead as authentic, motivated by genuine concern over shortfalls in shared knowledge and by a psychological need to have suppositions confirmed.

The overall effect, then, of the suppositions and questions in the poem is to suggest that the poet's main concern is to receive reassurance that his memories of the arrival of Spring in Soria do in fact correspond in detail to the current configuration of the natural scene. He is anxious to be 'brought up to date' as it were. It is worth keeping in mind here that, when an utterance contains several elements, the focus is normally on one of them, while the remaining elements are treated as presupposed information. This focusing occurs typically when a state or event is presumed to have occurred, but a particular element of it—which, in syntactical terms, may be subject, object, verb, adjective or adverb—is not fully known to the speaker. In particular, 'when optional adverbs are present in a declarative clause, the focus of assertion tends to be obligatorily attracted to them. Such obligatory focus also occurs in yes-no questions'.[70] This observation precisely fits Machado's elicitations in this poem, many of which contain temporal adverbs; the sort of thing he wants to know is whether the storks have already started arriving, (or will it be later?); are the farmers sowing (or still occupied in other tasks?); what is not questioned is whether these

[70] Talmy Givón, *Syntax: a functional typological introduction*, II (Amsterdam: Benjamin, 1990), p. 784.

events are going to occur or not. A dual effect is thus created; the uncontroversial (that is, presupposed) status of the content of the description as a whole is established, but, at the same time interrogative emphasis is placed on one particular detail. Although substantiating this claim would involve a very detailed stylistic analysis of the passages concerned, I would argue that most readers of 'A José María Palacio' will interpret as the focal points of the elicitations—the features the poet is particularly seeking confirmation of—precisely those adverbs that define a particular temporal perspective and those adjectives and adjectival expressions that function as classifiers, specifying which particular sub-class the poet is interested in. It will not have escaped notice that such classifying expressions, in this poem, typically have to do with passage of time, growth and change. A sequence from the central section of the poem provides a number of examples:

> ¿Hay zarzas FLORECIDAS
> entre las grises peñas [...]?
> Por esos camapanarios
> YA habrán ido llegando las cigüeñas.
> Habrá trigales VERDES
> y mulas pardas EN LAS SEMENTERAS
> y labriegos QUE SIEMBRAN LOS TARDÍOS
> con las lluvias DE ABRIL. YA las abejas
> libarán del tomillo y el romero.
> ¿Hay ciruelos EN FLOR?

This deliberate drawing of attention to time and the seasonal cycle also has the effect, of course, of underlining the physical separation of the poet from the scene he is imagining. The lack of synchronization in the arrival of Spring, explicitly mentioned in the poem, between Soria and the poet's actual location (Baeza) not only provides a justification for the queries and requests for confirmation, but also continually draws our attention to the setting of poet's present life 'in another country' as it were. Indeed, the temporal-spatial dislocation and emotional de-centredness evinced in this poem are characteristic traits of the nostalgic cast of mind of an émigré, anxious to be reassured by one still 'at home' that everything continues as it was, that his cherished memories continue to match a real state of affairs.

In adopting and exploiting in this way an archetypal model of human experience of loss and time, just as in contriving, in a psychologically convincing manner, to convey the substance of the poem in the form of information that is, potentially at least, redundant or irrelevant, we could say that Machado successfully negotiates an aesthetic tightrope, sustaining pathos without falling into banality. Moreover, it is this very flirting with communicative inauthenticity that conveys sincerity by revealing the presence of feelings complex enough to oblige the poet to bend some communicative rules. It is the final lines, however, that hold the poem's structure together, justifying the discursive idiosyncrasies that precede it and achieving a universal relevance by concentrating on intersubjectively communicable aspects of private experience, thus inviting readers to recognize an affinity with their own sensibilities. In contrast to the final broadening of the frame of reference found in poems such as 'El hospicio' or 'A un olmo seco', Machado ends here by intensifying the impression of private communication and insisting that the epistolary form is not a mere convention but a medium of authentically private exchanges that ordinary readers are privileged to 'overhear'. With the highly effective—and affective—switch of syntax and utterance type, at which the poet is so adept (note also the characteristic combination of a periodic sentence with effects of parallelism) the poem closes with a direct exhortation to Palacio:

> Con los primeros lirios,
> y las primeras rosas de las huertas,
> en una tarde azul, sube al Espino,
> al alto Espino donde está su tierra...

The poet mentions a name, presumably that of a local topographical feature (it is a church, in fact), which is clearly familiar to his friend, but not necessarily to readers at large. Even more enigmatically (for the general reader) there is a puzzling instance of zero anaphora in the use of a pronominal referring term, 'su tierra', of the type that is normally co-referential with a fuller description used in preceding text. To use such an expression without support in the text implies that the referent is straightforwardly recoverable in the speech situation itself as something salient in the shared knowledge of the participants. It is clearly assumed here that Palacio knows whose plot of ground the poet is referring to, but the ordinary reader will be confronted by the sort of reference assignment problem frequently encountered by overhearers of real-life conversations. In the case of such 'absentee antecedents' some inferential help in interpreting the anaphor in question is often provided by the reader's semantic / pragmatic schema (or cognitive framework).[71] Here, most readers will know that flowers are often placed on graves, themselves associated with 'tierra'; but the identity of the grave's occupant remains a matter of speculative inference.

The inferential aid we are invited to use here is our own knowledge or experience of such circumstances—in a word, empathy. Machado is clearly alluding to a bereavement; the hints, in the poem, of the traditional topos of former happy experiences evoked in a context of loss, the exilic presupposition of debarment from the heart's true home, and, above all, the impression given that the greater part of the poem functions as an extensive explanation or 'pre-sequence' for the request made to the poet's 'good friend', to lay the flowers on his behalf, all point to certain conclusions about the poet's state of mind and the sort of experience that might have precipitated it. The final phrase of the poem thus hits home in a particularly powerful way: after taking solace in thoughts of spring, 'tan bella y tan dulce', dressing the bare winter land in vivid colours and textures, the poet lifts the superficial covering aside. In mournful contrast to the bright show of flowers and the external signs of warmth and regeneration, he lets us see the cold underlying earth, the irrevocable finality of death and the bleakness of his inner feelings.

---

[71] See Francis Cornish, *Anaphora, Discourse and Understanding* (Oxford: Clarendon, 1992), p. 144.

Even in this apparent insistence on personal circumstances Machado is showing his ability to establish and exploit communicative links. The point at which the privatistic anaphor occurs is that of greatest interactive involvement, not simply because it depends on recursively shared knowledge—the poet assumes that his friend knows what it is his thoughts constantly return to—but also because, in on-going discursive exchanges, the use of such a referring expression often signals the establishment of a new topic (or reversion to a previous one).[72] It is as if Machado closes the poem for the reader precisely at the point where he wishes to continue (or renew) a private conversation with his friend, emphasizing yet further that the poem's situation of utterance, despite its conventionalized nature, is itself being held up as an exemplary model of the understanding made possible through dialogue.

2.4 DISSENTING VOICES

As we have seen, many of the poems of *Campos de Castilla* aim at creating a situation of address and engaging the reader's attention and cooperation as if in a face-to-face interaction. Even so obviously rhetorical a device as addressing inanimate entities can have the effect of thematizing the situation of utterance, since a shift in footing occurs, a breakthrough from one layer of the interaction to another.[73] In 'Campos de Soria', for instance, the effect of apostrophizing features of the landscape, as in '¡Colinas plateadas, / grises alcores, cárdenas roquedas [...]!' or 'Soria, ciudad castellana / ¡tan bella! bajo la luna!' is perhaps merely to stress that they have special personal connotations for the poet. On the other hand, the apostrophe of the poem's final lines

> ¡Gentes del alto llano numantino
> que a Dios guardáis como cristianas viejas,

---

[72] See Givón, *Functionalism*, p. 78, and *Syntax*, p. 709.
[73] See Bell, *The Language of News,* p. 97.

que el sol de España os llene,
de alegría, de luz, y de riqueza![74]

changes the reader's participant status from that of addressee to that of auditor; consequently, attention is drawn to the text as performance discourse (the poet availing himself of the licence of performers to address imagined interlocutors rather than the audience). A sense of structured—ritualized—closure is created (a benediction, in fact), and the authenticity of the poet's emotional attachment to the region and its historical heritage is emphazised.

Although the language of the poems is often rhetorically stylized, the means employed to establish and sustain a communicative bonding are essentially the same as those used in everyday language situations; looking at this question from the opposite perspective, we could say that Machado's verse amply bears out the contention of Deborah Tannen that many strategies which have been thought quintessentially literary are frequently used in ordinary conversation with the aim of reflecting and creating interpersonal involvement between speaker and hearer. As well as figures of speech and particular discourse types, such as narratives, strategies of involvement also include patterns of repetition and use of imagery and detail to build scene-pictures and enable audiences to imagine how the speaker feels.[75] In literary texts as much as in everyday talk involvement strategies send 'a meta-message of rapport'[76] and confirm that audiences are taking part in coordinated interaction and colluding in the joint creation of meaning rather than passively attending. It is important, however, not to think merely in terms of technical expertise in ensuring efficient communicative exchange. Involvement, whether on the interpersonal level or in terms of the speaker's or writer's involvement with the topic, should be thought of as creating 'the internal, even emotional connection individuals

[74] *Campos de Castilla*, p. 138.

[75] See Deborah Tannen, *Talking Voices: repetition, dialogue and imagery in conversational discourse* (Cambridge: Cambridge University Press, 1989), pp. 9-30.

[76] Tannen, *Talking Voices*, p. 149.

feel which binds them to other places, things, activities, ideas, memories and words.'[77]

One of the most effective of such strategies in ordinary conversations—and one that Machado consistently exploits in the poems of *Campos de Castilla*—is the incorporation of dialogue and dialogic effects. This may take the form, at one end of the scale, of directly represented speech exchanges and instances of so-called reported speech, or, at the other, of exploitation of polyphony, the co-presence in discourse of other texts or voices. Following Bakhtin, we have become accustomed to regarding all language use as inherently dialogic in that every utterance carries 'the echoes and reverberations of other utterances to which it is related by the communality of the sphere of speech communication'.[78] All texts call up prior texts and our mouths, as William Foley puts it, are full of the words of others.[79] While dialogic elements are inherent in language, there are differences in the degree to which writers make conscious use of the interplay of different voices and the different cultural, social and linguistic environments they evoke. One of the most marked changes in *Campos de Castilla,* compared to Machado's earlier poetic manner, is precisely a switch from the largely internal dialogues and self-questioning sequences of *Soledades. Galerías. Otros poemas* to a treatment of language—or rather discourse—as heteroglossic, a historically transmitted medium of social interaction, in which the multiple voices of different social groups and classes, generations and institutions do not merely combine, but also compete and conflict. Not only is there a consistent tendency to use phrases, motifs and formulas already established in the national cultural and linguistic heritage, but there is also a high incidence of passages of direct address to named persons and entities, and of embedded pieces of dialogue or reported speech, together with a variety of techniques for

[77] Tannen, *Talking Voices,* p. 12.

[78] M. Bakhtin, *Speech Genres and Other Late Essays*, edited by Caryl Emerson and Michael Holquist, translated by Vern McGee (Austin: University of Texas Press, 1986), p. 91.

[79] Foley, *Anthropological Linguistics*, p. 361.

introducing such modes. It is worth devoting a little attention to the effects Machado achieves through these related devices.

One clear indication of a measure of concern in *Campos de Castilla* with linguistic culture in its socio-historical dimension is the inclusion of axioms, aphorisms, proverbs and similar verbal formulas, not only in the series of 'Proverbios y cantares' but in other contexts as well. One poem, for instance, is entitled 'En abril, las aguas mil' and the central section of 'Campos de Soria' reproduces the motto on the city's coat-of-arms, 'Soria pura, cabeza de Extremadura'. In general terms, proverbs and similar expressions can be thought of as standardized utterances that are recontextualized in the present to provide a valid viewpoint on the current situation through their supposed value as received wisdom, moral truth or widely-shared public opinion. What is immediately noticeable, however, with Machado's verse 'proverbios' (which, though original, have the form and register of traditional examples) is that such normative authority and the voices that claim it seem to be incorporated and, in Bakhtinian terminology,[80] re-accentuated precisely so they can be challenged. For instance, the second poem of 'Proverbios y cantares' starts by calling into question the sort of conventional wisdom often expressed through the conceptual metaphor Life is a Journey:

> ¿Para qué llamar caminos
> a los surcos del azar?
> Todo el que camina anda,
> como Jesús, sobre el mar.[81]

As a poet who himself well knows how to use basic cognitive metaphors to very good effect, Machado is perhaps particularly aware of their dangers as well as their advantages. The appropriate question to ask, as Jacob Mey has pointed out, is not what does a metaphor mean, but 'how effective is a particular metaphor in a particular context (e.g. solving a problem, obtaining consensus,

---

[80] Bakhtin, *Speech Genres*, p. 89.
[81] *Campos de Castilla*, p. 214.

elucidating difficult subject matter, and so on)?'[82] In forcefully asserting that the 'camino' metaphor is mistaken and that 'surcos del azar' would be a more appropriate mapping of the course of human life, Machado is not merely questioning the appropriateness of the journey metaphor as a cognitive instrument. There is also a strong hint of reproof to those whose uncritical re-use of such metaphors is a substitute for genuine reflection, thus perpetuating faulty conceptions and avoiding important issues.

The question of Machado's attitude to the appropriation of traditional forms will be taken up again shortly; for the moment it is worth staying with the relation of mechanisms of critique to the incorporation of other voices. The lines just quoted evoke and engage with another discourse, that of conventional attitudes and received wisdom, in a markedly dialogic way. The question containing the verb 'llamar' functions as a direct challenge, suggesting that the poet is making a meta-linguistic counter-move to an immediately preceding utterance. The effect is to conjure up an opposed point of view, a dissenting voice, with some force and vividness; Machado's words, that is, 'demand to speak toward *someone* as well as against an opposing position'.[83]

The effect of directly taking issue with opposed viewpoints is memorably achieved in a number of poems of *Campos de Castilla.* At the same time, we should not overlook a more subtle device: the incorporation of routinized or formulaic expressions, often of official or semi-official provenance, to introduce a note of ironic deprecation. One such telling moment is the characterization of an accused man in the dock as 'devoto de María, / madre de pecadores', in a poem, 'Un criminal',[84] in which it is strongly suggested that Church-controlled education inhibits the development of moral character and thus weakens resistance to criminal urges. Another is Machado's prediction, in 'El mañana efímero', that the vacuous Spain he despises 'aún tendrá luengo

---

[82] See Jacob L. Mey, *Pragmatics: an introduction* (Oxford: Blackwell, 1993), p. 62.
[83] See Leith and Myerson, *The Power of Address*, p. 87.
[84] *Campos de Castilla*, pp. 125-26.

parto de varones'.[85] It is as if he is suggesting that the persistence of expressions that are routinely repeated without regard to changing contexts and needs is itself a symptom of intellectual or moral degeneration.

The effect of challenge or contestation is very characteristic of Machado's incorporation of other discourses, whether verbatim quotations or other modes of reproduction. The inclusion in a poem, for instance, of the actual words uttered by someone almost invariably serves to confirm the critical attitude the poet has already established through description of the scene. Such is certainly the case with the comment 'va sin remedio al palo' of the court usher in 'Un criminal', a prediction that betrays a complacently fatalistic view of transgression and punishment on the part of the speaker and thus both ironically echoes the poet's attribution of the crime to social, educational and environmental determinants and reinforces the poem's satirical depiction of an ossified and irrelevant judicial system.[86] A similar effect is achieved, sharply reminding the reader of the 'turno pacífico' in Restoration electoral politics, by the even more cynical prognostication of one of the local worthies gathered in a Baeza 'botica' in 'Poema de un día':

> —Pasados los carnavales,
> vendrán los conservadores
> buenos administradores
> de su casa.— [87]

---

[85] *Campos de Castilla*, p. 211.

[86] For an account of the presence in *Campos de Castilla* of the reforming theories associated with the currently influential Italian positivist school of criminology, see Robin Warner, 'Questioning the Rules: concepts of deviance and conformism in *Campos de Castilla*', in D. Gareth Walters (ed.), *Estelas en la mar: essays on the poetry of Antonio Machado* (Glasgow: University of Glasgow, 1992), pp. 62-53. I am grateful to Dr Rhian Davies for subsequently drawing my attention to the regular appearance of translations of essays by members of the group such as Ferri and Lombroso, together with commentaries on their theories, in *La España Moderna* in the decade preceding Machado's composition of poems such as 'Un criminal'.

[87] *Campos de Castilla,* p. 195.

It is entirely in keeping with Machado's intentions that the remarks quoted here are very shortly followed, to powerful ironic effect, by a proverbial expression 'ni gobierno que perdure ni mal que cien años dure'. In fact, the consistent note of social criticism involved in such appropriations of others' utterances in *Campos de Castilla* puts us in mind of Volosinov's view that dialogism is a vehicle of ideological tensions, since 'between the reported speech and the reporting context dynamic relations of high complexity are in force'. Such tensions, especially when the presence of a third person to whom the reported utterances are being relayed is taken into account, reflect 'the impact of organized social forces on speech reception'.[88] Direct quoting is not Machado's usual approach to reported dialogue, however. More typically, it is made clear that the quoted speech does not correspond to something actually uttered using the words as given, but rather that the source utterances have been substantially adapted and conflated. The most extreme example is the representation of Iberian Man at prayer that takes up a large part of 'El Dios Ibero'. The incorporated discourse is openly parodic and is even made to end with a gesture of explicit self-condemnation:

> ¡Señor, hoy paternal, ayer cruento,
> con doble faz de amor y de venganza,
> a ti, en un dado de tahúr al viento
> va mi oración, blasfemia y alabanza![89]

The mock quotation here should not be regarded as a mere device to emphasize the shortcomings of devotional practices in the country at large, but more as a way of engaging the reader in debate about

---

[88] V.N. Volosinov, *Marxism and the Philosophy of Language* (New York: Seminar Press, 1973), p. 117. Bakhtin also observes that even punctiliously accurate quotation of another's words can be framed in such a way as to bring about fundamental changes in meaning—see M. Bakhtin, *The Dialogic Imagination*, edited by Michael Holquist, translated Caryl Emerson and Michael Holquist (Austin: University of Texas Press, 1981), p. 340. Deborah Tannen quotes a Woloff proverb to similar effect: 'everything can be moved to another place without being changed—except speech' (Tannen, *Talking Voices*, p. 101).

[89] *Campos de Castilla,* p. 109.

moral and spiritual values. By openly renouncing any claim to superficial veracity in his reporting, the poet is claiming a deeper authenticity in terms of the underlying sincerity of his denunciations and the normative rightness of the values on which they are based. An equally striking example of critical generalization is found in 'Los olivos', embedded in Machado's appalled and angry description of the of the town square of Torreperogil (Jaen). Noticing a pitiful figure who 'parece mirarnos con la boca' he observes:

> […] será el loco del pueblo
> de quien se dice: es Lucas
> Blas o Ginés, el loco que tenemos.[90]

By conflating in this way a number of complacent comments made by different speakers on different occasions and in different locations, Machado evokes a depressingly generalized picture of material, social and intellectual backwardness—a judgement, it goes without saying, that applies to the privileged speakers rather than to the unfortunate human product of the conditions of deprivation in which they acquiesce.

As we have seen, there is a tendency in Machado's work to represent not so much the words of others as their thoughts, feelings and beliefs. Nigel Fabb's contention that, in literary representations of psychological states and linguistic behaviour, attribution (to someone other than the speaker) and attitude (toward the represented utterances) are more important than questions of absolute truth and falsity, is very relevant here. Attitudes 'are arrayed along a scale ranging from doubt to certainty' and speakers can, moreover, dissociate themselves from the thoughts communicated, whether in mild disbelief or fierce disapproval.[91] An attitude of dissociation on the part of the speaker, we should

---

[90] *Campos de Castilla,* p. 204.

[91] See Fabb, *Linguistics and Literature*, p. 255, and p. 264. In speech act terms, John Searle similarly sees the question of the truth status of reproduced utterances as depending on whether the speaker opts to commit himself to a belief or merely report it (see Searle, *Expression and Meaning*, pp. 157-61).

recall, is a plausible way of accounting for the creation of irony. Ironic utterances, that is, can be regarded as an echoic interpretation of the thought of a certain type of person, or of people in general. While ironic dissociation is generally associated with a disapproving attitude, there are no straightforward prescriptions in this area, and a speaker can use an echoic utterance to convey a whole range of attitudes and emotions, ranging from outright acceptance and endorsement to outright rejection and dissociation.[92]

It is with this function, as a signal to the reader to be alert to the expression of attitudes and emotions, that the extensive use of exclamation marks in *Campos de Castilla* is, in the last resort, to be understood. As we have seen, Machado often uses 'admiraciones' to convey a strongly personalized aesthetic and emotional identification with a contemplated landscape. Another frequent use, however, is to point up ironic contradictions, as in the interjection '¡Oh, tierra triste y noble!' that, in 'A orillas del Duero', initiates reflections on the entropic degeneration of historical qualities of greatness into their opposite, or the exclamatory list of contradictions in 'Orillas del Duero' that concludes '¡[…] tierra inmortal, Castilla de la muerte!'[93] A similar reaction to a glaring contradiction (neatly characterized by one commentator as a 'snort of derision')[94] is apparent in Machado's account of the ludicrous (if traditional) progression of Don Guido from roué to devout penitent:

> […] llevando un cirio en la mano
> —¡aquel trueno!—,
> vestido de nazareno.[95]

Occasionally the inherently dialogic quality of ironic exclamation can produce the equivalent of what in prose fiction is sometimes termed free indirect discourse, a focalization of the

[92] See Sperber and Wilson, *Relevance*, pp. 238-40.
[93] See *Campos de Castilla*, p. 103 and p. 112 respectively.
[94] Nicholas G. Round, '*The Three Caballeros: Don Guido and his relatives*', in D. Gareth Walters (ed.), *Estelas en la mar*, pp. 83-99, at p. 88.
[95] *Campos de Castilla,* p. 207.

thoughts and feelings of a depicted character. The motives of the sexually-frustrated parricide in 'Un criminal' are a clear example:

> Quiso heredar. ¡Oh guindos y nogales
> Del huerto familiar, verde y sombrío
> Y doradas espigas candeales
> Que colmarán los trojes del estío![96]

A similar effect can be detected in poems such as 'La saeta', the text of which appears entirely within exclamation marks; in a free, allusive style, Machado reproduces a genre-stereotyped discourse (the text of the original 'saeta' appears as an epigraph) of religious sentiment side by side with his own mixed feelings of recognition and disapproval.

> ¡Oh, la saeta, el cantar
> al Cristo de los gitanos,
> siempre con sangre en las manos,
> siempre por desenclavar![97]

It would be pedantic to insist on mentioning every one of the many and varied techniques in *Campos de Castilla* for introducing dialogue and polyphonic effects (for instance, there is at least one highly effective example, the poem 'Recuerdos', of self-quotation from earlier poetry, a device used to illustrate the inhibitive effect of the poet's Soria experience on the power of childhood memories as a source of poetic inspiration).[98] There is one strategy, however, that is particularly worth mention, combining evocation of others' utterances with a strong element of critique linked to an appeal to consensual norms and values. The strategy in question, the connection of which to reproduced discourse is not always recognized, is the use of negative utterances in an argumentational context. As Leith and Myerson observe, in an analysis of Wordsworth's sonnet 'Upon Westminster Bridge', a negative grammar need not imply a negative state of mind; indeed, negatives

---

[96] *Campos de Castilla,* p. 126.
[97] *Campos de Castilla,* p. 199.
[98] *Campos de Castilla,* pp. 173-74.

can have a very positive effect in creating an intrinsic quality of responding, of taking issue with and making a rejoinder to an opposed position. Negative turns of phrase thus 'tend to allow for other voices, voices which could contest the judgements being made'.[99] From the point of view of discourse in general, it is worth noting that the use of negatives in argumentational discourse seems to presuppose an assertion by somebody of the corresponding affirmative, and thus tend to occur 'when the writer/speaker assumes the addressee has some reason to believe the opposite, either from something in the preceding text or because of assumptions made about the addressee's state of knowledge.'[100] Machado is particularly adept at introducing negatives that conjure up the point of view associated with the corresponding affirmative; his trenchant denial of the traditional or 'romantic' view of madness, for instance, strongly presupposes that many continue to hold and express such a view:

> No fue por una trágica amargura
> Esta alma errante desgajada y rota:
> Purga un pecado ajeno.[101]

Similarly, Machado's vigorous statement of belief in the possibility of change and regeneration conjures up and reproves the apathetic and fatalistic passivity—combining unthinking acceptance of what is with a failure to conceive of the future in any authentic way as an outcome of resolve and effort—that informs the attitudes and utterances of too many of his fellow countrymen:

---

[99] Leith and Myerson, *The Power of Address*, p. 108.
[100] Coulthard, 'Forensic Discourse Analysis', p. 251. The dialogic nature of negative utterances is also recognized in Ducrot's polyphonic theory of language; his view is summarized by Torres Sánchez as: 'las oraciones negativas [...] pueden interpretarse como la refutación metalingüística de de una enunciación primaria "positiva", que se evoca para ser rechazada.' See M. Torres Sánchez, *Aproximación pragmática a la ironía verbal* (Cádiz: Universidad de Cádiz, 1999), p. 78.
[101] *Campos de Castilla,* p. 122.

> hombres de España, ni el pasado ha muerto,
> ni está el mañana—ni el ayer—escrito.[102]

One of the best examples of such argumentationally-evoked dialogism is provided by the close of 'La saeta'.

> ¡Oh, no eres tú mi cantar!
> ¡No puedo cantar, ni quiero
> a ese Jesús del madero,
> sino al que anduvo en el mar![103]

The use of 'sino' is particularly revealing here, since this conjunction is the argumentational connector par excellence in Spanish. In discursive (as opposed to syntactical) terms it serves to indicate that an utterance is intended as justification of a (preceding) wholesale rejection of another's belief or point of view. In this particular instance 'sino' introduces a forceful riposte to those who would have us believe a whole range of related things, including the notion that a person's first loyalty should be to the traditions and beliefs of his 'tierra' and his 'mayores', that manifestations of popular culture are exempt from criticism, that closed, repetitive cycles are preferable to radical change, and that religious faith springs from fervent pity for suffering rather than from faith in the renewal of life and the opening up of new possibilities and horizons.

2.5 TEXTS THEN AND NOW: 'LOS OLIVOS'

We have already seen that a work such as Neruda's 'Explico unas cosas' depends for much of its meaning on its audience's familiarity with a background of political and social conflict that affected daily life or, for those outside Spain, was continually reported in the press, shown on cinema newsreels, and so on. Sixty years later this particular area of contextual knowledge is far less readily accessible to readers of the poem, with a consequent risk of some loss of meaning. With the increasingly rapid pace of social and cultural change, even the relatively short time-lapse of two generations is

---

102 *Campos de Castilla,* p. 109.
103 *Campos de Castilla,* p. 199.

often sufficient to pose a particular challenge for discourse-based approaches to literature. Instead of aiming to elucidate timeless meanings definitively fixed in texts inherited from the past, discourse analysis tends to see meaning in terms of collaboration in contextualized sense-making on the part of producers and receivers. of utterances The problem is thus one of overcoming a potential opacity or disturbance of communication when interpreting utterances whose meaning is shaped by knowledge contingent on a here-and-now that is not our own. The importance of context for understanding implicit meanings and inferences is further magnified, moreover, when literary texts are conceived of as verbal art and thus as performance discourse. The challenge for the commentator becomes one of reconstructing the shared conventions of performance as well as the mutual 'knowledge of the world' of performer and audience.

It is interesting to consider as an example of such problems a text written against the political background of the initial months of World War I, Antonio Machado's 'Los olivos', a poem which, in parts, poses problems of interpretation of a kind to remind us with some force that our contextual environment is not that of the author. It will become apparent, however, that reconstituting the original presuppositions underlying this piece of discourse is a more complicated task than simply ascertaining the events that occurred and issues that were salient in the Spain of its day. In the words of one theorist with a particular interest in this topic, it involves 'making the effort to set in motion once again the disturbed communication between the author, his contemporaries and us'.[104]

One well-established and influential conceptual framework for consideration of the issues that arise in the interpretation of texts transmitted from a relatively distant epoch (and indeed, for considering the whole question of the relationship between language and epistemological concerns) is the philosophical hermeneutics developed by Hans-Georg Gadamer, and its modification in the theory of communicative action of Jürgen Habermas. It is a framework, moreover, that is particularly well

---

[104] Habermas, *The Theory of Communicative Action,* I, p. 133.

suited to our present purposes, in that the task of hermeneutics is conceived as one of shedding light on ordinary processes of understanding rather than on systematic investigation and analysis of data.[105] Hermeneutics 'watches language at work, language as it is used by participants'[106] and thus regards written texts as utterances in context and requires interpreters to 'take up the attitude of responsible subjects, becoming virtual participants in a dialogic correspondence'. Entering the text is thus a time-bridging process of restoring communicative understanding with the author and his audience.[107]

Habermas sums up the range and complexity of the contextual information that constrains meaning for a writer's contemporary audience and thus sets special tasks for the 'posthumous interpreter' in the following terms:

> The interpreter has to clarify the context that must have been presupposed as common knowledge by the author and the contemporaneous public if the difficulties with which the text presents us today did not arise at that time, and if *other* difficulties could arise for contemporaries that now appear trivial to us. The meaning of the text can be disclosed only against the background of the cognitive, moral and expressive elements of the cultural store of knowledge from which the author and his contemporaries constructed their interpretations.[108]

In this view, it is clear that the interpretation of literary texts of the past is not a matter of aiming at objective scrutiny of items preserved as museum pieces; such an approach is, in any case, impossible, since 'there is no such thing as an acontextual viewpoint'[109] and 'understanding what is said requires participation and not merely observation'. The act of interpretation, that is, has contemporary relevance since it involves the transmission and

---

[105] See Jürgen Habermas, *Moral Consciousness and Communicative Action* (Cambridge: Polity Press, 1990), p. 21.

[106] Habermas, *Moral Consciousness*, p. 25.

[107] Habermas, *The Theory of Communicative Action*, I, pp. 135-36.

[108] Habermas, *The Theory of Communicative Action*, I, p. 132.

[109] Jürgen Habermas, *Between Facts and Norms: contributions to a discourse theory of law and democracy* (Cambridge: Polity, 1996), p. 98.

application of cultural knowledge from past to present: 'every understanding of a text represents an actualizing appropriation of the meaning of the text by the interpreter with a view to possible situations in his world'.[110] The version of hermeneutics proposed by Habermas is particularly appropriate in the case of Machado's writing because of the former's emphasis on the critical monitoring of cultural traditions as well as the effective transmission of them. One of the most consistent features of *Campos de Castilla* is the way a sense of history and traditions, of the present as permeated by the past, is not merely conveyed in the poems but consciously reflected on and evaluated in terms of its current relevance. The contemporary interpreter of these poems, then, is often in the position of reconstructing a context which is itself informed by a conscious awareness of earlier historical contexts and utterances. This double hermeneutic can create an extra layer of complexity, but can also create empathy in our attempt to join the poet's dialogue with his contemporary readers while reconsidering in our own context the values and perspectives he sought to re-evaluate in his own.

While this is not the place for an overview of Habermas' theoretical project, or even for an outline of his adaptation of speech act theory to a broad model of social communication, some areas of particular relevance to Machado's outlook and compositional practice are worth mentioning. For instance, the Spanish writer's concern with the value—and limitations—of rationality can acquire a clearer focus through the concepts of a philosopher who has been termed the last great rationalist.[111] Again, we might note that Habermas proposes a discourse ethics based on overcoming egocentric viewpoints to achieve intersubjectively established consensus, and views language as having an inherent potential for bringing about rationally-motivated agreement: 'to understand an

---

110 Habermas, *The Theory of Communicative Action*, I, p. 135.

111 Indeed, one Spanish commentator has pointed to parallels between theoretical formulations by members of the Frankfurt School, including Habermas, and Machado's estimation of cognitive reason. See Luis Martínez de Velasco, 'De la lírica intemporal a la acción comunicativa', in J. L. de la Iglesia *et al.* (eds), *Antonio Machado y la filosofía* (Madrid: Orígenes, 1989), pp. 97-125.

expression means to know how one can make use of it in order to reach an understanding with someone about something'.[112] Machado, one suspects, would have concurred with the view that 'reaching understanding is the inherent telos of human speech'.[113] In 'Desde mi rincón', a poetic response to the publication of Azorín's *Castilla*, he strongly asserts his faith in 'la palabra buena', a responsible discourse of moral argumentation aimed at consensus and concerted action on the part of those who genuinely believe it is possible to build a better future.[114] The importance attached by Machado to intersubjectively constituted processes of understanding extends even to purely lyrical modes of expression. In a much-quoted passage of 1917 he insists that his subjective feelings are not exclusively his own, that he is aware that 'en mi sentir vibran otros sentires, y que mi corazón canta siempre en coro, aunque su voz sea para mí la voz mejor timbrada'.[115] Machado goes on to define the relations between personal experience and expression in a way that curiously seems to anticipate Habermas' central concept of an intersubjectively shared lifeworld, the linguistically embedded stock of knowledge within which individual instances of reaching new agreement are shaped,[116] as well as his definition of the expressive mode of communication as discourse oriented to the subjectivities of an audience:[117]

> Que lo sea también para los demás, ese es el problema de la expresión lírica. Un segundo problema: Para expresar mi sentir tengo el lenguaje. Pero el lenguaje es ya mucho MENOS MÍO que mi sentimiento. [...]

---

[112] Jürgen Habermas, *On the Pragmatics of Communication*, edited by Maeve Cook (Cambridge, Mass.: MIT Press, 1998), p. 199.

[113] Habermas, *The Theory of Communicative Action*, I, p. 287.

[114] In a letter to Juan Ramón Jimenez commenting on this poem Machado insists on the need for consensus: 'la conquista del porvenir sólo puede conseguirse por una suma de calidades. [...] Si no formamos una sola corriente vital e impetuosa, la inercia española triunfará'. See *Obras*, p. 1000.

[115] *Obras*, p. 787.

[116] See *The Theory of Communicative Action*, II, p. 125.

[117] 'Stylized disclosure of experiences to which the speaker has privileged access, with a view to the subjectivities of the audience' (Habermas, *The Theory of Communicative Action*, I, p. 81).

> Antes de ser NUESTRO—porque MÍO exclusivamente no lo será nunca—era de ellos, de ese tercer mundo que no es objetivo ni subjetivo [...] del mundo de LOS OTROS YOS.[118]

Where Machado's critical view of traditions is concerned, it is worth noting that whereas Gadamer's preferred model is the established classical text from which there is something—a truth or a timeless meaning—to be learned and communicated, Habermas allows for retrospectively critical approaches and reminds us that understanding does not require being in agreement, that canonical texts need not be treated deferentially as embodying superior knowledge.[119] Habermas, indeed, puts some emphasis on the importance of critical monitoring of traditions rather than unquestioning reduplication, envisaging the possibility of a 'non-alienated, solidary social life within the horizons of traditions that have been self-consciously appropriated and critically passed on'.[120] Machado is often thought of as anti-traditional, implacably opposed to the persistence of 'sagradas formas y maneras',[121] but, his objection, one might suggest, is not so much to traditions in themselves as to attitudes deeply ingrained in the national character that result in complacent, unthinking reduplication of a status quo predicated on the past.

As with a number of poems of Machado, 'Los olivos'[122] creates the situation of utterance of a traveller presenting his observations and reflections during the course of a journey (in this case in a 'lento carricoche' linking towns in the province of Jaén). The poem is in two distinct parts. The first, inspired by landscape traversed in the stage from Úbeda to Torreperogil, contrasts the productively hard-working life of poor peasants, characterized as honest toilers close to nature, with the unproductive idleness or black-market activities of the 'señores devotos y matuteros' and their bandit

[118] *Obras*, pp. 787-88.
[119] Habermas, *The Theory of Communicative Action,* I, pp. 134-35.
[120] Habermas, *Between Facts and Norms*, p. 98.
[121] *Campos de Castilla*, p. 211.
[122] *Campos de Castilla,* pp. 202-205.

cronies. The second part begins by recording the poet's reactions to the small town of Torreperogil itself:

Allá, el castillo heroico.
En la plaza, mendigos y chicuelos:
una orgía de harapos…
Pasamos frente al atrio del convento
de la Misericordia.
¡Los blancos muros, los cipreses negros!
¡Agria melancolía
como asperón de hierro
que raspa el corazón! ¡Amurallada
piedad, erguida en este basurero!…
Esta casa de Dios, decid, hermanos,
esta casa de Dios ¿qué guarda dentro?

The coach resumes its journey, bringing a pleasantly fertile landscape once more before the poet's eyes, but the sights and sounds of Torreperogil seem to intrude into and undermine his approving contemplation:

La tierra da lo suyo; el sol trabaja;
el hombre es para el suelo:
genera, siembra y labra
y su fatiga unce la tierra al suelo.
Nosotros enturbiamos
la fuente de la vida, el sol primero,
con nuestros ojos tristes,
con nuestro amargo rezo,
con nuestra mano ociosa,
con nuestro pensamiento,
—se engendra en el pecado,
se vive en el dolor. ¡Dios está lejos!—

As often happens with the poems of *Campos de Castilla,* we are presented with a variety of utterance-types and even voices, since there is at least one occasion when the 'speaker' of a piece of the text is clearly not meant to be identified with the 'I' of the poet. Obviously, a familiarity with the poet's sensibilities and sympathies, as expressed in his work as a whole, would help the reader to estimate with greater confidence the point of what he is saying, but there is no reason for supposing the poem is not meant to be fully comprehensible on its own terms. The most revealing feature of the description of the town is the consistent motif of contrast or contradiction, expressed in a series of oppositions: 'Castillo heroico' / 'mendigos'; 'blancos muros' / 'cipreses negros'; 'amurallada piedad' / 'este basurero'. This effect is not confined, moreover, to contrasted pairs of nouns, but is reinforced by basic cognitive contrasts, such as the roughness of the 'asperón' against the softness of the heart, and the separation of the castle 'allá' from the square, the locus of immediate perception 'here'. Perhaps the most telling detail is the phrase 'una orgía de harapos', a powerful oxymoron yoking connotations of wealth-fuelled excess with evidence of squalor and poverty. These features, together with the allusion to the strong feelings the scene produces in him, give Machado's utterances an overall character of denunciation or protest. Such an illocutionary force presupposes, of course, that the speaker holds a set of normative beliefs in accordance with which moral judgements can be made, and that readers will broadly be in agreement with them. Another, and very important assumption underlying this sort of illocution is that the wrong is capable of being righted; protests or denunciations, that is, are also calls for action. In this particular case we should note that the localized setting has an exemplary status, (it is carefully identified at the start as a 'triste burgo de España') making the appeal one for consensus in setting in motion a programme of national reform.[123]

This broad illocutionary trend sets a framework within which to interpret the poem even though there is a certain potential opacity. To switch, as Machado does here, from the implicit 'I' of a poet-observer to an explicit but ill-defined 'nosotros' is to court ambiguity and suggest a range of possible interpretations. The pronoun 'nosotros' is notoriously ambiguous in its scope of reference, since it can just as easily be used to exclude as include

[123] In a letter to Unamuno of 1913, Machado claimed, more in anger than in irony, that there was more to be learned from the contemplation of such places (and the attitudes that produced then) than from the lectures he attended in Paris (*Obras*, p. 1014).

groups in various relations to the speaker. Here, for instance, it is not clear whether reference is being made to the writer and his readers or to the writer and his fellow-travellers in the coach (the elided subjects of the first-person-plural verb forms in the poem up to this point can be taken as referring to this group). On the other hand, and assuming that there is a consistency of feelings and attitudes in the poem, the contrastively explicit 'nosotros' and the self-incriminating assertions that follow might suggest that the poet is no longer speaking to us 'in his own voice', but is critically presenting the discourse of others. Such a switch, in fact, has already occurred earlier in the poem, with the reporting (already analayzed in this chapter) of a stereotypical comment on a mentally retarded youth in the town square, 'es el loco que tenemos'. Moreover, since the poet has previously directed a 'rhetorical' question to the 'hermanos' of the Convento de la Misericordia in the town, it would be appropriate to evoke satirically an answer of sorts, exposing the sin-obsessed mindset and non-productive life-style of a religious order and criticizing what he sees as the pernicious influence of religious institutions and devotional attitudes—and the prestige they continue to enjoy—on Spanish national life. Again, it is possible Machado is dramatizing the gloomy mood the town has produced in him, and is speaking for a whole class (from which he does not exclude himself), contrasting the selfish and artificial preoccupations of professionals and entrepreneurs, priests and intellectuals, all those who do not labour on the land, with those who do, their honest and productive toil attuned to natural life-processes.

What is clear, however, is that the main thrust of his thoughts remains consistently directed to the obscene contrast between the poverty and social deprivation of the town and the irrelevant rituals of the (presumably comfortably-endowed) 'convento' and its inmates. The close of the poem repeats the accusing question '¿qué guarda dentro?', implying even more strongly that the answer is a negative one, that the outward manifestation and physical setting of the religious life lacks any inner spiritual substance:

Esta piedad erguida
sobre este burgo sórdido, sobre este basurero,
esta casa de Dios, decid ¡oh santos
cañones de Von Kluck!, ¿qué guarda dentro?

This time, however, the question is linked to an allusion to the German general von Kluck, best known to posterity for a strategic miscalculation in the advance on Paris. We are dealing here, however, with a typical example of discrepancy between the easily accessible contextual knowledge of Machado's original audience and that of readers of today. During the early phase of the war, before it settled into the routine carnage of entrenched confrontation, there was still scope for speculative commentary on the broad moral issues of modern warfare. One such issue was the legitimacy of subjecting churches to the destructive power of modern weaponry. The damage to the cathedral of Reims, for instance, was widely discussed, and indeed, in the poem 'España en paz' Machado complains that 'Germania arruina templos'.[124] Contemporary readers, especially given Spanish neutrality in the conflict, would be aware of the context of debate around this issue and quick to catch the irony of the adjective 'santos' applied to church-destroying artillery-pieces.

What is particularly interesting about this poem is that it is quite possible that the element of uncertainty as to the moral perspective or point of the closing lines is not simply the result of our difficulty in engaging with the original context, but was intended as such in the first place. The poet, that is, may be using it as a device for encouraging a re-evaluation of beliefs and attitudes and drawing attention to the need for a critical approach to traditions and established ways of thinking. Machado frequently criticizes the emptiness of 'la fe de mis mayores' and other traditional features of national life to which many in the Spain of his day fondly clung, but his real target is not so much the degeneration of traditional institutions as the thoughtless mental reflex of equating national identity with resistance to change. Such an attitude, in its extreme form, is manifested in an inability to conceive of the future as

[124] *Campos de Castilla*, p. 248.

anything other than a repetitive extension of the present, itself conceived as faithful maintenance of what is inherited from the past. What Machado satirizes as 'el mañana efímero' is just such a mock-future of repeated cycles—an 'eterno retorno' in Claudio Guillén's telling phrase[125]—which is the complete opposite of a future conceived in terms of purposeful human agency and dynamic change.

The uncertainty as to the source of perspectives voiced in the poem is also apparent in other stylistic features. With some of the utterances marked as exclamations, for instance, there is little guidance as to their force. Exclamations have the basic function, in Machado's poetry in general, of drawing the reader's attention to something that provokes an emotional reaction in the poet. However, when the reader encounters the line

> ¡Los blancos muros, los cipreses negros!

there is no explicit clue as to whether the poet is admiring something beautiful, recoiling from something ugly, enjoying something amusing, or any number of other possible types of affective response. The reader, that is, has to reconstruct the tone of the exclamation by inferring it from the contents of a description that, as it stands, seems to have no particular evaluative connotations. The reporting mechanism 'de quien se dice', used to incorporate the dismissive remarks made about the pitiful mentally-retarded youth who gawps open-mouthed at the stagecoach, is similarly somewhat non-committal, since 'decir' is the most neutral of reporting verbs and there is no individual characterization of a speaker to provide the reader with clues. Machado, in such instances, seems to be forcing readers to deduce or construct an evaluation that will make sense of states of affairs that are presented in a more or less neutral way. The reader, that is to say, is required to reflect on and reinterpret descriptions that are not marked as

---

125 Claudio Guillén, 'Proceso y orden inminente en *Campos de Castilla*', in José Ángeles (ed.), *Estudios sobre Antonio Machado* (Barcelona: Ariel, 1976), pp. 195-216.

exceptional. Both the examples just considered (and others in the poem) of apparently neutral presentation reveal themselves, on closer inspection, to refer to words and things that are widely-encountered and embody the continuance of traditional settings, institutions, ways of behaving and habits of thought. In essence, by forcing the reader to re-evaluate states of affairs that are normally unreflexively presupposed, Machado is raising to consciousness and problematizing the dangers of unquestioning acceptance of what is, especially when it is accepted precisely because it 'always' has been. The close of 'Los olivos', with its bellicose metaphor for resolute commitment to the dismantling of obstacles to progressive reform, is perhaps a deliberate attempt to shock, conjuring up as it does the image of violent destruction of a church, to the poet's evident approval (in the final lines of a poem written in the same period, 'El mañana efímero', the spirit of national regeneration similarly holds 'un hacha en la mano vengadora').[126] On the other hand, the extent to which the conflict of 1914-18 was to bring momentous and irreversible changes in Western society and its values was possibly starting to become apparent, and Machado is perhaps merely attempting to conclude the poem with a striking motif of the inevitability of change even in a country in which resistance to it was as deeply entrenched as in the Spain of his day.

[126] *Campos de Castilla*, p. 212.

3. THE POWER OF THEATRE: LORCA

3.1 VALLE-INCLÁN AND LORCA: THE LANGUAGE OF MELODRAMA

The thirty-five-year-old Lorca, with the success of *Bodas de sangre* behind him and already shaping the ideas for *Yerma*,[1] seems to have been so unimpressed by Valle-Inclán's evocation of rural Galicia in his theatre that, perhaps unwittingly, he paid the older writer the supreme insult of comparing his work with that of the contemporary dramatists he most despised:

> [...] algo pésimo, algo tan falso y malo como los Quintero en Andalucía. Si te fijas, toda la Galicia de Valle-Inclán, como toda la Andalucía de los Quintero, es un Galicia de primeros términos: la niebla, el aullido del lobo.[2]

These comments were made in August 1933, three months before Margarita Xirgu's company staged Ramón del Valle-Inclán's Galician 'tragicomedia de aldea', *Divinas palabras*, in the Teatro Español, and it is possible Lorca had in mind the somewhat ponderously fatidic *El embrujado*, written in 1913, which had been staged in Madrid two years earlier. On the other hand, his comments may have been based on a well-attended and widely

---

[1] See Ian Gibson, *Federico García Lorca,* II (Barcelona: Grijalbo, 1987), p. 249.

[2] The interview, in *La Mañana* (León), 12 August 1933, is notable for some trenchant remarks on the commercial theatre ('por y para puercos'). Buero Vallejo suggests Lorca's remarks reflect his espousal of a theatre aesthetic very different from Valle's *esperpento* approach. See A. Buero Vallejo, *Tres maestros ante el público* (Madrid: Alianza, 1973), pp. 121-22.

reported public reading of *Divinas palabras* (24 March 1933).[3] At all events, it seems fair to wonder whether a comparison of the two dramatists' treatment of a stock theatrical situation, the flight of adulterous lovers, might serve to redress the balance a little.

Given the artistic originality—for its time and place—of Lorca's *Bodas de sangre,* it can sometimes be forgotten that there are certain elements of the play that represent more of a continuation of the Spanish theatrical tradition than a break with it. We thus have the curious situation that, in 1933, and in a work consciously designed to challenge the lamentable standard of the current commercial theatre, Lorca reproduces a set of verbal and gestural clichés that Valle-Inclán had parodied more than a decade earlier with similarly renovatory intentions.

The third act of Lorca's play begins with the justly celebrated woodland scene highly suggestive of primitive supernatural forces, with poetic dialogue between two woodcutters and then between a chillingly bloodthirsty Moon and a sinister Mendiga. When the Novia and Leonardo appear they have already eloped, but their decision to run away together has not been presented on stage, since the action has focused on the shattering discovery of the bride's absence from the wedding celebrations. As if Lorca had been unwilling to lose through this undeniably effective strategy the opportunity to include one of the most dependably successful types of scene in the Spanish theatre, the escaping couple now enact a stereotypical alternation of doubts and impulsiveness, of the sort ridiculed by Valle-Inclán in the eleventh scene of *Los cuernos de Don Friolera.*[4] In both plays the exchanges revolve around a drawn-out series of declarations and protestations to do with the conflict between the irresistible force of passion and the demands of duty and responsibility, with fear of pursuit and retribution, on the one hand, and of living in dishonour on the other. If we set together

---

[3] See Juan Aguilera Sastre, 'La versión escénica de *Divinas palabras* en el estreno de 1933', in Manuel Aznar and Juan Rodríguez (eds), *Valle-Inclán y su obra* (Barcelona: Associació d'Idees, 1995), pp. 553-62, at p. 553.

[4] See Ramón del Valle-Inclán, *Martes de carnaval*, edited by Ricardo Senabre (Madrid: Espasa-Calpe, 1990), pp. 205-215; and Federico García Lorca, *Bodas de sangre*; *Yerma* (Madrid: Espasa-Calpe, 1973), pp. 104-110.

the speeches of Lorca's fated lovers and those of Valle's somewhat less glamorous fugitives, the similar dependence on stereotyped sentiments and motifs is very apparent. Both couples insist they are helpless in the grip of passionate feelings, which, in the women's case, makes it impossible for them to think clearly: '¡la cabeza se me vuela!' (Loreta), '¡qué fuego me sube por la cabeza!' (Novia). Both believe they are fated to die '¡mi destino es morir degollada!' (Loreta), 'es justo que yo aquí muera' (Novia). The Novia affects to wish for her own death in order to preserve her still technically intact honour, and protests she will go with Leonardo only 'a la fuerza', at which he reminds her '¿quién bajó / primero las escaleras [...] quién le puso / al caballo bridas nuevas?', obliging her to acknowledge that it is the overwhelming force of her feelings rather than any compulsion on his part that is inexorably driving her. When Loreta similarly claims to prefer honour to life, Pachequín answers her accusation that he is dragging her to perdition with the smug rejoinder 'por la fuerza no apetezco yo cosa alguna' eliciting from her the admission that '¡me pedirías la vida y no sabría negártela, hombre fatal!'

Both women suffer pangs of guilt at having exposed the man they love to the vengeful fury of an aggrieved husband, and attempt to persuade him to save himself:

> Para ti será el castigo
> y no quiero que lo sea.
> ¡Déjame sola! ¡Huye tú!

> A mí poco me importa morir, pero me sobrecoge pensar que peligra la vida de un sujeto de las circunstancias de usted, Pachequín.

But in each case the lover gallantly insists that love has lent him the courage and resourcefulness to avert any danger:

> NOVIA. ¿Adónde me llevas?
> LEONARDO. A donde no puedan ir
> estos hombres que nos cercan.
> ¡Donde yo pueda mirarte!

PACHEQUÍN. ¡Así habla el amor! Por lo demás, un hombre es como otro, y servidorcito no le teme al Teniente.
DOÑA LORETA. ¡Es un sanguinario!
PACHEQUÍN. ¡Yo soy alicantino!

Perhaps the most obvious cliché in the *Bodas de sangre* episode is the motif of the woman melodramatically dramatizing her fear of loss of honour and respect in the eyes of her lover as well as those of society. Lorca's Novia creates a somewhat bizarrely over-emblematic image of a shamefully fallen wife when she exclaims (*sarcástica*):

Llévame de feria en feria,
dolor de mujer honrada,
a que las gentes me vean
con las sábanas de boda
al aire como banderas.

The amply-endowed Loreta, on the other hand, more appropriately worries that 'Una mujer es una carga muy grande' and, in spite of her swain's insistence that a beloved partner is 'un peso muy dulce', continues to fear that he will grow tired of her: 'luego sentirás el empalago [...]. Tu desvío sería para mi una puñalada traidora!'

Any spectator familiar with Valle's parodic treatment (Pachequín even boasts, alluding to the title of Eugenio Sellés's well-known nineteenth-century drama of adultery, that 'este nudo gordiano lo corto yo con mi navaja barbera') might find it a little difficult to empathize fully with the fears and desires of Lorca's couple, especially since one of the most telling similarities between the two scenes lies in the discursive structure of the dialogue. It would be necessary to examine unsuitably extensive stretches of dialogue to substantiate the claim in full, but even making allowances for the fact that Lorca's characters are speaking *romance* lines, it is noticeable that neither set of exchanges gives the impression of an emergent process of interaction. Instead of one topic being linked to the next in an on-going movement of persuasion and a gradual overcoming of initial doubts on the part of the woman, there is an arbitrary switching from one hackneyed sub-theme to another, giving the impression of actors jumping through a well-worn set of hoops. In the case of the exchanges between Pachequín and Loreta, of course, this effect is precisely what Valle-Inclán intends, but it is interesting to consider why Lorca should have chosen such a risky combination of clichés from melodramas of adultery in what is clearly meant to be an evocation, in verse dialogue, of violently erotic passion (one *acotación* specifies that 'toda la escena es violenta, llena de gran sensualidad').

It is possible that Lorca's aim was to suggest, through a conventional stereotyping of gestures and words, the helpless obedience of mere mortals to the dictates of the supernaturally powerful entities evoked in the scene as a whole; or again, he may have felt confident that genuinely poetic use of language could restore dramatic potency to the clichés of vacillation associated with the elopement situation. Certainly the greatest contrast between Valle's and Lorca's treatment of this stock situation lies in the verbal style. Both playwrights present characters engaged in puppet-like performance of pre-established gestures and formulas, but whereas Valle systematically mixes overblown rhetoric with prosaic banalities to create a ridiculously grotesque effect, Lorca's intention seems to be rather to suggest, through verbal imagery, the power of the elemental forces in whose orbit the characters move. Thus Lorca's figurative language consistently evokes urgently physical erotic attraction rather than romantic sentiments, while Valle depicts a relationship in which kitsch clichés have usurped genuine feelings.

While it is true that much of the dialogue in *Bodas de sangre* is couched in ritualized language, creating the effect of collective patterns of experience rather than the particular agendas of individuals, there are nevertheless a number of inconsistencies and loose ends associated with this particular scene. For instance, if Lorca aimed to create an effect of tragic irony by making the Novia's final fate that of a 'mujer perdida y doncella', because Death and her lunar accomplice deny the lovers time to attain physical fulfilment of the imperious erotic impulse that possesses them, the introduction of more conventional worries about honour is not altogether consistent with achieving it. The same concern for reputation motivates protestations, in the final scene, that can only seem (as the Madre, indeed, points out) an irrelevant distraction from the tragic course of events:

> NOVIA. Que quiero que sepa que yo soy limpia, que estaré loca, pero que me pueden enterrar sin que ninguna hombre se haya mirado en la blancura de mis pechos.[5]

This avowal is perhaps similar in its slightly puzzling effect to the Novia's earlier melodramatic exhortation to Leonardo to put an end to her shame, either by killing her as he would a snake or by placing 'en mis manos de novia el cañon de la escopeta', an appeal made only a matter of minutes before the two men fight to the death, each armed with the 'cuchillo' that is one of the most prominent fateful leitmotifs of the play.

Transgression of sexual taboos is, in fact, a consistent theme of Lorca's three 'rural tragedies' as well as of Valle-Inclán's later plays, reflecting perhaps, if in different ways, the persistent popularity in the Spanish mainstream theatre of the codes and attitudes traditionally associated with honour. The particular approaches adopted by the two dramatists, however, are diametrically opposed. In Valle's 'esperpentos' the traditional Spanish notion of honour and its status as a source of theatrical plots is consistently criticized, subverted or parodied. Two of the later plays do deal with the topic of honourable standards of conduct, but, in both, treatment of plot or character along lines associated with the honour tradition is carefully avoided. One of them, *Luces de Bohemia*, places the emphasis firmly on personal and professional responsibilities and commitments, while the traditional focus of attention on women's sexual behaviour is notably absent. Similarly, while the action of *Cara de plata* turns on the jealousies and rivalries inspired by a young woman who arouses the sexual appetite of a number of characters, her presentation as a passive trophy in a three-sided power struggle seems, in itself, a pointed rejection of established approaches.

---

[5] *Bodas de sangre*; *Yerma*, p. 119.

Other plays directly satirize the honour convention. *Divinas palabras*, Valle's first play in the *esperpento* style (although labelled 'tragicomedia'), introduces the linkage of dishonour and gross venality that is typical of his treatment of this theme. The adulterous wife, Mari-Gaila, is led into temptation precisely by her greed, and her sexual lapse coincides with the death of the grotesquely retarded nephew she has been exhibiting as a fairground freak; meanwhile (in a piece of comedy that is repeated in *Los cuernos de Don Friolera*) the aggrieved husband is distracted by over-consumption of alcohol from plans for bloody retribution. In *Divinas palabras* the parody of Calderonian intricacies of fitting punishment to transgression is particularly pointed in the husband's drunken fancy that he can avenge the wife's damage to his honour by sleeping with their daughter: 'pues que me da corona, vamos nosotros dos a ponerle otra igual en la frente'.[6]

This sort of theme is often associated at the level of dialogue with melodramatic *tópicos*, as if characters did not have choices and decisions to make, but can only repeat hackneyed formulas and gestures, interspersing them with the occasional expression of realistic if banal concerns that serve to point up the ridiculousness of their pieces of inflated self-dramatization. Pedro Gailo's reaction to his sister's revelations about his wife's conduct is a good example: he absurdly claims that he has no option but to exact the ultimate penalty, since his alleged poor state of health, 'resentido del pecho', means that he cannot simply give her a beating: 'las tundas no bastan, porque se me vuelve'. Mental contemplation of the imminent act of slaughter launches him into a lurid depiction of himself as a condemned murderer:

> ¡[…] me subirás a la horca! ¡Me hilan el cáñamo las malas lenguas, y llaman sobre mí el verdugo! ¡Por perdido me cuento! ¡Tendrás, Marica, un hermano ahorcado! ¡Esta noche saco los filos al cuchillo![7]

---

[6] Ramón del Valle-Inclán, *Divinas palabras*, edited by Luis Feijoo (Madrid: Espasa-Calpe, 1991), p. 279.
[7] See *Divinas palalabras,* pp. 251-52.

The contrastive alternation of pompous descriptions of military intransigence in matters of honour, full of theatrical artificiality and exaggeration, with expressions of practical concerns of the most prosaic or banal nature is, of course, the structuring principle of the dialogue in Valle's most complex 'esperpento de honor', *Los cuernos de Don Friolera.* It should not be supposed, however, that this technique is exclusively one of distancing, reducing a character to the status of a puppet-like automaton, incapable of inspiring the audience's serious regard; it also allows the dramatist to create two seemingly contradictory effects simultaneously. In some ways the audience is meant to follow the lead of the puppeteer in the play's prologue, who, in the words of Don Estrafalario, 'solo trata de divertirse a costa de Don Friolera'.[8] On another level, however the spectators are given a glimpse of the human substance of Lieutenant Pascual Astete, whose peaceful and profitable life as a middle-aged officer in the Customs Corps has been cruelly shattered by 'el honor teatral y africano de Castilla'.[9] The closing scene of the play's central action offers a good example of such ambivalence; unsettling shifts of perspective are frequent and the audience's reaction often hovers between sympathy evoked by a plausible spectacle of suffering and ironic consciousness of extreme theatrical artificiality. Friolera confesses he has got drunk 'para olvidar', to obliterate the mental image of his daughter, effectively an orphan, tearfully embracing the corpse of her adulterous mother, who lies 'con una bala en la sien'.[10] This luridly emblematic depiction earns him the congratulations of the colonel for his exemplary upholding of the honour of the corps, but the shattering news of what has really occurred leaves the audience with a final impression of Friolera not simply as a cardboard figure of fun but also as a human being whose grip on reality has been broken, with tragic consequences, by pressures to conform to a code of conduct that is itself inhumane and unrealistic:

---

[8] *Martes de carnaval*, p. 123.
[9] *Martes de carnaval,* p. 121.
[10] See *Martes de carnaval*, pp. 219-20.

DOÑA PEPITA. ¡Qué drama! ¡No mató a la mujer! ¡Mató a la hija!
DON FRIOLERA. ¡Maté a a mi mujer! ¡Mi hija es un angel!
DOÑA PEPITA. ¡Mató a su hija, Pancho!
EL CORONEL. ¿Ha oído usted, desgraciado?
DON FRIOLERA. ¡Sepúltate alma, en los infiernos!
EL CORONEL. Pepita, que le sirvan un vaso de agua.
DON FRIOLERA. ¡Asesinos! ¡Cabrones! ¡Más cabrones que yo! ¡Maté a mi mujer! ¡Mate usted a la suya, mi Coronel! ¡Mátela usted, que también se la pega![11]

These excerpts should be sufficient to make clear that Valle is not simply satirizing the melodramatic tendencies he sees as a debilitating long-term flaw of the Spanish theatre; he is also incorporating them in an innovatory theatrical discourse of conflicting voices, thus challenging established assumptions about character, language, and the relation of both to the audience and to social reality. Lorca, on the other hand, seems more interested in adapting and refining melodramatic techniques to achieve a more expressive theatrical language and more effective emotional characterization. The essential difference, then, is that Valle-Inclán, in his later plays, adopts a critical position with regard to melodrama, presenting it in an entirely unflattering light as an artificial—and superficial—exaggeration of emotions, motives and situations, whereas Lorca seems more interested in exploiting the strengths of melodrama as an expressive style and as a technique for focusing on moral issues. We will return shortly to this aspect of Lorca's mature plays, but for the moment it is worth considering a very instructive if fortuitous textual comparison. The first example, from Valle's *Cara de Plata*, is a confrontation between one of the sons of an aristocratic landowner and the powerful local abbot, who finds what had hitherto been a right of way blocked:

CARA DE PLATA. Señor Abad, que no hay vereda.
EL ABAD. Joven Absalón, no me detengas con chanzas [...].
CARA DE PLATA. ¡Ojalá fueran chanzas! [12]

---

[11] *Martes de carnaval*, p. 220.

[12] See Ramón del Valle-Inclán, *Cara de Plata*, edited by Antonio Risco (Madrid: Espasa-Calpe, 1992), pp. 66-67.

While in the second scene of *Yerma*, the protagonist's husband protests about the gossip provoked by her unwifely penchant for walking abroad:

YERMA. ¡Puñalada le den a las gentes!
JUAN. No maldigas. Está feo en una mujer.
YERMA. ¡Ojalá fuera yo una mujer![13]

Both are examples of a type of verbal irony that involves direct rejection by one character of the presupposition underlying another's utterance, a dialogue device of tested efficacy in bringing situational tension to life. The Valle-Inclán example does not go much beyond this basic function, although Cara de Plata's use of a politeness strategy is dramatically effective. His apparent attempt to mitigate his refusal and attend to the want of the Abbot to be considered a person of consequence by insinuating personal regret for a course of action that has been unavoidably imposed on him, stems, in reality, from the never-back-down attitude of a young blood who is determined to prove his previous boast 'si no pasan los que caminan a pie, no pasarán los que vienen a caballo' is his bond.[14] Yerma's strategy is more complex in terms of hinting at her psychology. There is an implied rhetorical self-characterization in the background here, of the type that consists of denying undoubted facts (in this case the fact of her biological gender) in order to foreground a quality she wants to be perceived as more deeply relevant. At first sight, then, Yerma is creating an implicature along fairly orthodox Gricean lines: since what she says is ostentatiously untrue (that is, she is flouting the maxim of quality), there must be another meaning that can be deduced in the context that allows her comment to make sense. For Yerma of course, the context (as always) includes presumed mutual knowledge of her childlessness and the dissatisfaction this causes her. In terms of the current dispute with her husband, she is implicating (possibly not without an element of blame) that if she had a child to occupy her she would

[13] Federico García Lorca, *Yerma,* edited by R. Warner (Manchester: Manchester University Press), 1994, p. 52.
[14] *Cara de Plata,* p. 65.

willingly accept the restrictive norms circumscribing women's behaviour. On the other hand, we might even suspect that Yerma is speaking quite literally, that her psychological truth is simply at odds with the external facts and she is genuinely convinced that she is not in any 'real' sense a woman. Whatever interpretation is favoured, the audience will appreciate that Yerma has found a powerfully paradoxical way of naming the inner contradiction of her life and the pain it causes her.

Since the main concern here is with melodramatic style of dialogue there is little point in providing any detailed account of melodrama in general, especially since it is clear Lorca was not particularly interested in offering straightforwardly sensationalized fables of vice and virtue, conflicts motivated externally rather than through characters' divided nature, extravagant peripeties, coups de théâtre, or any other of the superficial features associated with the genre in the nineteenth century (and, in Spain, well into the twentieth). What is of more particular relevance is the structural definition of melodrama as a full and explicit acting out of the moral and emotional meaning of situations and gestures, the use of verbal and stage signs for techniques of nomination, that is, 'the full enunciation of how and what one is'.[15]

Where his major stage works were concerned, of course, Lorca was determined not only to reach a level of achievement aesthetically superior to that of the mainstream Spanish theatre of his day, but, as a number of his comments to journalists and theatre professionals make apparent, to use the stage as a stimulus to serious debate on important moral issues.[16] Melodramatic dialogue, with its propensity for making explicit the moral significance of situations and actions and its tendency to highlight ethical tests of character ('the intensity of moral claim impinging on characters' consciousness'),[17] offered some useful options in this respect. We have seen how the linking of such a style with the typically Spanish

[15] Peter Brooks, *The Melodramatic Imagination* (New Haven: Yale University Press, 1976), p. 44.

[16] For a discussion of Lorca's views on the theatre as a forum for raising such issues, see my comments in *Yerma,* pp. 2-5.

[17] Brooks, *The Melodramatic Imagination*, p. ix.

concern with *honra* has a perhaps intrusive effect in *Bodas de sangre*, which in many ways seems designed to evoke a tragic frame of reference that is more anthropological than social. It is worth noting, however, that at the beginning of the episode of the fleeing lovers just discussed, our attention is drawn precisely to this universalized tragic ethos, with its suggestion of the inexorable working of timeless forces, by the inclusion, in the speech of the Novio, of a verbal device very characteristic of melodrama. The device in question could perhaps be termed meronymic redefinition, since it consists of explicitly enunciating the functioning of a body part as theatrical sign: '¿Ves este brazo? Pues no es mi brazo. Es el brazo de mi hermano y el de mi padre y el de toda mi familia que está muerta.'[18]

This sort of melodramatic dialogue-effect, we should note, is not limited to moral re-naming of parts of the body, but appears in a more generalized form as emphatic re-definition of personal feelings and circumstances. What is involved is a rhetorical formula—consisting of a denial of superficially plausible facts or opinions as a prelude to the assertion of deeper truths—that is used more consistently, and to consistently good effect, in later plays such as *Yerma* and *La casa de Bernarda Alba.* Yerma, for instance, is quick to redefine her true feelings to the young mother María: 'no es envidia lo que tengo; es pobreza', or to retort to the older woman who enjoins her to think of the comfortable long-term perspective of a childless life: 'Yo no pienso en el mañana: pienso en el hoy'.[19] Similar redefinitions are used in *La casa de Bernarda Alba* to emphasize the dangerous disparity between the 'official' version of the situation in the household and what is really going on. The jealously-observant Martirio's reply to Adela's expressions of admiration at the brightness of shooting stars, pointedly hinting at the real cause of her sister's star-struck mood, is a typical example of this sort of challenge.

---

[18] *Yerma*, p. 101.

[19] See *Yerma*, p. 66, p. 74.

> A mí las cosas de tejas arriba no me importan nada. Con lo que pasa dentro de las habitaciones tengo bastante.[20]

From a more specifically discursive point of view, it is worth noting that the contradictory polarization (itself a central motif of melodrama at large) achieved by this device is almost invariably, as befits effective stage dialogue, embedded in presuppositions and implicatures rather than explicitly realized in the canonical form of a negative utterance followed by the conjunction 'sino' that formally marks this type of argument (indeed, the latter form is, in any case, a feature more of written than spoken language). Thus the irresolvable conflict between Yerma's central life-roles of wife and mother—on the one hand she sees motherhood as her sole reason for being, on the other her self-integrity depends on unswerving monogamy—is typically expressed through implied rather than explicit naming of the dilemma on whose horns she is caught. A striking example occurs at the end of the play's fifth scene, when, yet again, we find Yerma defending herself angrily against accusations that her behaviour encourages rumours of interest in other men. In spite of her previous claim to Dolores that her husband is too heavily preoccupied with work and the profitability of his land to be interested in having sex with her, let alone having children, she makes it clear that she has no option but to play the hand that life has dealt her, and that to choose any other course would be a betrayal of her own deepest nature. Therefore, in spite of evidence to the contrary, she insists—or deludes herself—that somewhere within him there is a 'real' Juan, a loving husband and potent father of children, whom it is her task to search out and bring to life.

> JUAN. Ni yo sé lo que busca un mujer a todas horas fuera de su tejado.
> YERMA. *(En un arranque y abrazándose a su marido.)* Te busco a ti. Te busco a ti, es a ti a quien busco día y noche, sin encontrar sombre donde respirar. Es tu sangre y tu amparo lo que deseo.

---

[20] Federico García Lorca, *La casa de Bernarda Alba*, edited by H. Ramsden (Manchester: Manchester University Press, 1983), p. 70.

The deeper truth of her being, however, her life's inner meaning, is one that she is afraid to name openly. When she finally does name it, it comes as a shattering moment of recognition that precipitates the final catastrophe:

> Marchita sí, ¡ya lo sé! ¡Marchita! [...] Desde que me casé estoy dándole vueltas a esa palabra, pero es la primera vez que la oigo, la primera vez que me la dicen en la cara. La primera vez que veo que es verdad.[21]

At the very end of the play, when she has killed the man who is her only hope of redemption through a child, Yerma again acknowledges her identity is her destiny, 'Marchita, marchita pero segura. Ahora sí lo sé de cierto'.[22] This is indeed the sort of nomination Brooks has in mind when he describes melodramatic anagnorisis as 'the recognition, the liberation from misprison, of a pure signifier, the token for an assigned identity'.[23]

There is a strong link, in *Yerma*, between the recurrent allusions to the notion of explicit expression—and equally, of explicit non-expression—and the central themes of the play. Much of the dramatic tension derives precisely from the unwillingness and downright refusal, on the part of most of the characters, to allow meanings and identities to be openly named. Rarely can a play have contained so many injunctions from one character or another to 'callar', or explicit refusals to speak out clearly; this tendency is by no means limited to the acrimonious mutual accusations between Yerma and her husband. In every scene of the play, one or more characters, even minor ones such as the squabbling *lavanderas* or the old women with whom Yerma visits the graveyard, at some point demand silence. In almost every case what is involved is a refusal to listen to or enunciate judgements and definitions that are dark and dangerous:

---

[21] *Yerma*, p. 88.
[22] *Yerma,* p. 90.
[23] Brooks, *The Melodramatic Imagination*, p. 53.

YERMA. Yo no sé, pero dímelo tú por caridad. (*Se arrodilla.*)
VIEJA. ¡Ay qué flor abierta! ¡Qué criatura tan hermosa eres! Déjame. No me hagas hablar más. No quiero hablarte más. Son asuntos de honra y yo no quemo la honra de nadie. Tú sabrás. De todos modos, debías ser menos inocente.[24]

For all that the atavistically honourable (and somewhat prudish) Yerma fails to catch her drift, the audience cannot fail to notice that the Vieja is, in fact, hinting very strongly at what she is careful not to name explicitly. (In Gricean terms, her comments on 'honra' implicate—since they would otherwise be irrelevant—that the remedy she has in mind involves damage to someone's honour, that is, an illicit sexual liaison.) This by no means alters the significance of her—and others'—apparent adoption of a 'sealed lips' policy. The space in which the characters of *Yerma* move is one of dialectical interplay of norms and deviance, of taboos and transgressions, whether conscious or unconscious, external or internalized, and their verbal strategies appropriately reflect uncomfortable awareness of this tension between the governing principles of their world.

The melodramatic expression of opposed polarities is also a feature of *La casa de Bernarda Alba*, with the difference that the eponymous protagonist is no longer, as in *Yerma*, a character who is unable to reconcile the demands on her of the equally strong but by no means compatible forces of nature and society. We encounter instead a character who attempts to impose her own definition of the particular situation and life in general in accordance with only one set of forces—the values and codes of conduct of an ultra-traditional and moralistic society. While in Lorca's rural plays in general there is a tendency for traditional definitions of norms of conduct and social organization to find expression in what seem to be popular axioms and proverbs, in *La casa de Bernarda Alba* the eponymous matriarch constantly expresses the hierarchical power vested in her not through issuing directives—although the fondness for demands for silence noted in *Yerma* remains in evidence—but through the apparently impersonal and thus more effective strategy

[24] *Yerma,* p. 46.

of defining reality. Her first speech (apart from an inevitable '¡silencio!') contains a number of examples of the sort of highly-polarized moral definition (the antithetical terms either fully explicit or clearly to be inferred) that is often found, as we have seen, in the language of melodrama:

> Menos gritos y más obras. Debías haber procurado que todo esto estuviera más limpio para recibir el duelo. Vete. No es éste tu lugar. *(La Criada se va sollozando.)* Los pobres son como los animales. Parece como si estuvieran hechos de otras sustancias.[25]

The whole play, in fact, becomes a struggle over which—or whose—definitions are to count, and the definitions themselves are implacably opposed: is the house an oppressive prison or a protective home, are its inhabitants a close-knit family or a nest of warring vipers, are the visits of Pepe el Romano an observance of courting customs or a cover for sexual transgression? Accordingly, the play's principle resource for creating dramatic tension and conflict in particular episodes—and theatrically it is a highly effective one—is to present the interplay of various discursive strategies of power and discursive strategies of challenge to the legitimacy of that power.

Episodes such as the violently direct final rejection by Adela of Bernarda's parental authority, or the moment when Martirio's progressively more pointed hints to Adela erupt into nails-drawn confrontation, predictably exploit overtly melodramatic techniques. In the first instance, there is a full 'acting out' of the situation by matching action with the naming of its moral significance, such as when Adela declares, on breaking her mother's stick in two, 'esto hago yo con la vara de la dominadora'.[26] In the second there is a characteristic use of the device of polarized re-definition we have already noted (with 'mujer' being used in the sense of rival for a man's affections):

---

[25] *La casa de Bernarda Alba,* p. 9.
[26] *La casa de Bernarda Alba,* p. 88.

> Mi sangre ya no es la tuya, y aunque quisiera verte como hermana no te miro ya más que como mujer.[27]

It is in the less obviously confrontational episodes, however, that some of the more telling blows are struck in the minor verbal skirmishes in which the play abounds. The visit of Prudencia, for instance, for all its formality and politeness, is full of little gossip-gathering provocations (such as 'en mi tiempo las perlas significaban lágrimas'). A little later there is a telling moment when Bernarda's prescriptions and definitions touch (as part of a reprimand to Angustias) on the interactive ground rules of marriage in a way that almost moves us to sympathetic understanding of how she has become what she is, in that it suddenly illuminates the extent to which all the characters, including the domineering matriarch herself, are trapped in an intersubjective network of asymmetrical relations of power: [28]

> BERNARDA. No le debes preguntar. Y cuando te cases, menos. Habla si él habla y míralo cuando te mira. Así no tendrás disgustos.
> ANGUSTIAS. Yo creo, madre, que él me oculta muchas cosas.
> BERNARDA. No procures descubrirlas, no le preguntes, y, desde luego, que no te vea llorar jamás.
> ANGUSTIAS. Debía estar contenta y no lo estoy.
> BERNARDA. Eso es lo mismo.[29]

This is the only tragedy of Lorca, moreover, in which servants are given social, that is, a class significance beyond their traditional and conveniently useful theatrical functions, and the ambivalent position of La Poncia is skilfully exploited in this respect. The family servant, who represents a 'middle-ground' perspective in the play, knows that social rules were made to channel natural impulses and needs rather than suppress them altogether, and conducts intricate debates with Bernarda, revolving around competing

---

[27] *La casa de Bernarda Alba*, p. 86.
[28] Or in Foucauldian terms, 'the multiple flexibility of subjection'. See Paul Julian Smith, *The Body Politic: gender and sexuality in Spanish and Spanish-American literature* (Oxford: Clarendon, 1989), p. 115.
[29] *La casa de Bernarda Alba*, p. 74.

linguistic constructions of reality and the close links between discourse, moral values and power. These conversations frequently take on patterns of discursive reflexivity, as Bernarda consistently has to defend herself against insidious accusation that her world-picture is a word-picture, a construct designed to confer legitimacy on her exercise of control. In the following example (as in many others) she forced to fall back on her class prerogative of naked assertion of power:

> BERNARDA. ¿Es que quieres que las entregue a cualquier gañán?
> LA PONCIA. Debías haberte ido a otro pueblo.
> BERNARDA. Eso. ¡A venderlas!
> LA PONCIA. No, Bernarda, a cambiar… Claro que en otros sitios ellas resultan las pobres.
> BERNARDA. ¡Calla esa lengua atormentadora!
> LA PONCIA. Contigo no se puede hablar. ¿Tenemos o no tenemos confianza?
> BERNARDA. No tenemos. Me sirves y te pago. ¡Nada más![30]

In the counterpart of this conversation, in the third act, the discursive polarity is, as it were, reversed; it is Bernarda who repeatedly challenges her family servant to justify her warnings of impending disaster, and Poncia who avoids saying any more on the matter, knowing that she has done her duty by saying as much as she can:

> BERNARDA. Mis hijas tienen la respiración tranquila.
> LA PONCIA. Eso te importa a ti que eres su madre. A mí con servir tu casa tengo bastante.
> BERNARDA. Ahora te has vuelto callada.
> LA PONCIA. Me estoy en mi sitio y en paz.[31]

As Poncia now clearly realizes, Bernarda has made the fatal mistake for any tyrant—she has come to believe her own propaganda. The reversing of discursive strategies is a subtle way of revealing this error to the audience and preparing for the final violent outcome.

---

[30] *La casa de Bernarda Alba*, pp. 20-21.
[31] *La casa de Bernarda Alba*, p. 78.

After this conversation, the nomination with which the play closes, Bernarda's last attempt to define reality as in accordance with her own grotesquely skewed priorities, 'la hija menor de Bernarda Alba ha muerto virgen',[32] will be instantly recognized as the pathetic reflex of a ruler whose power has largely collapsed.

3.2 BALLAD AS DRAMA

The claims made here for the productiveness of a discourse studies methodology could never be fully justified without being tested on what is probably the most written-about and analyzed collection of poems in the Spanish language—Lorca's *Romancero gitano*. While there is probably not much scope, where these poems are concerned, for arriving at radically new conclusions, it is worth exploring ways of providing a new focus on or a firmer underpinning for interpretations the main lines of which have already been put forward. Critical commentary on Lorca's work has sometimes indulged in psychological biography and the interpretation of images and metaphors as surface clues to deeper personal and cultural meanings. While there is much to be said for the view of poets in general as truth-tellers in a deep sense, in touch with important intuitive experiences of the type increasingly ignored by the advance of technological civilization, it is dangerous to assume that the revelation of encoded meanings adds up to a sufficient account of a poem or a passage of verse. To emphasize generalized trends of signification is often to underrate the element of verbal creativity, the capacity of poets to treat words as living things with cultural histories, and find new combinations to make them come to life anew. One fruitful way of approaching Lorca's work is to pay close attention to individual texts as complexly coherent, as intersections of prosodic and conceptual artifice, skilfully combining traditional cultural resonances with the insights of a modern sensibility. Following this broad method of analysis, the focus here will be on the way the expression and structure of one particular ballad—'Romance de la luna, luna'—are geared to

---

[32] *La casa de Bernarda Alba*, p. 91.

evoking characteristic features of traditional oral performance, while at the same time making possible the achievement of aesthetic effects outside the traditional remit of the genre.

Although 'literary' adaptations and pastiches were not uncommon, we should remember that the live performance of popular ballads and 'coplas' persisted in Spain well into the first half of the twentieth century, and Lorca's readers would be very familiar with instances of such performances. To judge by his own comments on the work, Lorca's aims in writing the ballads of *Romancero gitano* were not to imitate superficial aspects of subject matter and language, but to exploit generic possibilities to the full.[33] Critical analysis should, accordingly, give due weight to the markedly performative mode of the ballads of *Romancero gitano* and the performer/audience situation of communication they call into being.

'Romance de la luna, luna', the poem with which the collection opens,[34] apparently one of the earliest to be composed,[35] contains many of the stylistic and thematic features that characterize the collection as a whole. An element that frequently attracts comment is the suspense and sense of mystery created by a laconic and fragmented presentation of both narrative line and description of scene or situation, a treatment which tends to foreground isolated details and give them an enigmatic quality, as if to invite symbolic interpretation. The intention here is to account for this effect by examining the linguistic form and the discursive structure of the text, in conjunction with a consideration of contextual features influencing readers' interpretation of it. A preliminary general point worth making, however, is that gaps in anecdotal information and narrative continuity are a consistent feature of the ballads in the collection. 'Romance sonámbulo', for instance, begins by evoking,

---

[33] The most relevant of Lorca's comments can be consulted, together with the text and useful textual notes, in Miguel García Posada (ed.), *Federico García Lorca: Primer romancero gitano; Llanto por Ignacio Sánchez Mejías* (Madrid: Clásicos Castalia, 1988). See also Federico García Lorca, *Romancero gitano*, ed. Derek Harris (London: Grant & Cutler, 1991).

[34] García Posada, *Primer romancero* gitano, pp. 103-104.

[35] See Garcia-Posada, *Primer romancero gitano*, p. 279.

in a mysterious green light, a set of objects and persons that are neither identified nor related in an explicit way:

> El barco sobre la mar
> y el caballo en la montaña.
> Con la sombra en la cintura,
> ella suena en su baranda [...].[36]

Although such lack of explanatory detail could be regarded, in its potential to create problems for interpretation, as a typically modern trait, it is, in fact, something often encountered in oral performances of traditional material. Even so traditional a work such as 'Lord Gregory', it has been noted, makes 'stringent demands on the audience's ability to comprehend the ballad as a narrative', since 'there are an enormous number of gaps to be filled in'.[37] Such performances tend to have their own sequential logic, in which structured connectedness between discursive episodes and even between individual utterances relies on knowledge shared by the performer and audience as to generic topics and conventions. In a similar way, 'Romance sonámbulo' depends on the recognition of motifs to do with smuggling to provide a framework for interpreting the laconic narration of events and the pared-down pieces of dialogue between unidentified speakers which make up most of the poem. The principal aim of the performers, of course, is to maximize involvement and rapport with their audiences through a mode of presentation that is mimetic rather than an exposition of a narrative schema, and to concentrate on producing patterns of emotional interaction rather than explaining causes and describing situations in full.

Following a method already used in analyzing poems of Neruda and Machado, a useful place to start with Lorca's poem is to consider examples of deviation from 'normal' linguistic usage, since this has the effect of foregrounding the textual elements concerned. A number of features of *Romance de la luna, luna* are in some sense deviant, and therefore perceptually salient. For

---

[36] *Primer romancero gitano*, p. 120.
[37] Leith and Myerson, *The Power of Address*, p. 60.

instance, the first of the set of statements with which the poem opens demands our attention because it seems slightly anomalous or ill-formed in some way:

> La luna vino a la fragua
> con su polisón de nardos.

One way of explaining the slightly unsettling effect from a semantic point of view would be to say that there is a minor violation of selection restrictions;[38] 'la luna', that is, does not belong to the class of nouns (those denoting animate entities) that can turn up in Spanish as the subject of the verb 'venir' when it is followed by a prepositional phrase referring to a humanly-defined space. To make sense of it we have to interpret either 'luna' or 'vino' in some non-literal or transferred meaning. The most obvious interpretation, perhaps, involves taking 'luna' as some sort of animate being; indeed, readers will be aware that the moon has often been evoked in an anthropomorphic guise, associated with mythical beliefs, the irrational and the mysterious. A similar option of transferred meaning allows interpretation of 'polisón de nardos' in terms of scent. In both of the poem's opening lines, then, the effect of defamiliarization is sufficient to attract attention and create a certain sense of mystery, but not so pronounced as to hold up understanding. Some interesting further considerations emerge, however, if we switch our attention from deviant foregrounding to background features, that is, to linguistic choices that are not salient but which create presuppositions and expectations at a level often below that of conscious attention. The intriguingly humanoid behaviour ascribed to 'la luna' in the ballad's opening line results in our not paying particular attention to the choice of determiner for the nouns 'luna' and 'fragua'. Definite noun phrases in Spanish may be used for generic reference (as in, for instance, 'la vivienda' in a text about building costs and mortgage rates), but a more frequent use, as in English, is to label the entity referred to as

---

[38] Selection restrictions 'tell us, in effect, which pairs of lexemes can combine with one another meaningfully in various grammatical constructions' (Lyons, *Language and Linguistics*, p. 152).

already familiar to the reader or hearer in some way. In Halliday's account of its function 'it signals "you know which one(s) I mean"'.[39] This presupposition should be combined, in turn, with the operation of the Given/New principle of information sequencing. In the absence of indications to the contrary (such as intonation), it is assumed that what comes at the start of an utterance is being treated by the speaker as part of backgrounded information readily accessible to the hearer. Information that comes later in the utterance-unit, on the other hand, is being treated as 'non-recoverable' and to be attended to as new or unpredictable.[40] Thus we can interpret the ballad's opening line as informing us of the coming of an already familiar entity to an already familiar place (although the specification of that place in particular is perhaps worth taking note of), dressed in a way we should definitely pay attention to. The same sort of considerations apply to the lines introducing the other character in the scene:

El niño la mira, mira.
El niño la está mirando.

Here, however, the insistent repetition and parallelism have a reassuring, familiarizing effect, in spite of the fact that we do not know, as we seem to be expected to, which child the poet means.

Clearly all pieces of discourse have to start somewhere, and the apparent presupposition that readers are familiar with persons and things mentioned in the first words is a convention that all sorts texts ranging from news-reports to advertisements and fictional stories have in common. In this particular poem, however, it is worth noting that virtually all the noun phrases are of the definite type; the exceptions are a number of possessive pronouns, direct address nouns—[tú] 'luna', [tú] 'niño'—in a passage of dialogue, and a highly significant use of the indefinite article near the end of the poem:

---

[39] Halliday, *An Introduction to Functional Grammar,* p. 314.
[40] See Halliday, *An Introduction to Functional Grammar*, pp. 295-299.

Por el cielo va la luna
con un niño de la mano.

The use of the definite article as the determiner before most of the nouns in the poem undoubtedly has the effect of drawing us as readers into the world of the narrator / performer, situating us as members of a community of address who are familiar with the people and things referred to. The fact that one of these appears to be a supernatural being, an astral body become a human one, by no means weakens this effect, but rather encourages us to give a freer rein to our intuitive or mythical interpretation of experience.[41] However, the switch to '*un* niño' marks—if the expression is meant to be taken as co-referential with 'el niño', and there is nothing to prevent us making this natural connection—an abrupt removal of the foregrounded figure of the child from 'our' world, its replacement by angry or grieving adults, and its estranged relocation in a distant and unfamiliar setting. While, as a matter of principle, nothing has been said here about what these events might 'mean' as a narrative, the effect just described certainly accords with many lines of interpretation of what 'happens' in the poem.

Where the narrative thread is concerned, in fact, we might note that the traditional Spanish ballad licence in the choice of verb tenses is fully exploited. The alternation of present and past tenses is associated with unannounced transformations in the situation of address, as the performer switches between narration of events and mimetic evocation of scenes. This feature is again one that is associated particularly with oral performance, where the performer has the capacity to dramatize episodes through variations of intonation and gesture, as well as characterizing them through the use of deictic markers, such as the possessive pronouns already mentioned, the 'yo' of each voice and the 'tú' of the person addressed. Three voices are heard: that of the performer/narrator whose account of events begins and ends the poem, but whose role is anything but a neutrally detached one ('Cómo canta la zumaya, /

---

[41] The term 'mythical' is meant to include here both primitive-traditional formulations of basic human truths and particular classical (and some more recent) treatments of myths, the details of which Lorca often exploited allusively.

¡ay, cómo canta en el árbol!' he exclaims at one point), and what seems to be the voice of a gypsy child alone in a smithy at night, and that of the moon, who appears to him in the guise of a mysterious, metallically glistening woman. Their dialogue is itself a dramatically suspenseful one, constructed through a symmetrically matched series of warnings and injunctions. It is worth noting that, as we saw with Neruda's 'Explico algunas cosas', the use of the future tense to speak about the informational domain of the addressee can be appropriate only in certain specific situations of utterance. While the child, presumably, naively bases his warning on a presumption of the moon-woman's ignorance of the gypsies' imminent return, she, in contrast, uses the prerogative of prediction and warning belonging to someone whose superior power and knowledge ensure complete control of the situation.

> Huye luna, luna, luna.
> Si vinieran los gitanos
> harían de tu corazón
> collares y anillos blancos.
> Niño, déjame que baile.
> Cuando vengan los gitanos,
> te encontrarán sobre el yunque
> con los ojillos cerrados.
> Huye luna, luna, luna,
> que ya siento sus caballos.
> Niño, déjame, no pises
> mi blancor almidonado.

Another prominent feature, again one often found in traditional ballads, is that the utterances seem to imply a narration of events, in a similar way to the development of a scene in the theatre through dialogic exchanges. The urgent warning that concludes the passage of dialogue suggests that the child, fascinated by the dance of the mysterious moon-woman, is, with fatal consequences, about to transgress the apparition's personal space. Thus, when the narrator later reveals that the figure of the moon can be seen in the sky leading a child by the hand, the reader might well conclude the child has died. It is worth insisting, perhaps, that the abduction (or death) of the child is an inference rather than an explicit piece of storytelling, since there is no definite article to confirm the identity of this child with 'el niño' in the forge. There are gaps to be filled in and the audience needs to make the connections between voices and events.

A common feature of ballad dialogue is that the same or similar, parallel words or phrases are used by different protagonists to accomplish different ends. This is certainly the case with the passage of dialogue just examined, and indeed, one of the most prominent features of 'Romance de la luna, luna' as a whole, and one that is also closely associated with performance discourse in general, is the economical and effective use of patterning—whether prosodic, syntactical or informational—of the sort that creates what could be termed memorability. As well as a preference for sensorially striking images there is a consistent use of patterned structures to foreground important effects and make key pieces of information salient, as well as a shaping of events into the sort of sequential relationships which invite interpretation as a story (although not necessarily as a fully explicit one).

Where purely verbal patterning is concerned we find a number of instances of repetition, ranging from the rhythmical doubling—or tripling—of individual lexical items, such as 'luna, luna, luna' 'mira mira', 'vela vela', and examples of phrasal reminiscence such as 'Como canta [...] ay, cómo canta', or 'mira [...] está mirando', to more complex effects of verbal reiteration which are closely tied up with semantic or cognitive patterns. Parallel structures always have the effect of prompting audiences to infer parallel meanings between those structures, and the preponderance of such patterns in this poem is clearly meant to influence its interpretation. In addition, there are a number of cognitive parallelisms of a type that suggests linked events and processes. Besides the ones already mentioned in passing, we should note that we are told the gypsies may come, then they do come, and that the child's eyes will be closed, then they are closed. The parallel warnings, moreover, consign the moon-woman's heart to metal 'anillos y collares' and the child's body to the metal of 'el yunque' respectively, and while a horseman gallops over the plain, the gypsies ride through the olive grove—and so on.

The effect of such an abundance of parallelism —and we have seen that there are prosodic, syntactic and ideational examples in this poem—is not only to foreground certain motifs, but also to make the reader search for connections of meaning. It is worth wondering what sort of equivalence is suggested by the series of references to eyes being wide open, shut, half shut (the gypsies riding through the olive trees have 'los ojos entornados'), since it is clear that readers are being encouraged to perceive meaningful linkages between them. The last of such allusions, in the closing lines of the poem,

> El aire la vela, vela.
> El aire la está velando.

characterizes the air as 'velando', watching, staying awake, and, as we have noted, closely echoes in its formal structure the earlier description of the child's wide-eyed fascination:

> El niño la mira mira.
> El niño la está mirando.

Why should the ballad thematize eyes open or closed, wakefulness or oblivion? There is a clue, perhaps, in the fact that the actual words of the poem's close are a direct borrowing from a Granadine gypsy lullaby.[42] Repetition is, of course, a functional feature of lullabies, and indeed Lorca himself points to the sleep-inducing efficacy of a constantly repeated imaginary outward-and-return journey, an alternation of tension and relaxation.[43] This ballad, perhaps, is meant—possibly in a bizarre or slightly macabre way—to evoke for the audience the ethos of a 'nana'—the central presence of the child, the unresolved repetition-enhanced mystery,

---

[42] The text is given in García-Posada, *Primer romancero gitano* p. 107: 'Tengo una choza en el campo. / Tengo una choza en el campo, / el aire la vela, vela, / el aire la está velando.'

[43] See Lorca's lecture 'Canciones de cuna españolas', in Federico García Lorca, *Obras completas*, III, ed. Arturo del Hoyo (Madrid: Aguilar, 1989), pp. 282-300, at p. 291.

the warnings of dire consequences of keeping eyes open and not going to sleep, the hints of the child's seduced complicity in its own abduction by a supernatural being are all features traditionally associated with lullabies or bed-time admonitions. In combining genres in this way the performer is taking on constraints which go much further than the rules of the particular type of verbal art denoted by the term *romance*; in so doing, he is, of course, emphasizing—one might almost say showing off—an element of conscious artistic control, the expertise to subvert and sustain simultaneously the conventions of his expressive model. In a sense what Lorca is doing is exploiting the (apparent) tension between performance as reproduction, in the presence of an audience, of collectively-owned texts and conventions, and the post-Romantic tendency to emphasize the visionary-expressive powers of the autonomous artist.

It is worth asking at this point what is the nature of the audience for these poems. There is something of a legend concerning the popular reception, appreciation and repetition of some of these ballads (especially 'Romance de la casada infiel' or 'Romance de la Guardia Civil'). However, spite of the systematic incorporation of popular-traditional material and motifs, the whole approach is one designed to draw attention not so much to authenticity as to cultured artfulness and familiarity with an elitist cultural tradition that has always known how to imitate and exploit popular forms. The envisaged audience is similarly an educated and cultivated one rather than genuinely popular. To point this out is certainly not to criticize Lorca's motives; indeed, his approach is an honest one in that he conscientiously and openly applies his own middle-class, educated sensibilities and skills to a an existing creative ethos he clearly admires. Any attempt to produce 'authentic' simulacra could only result in pastiche; if a mildly satirical or tongue-in-cheek distance is apparent where certain *personae* of these ballads are concerned, we should remember that boastfulness and naivety are legitimate effects in any dramatizing performance discourse. What these poems reveal, perhaps, is a certain ambivalence with regard to the value of popular culture that ran through the nineteen-twenties and thirties in Spain. As Juan Carlos Mainer has remarked, this was an epoch in which 'lo popular—unos potes de barro, un romance tradicional, un cantar de Lope, una costumbre olvidada—se convirtió para jóvenes y no tan jóvenes en un modo de adhesión emocional al pueblo'.[44] What may be involved is a desire both to retain traditional, that is rural, low technology values, and to assimilate them at the same time into a modern outlook in a country which, in the first four decades of the century, was ambivalently poised—if not torn—between the past and the contemporary world.

3. 3 EXPERIMENT AND EXPRESSION: *ASÍ QUE PASEN CINCO AÑOS*

(i) A Problem Play

The question of how effectively a discourse studies perspective can be applied to non-realistic texts is a particularly interesting one. As well as the abandonment of established conventions of performance and genre, radically innovative modes of expression often entail setting aside norms of language use, and are thus likely to constitute something of a challenge for an approach which derives from the investigation of principles behind everyday discourse. One such unsettling element often encountered in experimental theatre is the occurrence of apparently dysfunctional pieces of dialogue, in the sense of exchanges that create difficulties for the audience where coherent interpretation is concerned. (The fact that the characters themselves often carry on with their anomalous 'conversations' as if unaware of any problem only adds to the unsettling effect.) The environment in which the characters are presented is often a defamiliarized one, and the audience's expectation that what is 'going on' can readily be inferred on the basis that words and actions on stage consistently reflect 'real-life' patterns of thought and behaviour frequently turns out to be misplaced.

Effects of this sort can be found in a number of Lorca's works for the theatre, written, for the most part, in the period 1930-1931. While they do not altogether justify the term 'surrealist' which is sometimes applied to them, these works certainly stand out within

---

[44] J.C. Mainer, *La edad de plata* (Madrid: Cátedra, 1981), p. 289.

his theatrical production as vanguardist or experimental in a number of respects,[45] and, where critical commentary on their overall structure and meaning is concerned, are often regarded as problematical. They include a number of fragments and short pieces, one act of a proposed three-act play and two substantial works (one of which, *El público*, is probably incomplete).[46] As the only major example of Lorca's 'teatro irrepresentable' in definitive form, and, while not as thoroughly experimental a work as *El público* in technique, one that certainly poses as many problems of interpretation (indeed, one commentator sees it as it as 'the most problematical and enigmatic' of Lorca's plays)[47] it is worth giving some careful consideration to *Así que pasen cinco años. Leyenda del tiempo*.

One of the most interesting aspects of the play's dialogue is that, both at the level of diction and that of interactive exchange, there are a number of unusual features that have an intriguing correspondence with the play's broader themes. Before investigating these features in detail, however, it is may be useful to devote some attention to the way *Así que pasen cinco años* raises broader questions to do with the theatre as a culturally embedded form of communication, as well as taking some account of the wide-ranging speculation the play has inspired where interpretations of its overall meaning are concerned. Since experimental works of this sort tend to engage more-or-less overtly with established modes and frames of signification, it is impossible here to avoid excursions into areas which are more the province of mainstream literary criticism, such as literary sources and theatrical models. Similarly, when dealing with a play in which highly-stylized elements of staging constantly make strong claims on the audience's attention, it is important to keep in mind that dialogue is only one element, if an

---

[45] See Andrew A. Anderson, 'The Strategy of García Lorca's Dramatic Composition 1930-1936', *Romance Quarterly*, XXXIII (1986), 211-229.

[46] See Federico García Lorca, *El público,* edited by María Clementa Millán (Madrid: Cátedra, 1991), p. 109.

[47] Paul Julian Smith, *The Theatre of García Lorca: text, performance, psychoanalysis* (Cambridge: Cambridge University Press, 1998), p. 71.

important one, in an overall theatrical language that comprises linguistic and non-linguistic modes.

Understandably, given the plethora of cultural movements and manifestos of its era, a varied set of models and influences have been attributed to Lorca's *Leyenda del tiempo*. The view favoured here is that it is more reasonable to situate the work within the broad framework of Expressionism as it was manifested in European theatre, cinema and other cultural forms, rather than seeking parallels with, say, the narrower and more exclusively French-oriented paradigm of literary surrealism.[48] In the broad sense, Expressionism denotes an anti-realist concern with essence rather than cause and with subjective perceptions rather than objective observation. To features of *Así que pasen cinco años* mentioned by Andrew Anderson that support placing it in the broad expressionist camp (episodic exposition, scenes set in different locations, each with its own set of somewhat strangely-costumed characters, eschewal of in-depth psychology except in the case of the protagonist, and stage settings that do not suggest reality, but rather seem constructs of the protagonist's waking or dreaming mind)[49] we might add an inherent propensity for various types of meta-theatrical effect and self-consciously stagy devices, since 'the more theatre concerns itself with analysis of the self, the more the latter becomes elusive, escaping into role-playing where the face dissolves into multiple masks'.[50] Another trait of expressionist

---

[48] Thus following a relatively recent tendency to re-vindicate what has been, in fact a persistent, if not always heeded line of critical interpretation where Lorca's 'experimental' works are concerned. See Margarita Ucelay (ed.), *Federico García Lorca: Así que pasen cinco años* (Madrid: Cátedra, 1995), pp. 40-46; and Andrew A. Anderson, 'Bewitched, Bothered and Bewildered: Spanish dramatists and Surrealism, 1924-1936', in C. Brian Morris (ed.), *The Surrealist Adventure in Spain* (Ottowa: Dovehouse, 1991), pp. 240-281. Anderson's overall conclusion is that Lorca's experimental, avant-garde theatre 'would seem to owe a good deal more to the German "ism" than to the French one'.

[49] Andrew A. Anderson, '*El público*, *Así que pasen cinco años* y *El sueño de la vida:* tres dramas expresionistas de Lorca', in Dru Dougherty and M. Francisca Vilches, (eds) *El teatro en España entre tradición y vanguardia* (Madrid: C.S.I.C., 1992), pp. 215-226, at p. 217.

[50] Christopher Innes, *Avant Garde Theatre* (London: Routledge, 1993), p. 43.

theatre found in Lorca's play is that dialogue often takes the form of ritual exchanges or the presentation of viewpoints in a debate on pre-determined topics, couched in language which reflects attitudes and states of mind rather than social background.[51]

The case for regarding the play as surrealist in any case sometimes seems to rest on a dubious assumption, namely that the movement had exclusive rights to the artistic and literary exploitation of both of the content of dreams and of psychoanalytical models of their nature. The reality is that a number of tendencies, schools and individual writers, belonging to what could be termed, if paradoxically, the avant-garde mainstream, were interested both in oneiric experiences—among internal cognitive states in general—and in the theoretical explanations of them developed by the Viennese circle. Indeed, those familiar with the German language (the case with many Expressionist writers) had something of a head start, since Freud's *The Interpretation of Dreams* and *The Psychotherapy of Everyday Life* were originally published in 1900 and 1901 respectively.

The dispute over which '-isms' are most influential in the play's gestation is not an altogether sterile one, since it has some bearing on an interpretation that has achieved a surprising degree of critical support or acquiescence: that the action is a dream of the central character.[52] While it is true that what is shown and is said on stage seems to be a manifestation of subjective perceptions and experiences rather than being organized from any objective or 'realistic' viewpoint, there is a good general reason for rejecting this view. To claim, as an explanation for unusual goings-on in a play (and in the absence of unequivocal indications that such an interpretation is intended), that it takes place in the dreaming mind of one of its characters, is to hold a view of the theatre at large

---

[51] See Michael Patterson, *The Revolution in German Theatre* (London: Routledge, 1981), pp. 51-54.

[52] This interpretation, largely based on the supposition that the audience is given to understand that no 'real' time elapses over the course of the events shown on stage, was first—and as Anderson ('Bewitched, Bothered and Bewildered' , p. 280) notes, influentially—put forward in R.G. Knight, 'Federico García Lorca's *Así que pasen cinco años*', *Bulletin of Hispanic Studies*, XLIII (1966), 32-46.

predicated simplistically on the mimetic-realist model. To insist there is a plausible 'explanation' for everything that happens is to take for granted the assumption, applicable at best to only one particular style of theatre, that the world evoked on stage must slavishly match the audience's notion of the 'real' one. The drawback of such a view, of course, is that whatever problems of interpretation plays such as *Así que pasen cinco años* may pose, they are obviously designed to challenge the standard currency of the realist model, not confirm it. When audiences are meant to take what occurs on stage as a dream they are generally provided with unmistakable clues; indeed, certain scenes of *Así que pasen cinco años* are marked by features of lighting, costume, décor and language style as having an 'unreal' dreamlike or hallucinatory quality, an effect which is rendered virtually pointless if the entirety of the action is meant to be taken as representing a unified oneiric experience.

To cast doubt on the claim that Lorca's *leyenda del tiempo* depicts a dream of the central character, however, is by no means to deny that the play's action may be intended as an illustration of or at least as a relevant comment on his inner experiences and states of mind; and there is certainly no intention to discount the link between such exteriorizations of a 'psychomachy'[53] and contemporary interest in psychoanalytical theories of dreams and the unconscious. Overall, it seems sensible—and analytically productive—to regard the dramatic space evoked by the play as one that imaginatively depicts the interconnection of inner and outer facets of experience.

(ii) An Expressionist Antecedent

Let us consider, for the moment a description of a play. It is constructed around one central character, and gestures, movement, scenery, costumes and the colour and intensity of stage lighting are of crucial importance in presenting the inner world of this protagonist. The other characters, the set and the action are not to

[53] Anderson, 'Bewitched, Bothered and Bewildered', p. 261.

be taken as some objective reality, but more as representations of the protagonist's varying subjective perception of himself and the world around him, on the assumption that the inner workings of the mind are organized on a theatrical basis. The action concerns the fantasies of a disappointed lover, and involves both diametric reversals in situations and relationships, and the systematic presentation of contradictions between different modes of perception or experience. The final scene shows the protagonist's definitive existential failure or emotional death, symbolized by the puncturing of a heart represented on the back of the stage.

The foregoing account would probably be recognized by anyone familiar with Lorca's *Así que pasen cinco años*; it is, in fact, based on a description, by the writer concerned, of an earlier play: *Theatre of the Soul,* one of the first forays by the Russian Expressionist writer-director Nikolei Evreinov into a type of experimental theatre he termed 'monodrama'.[54] The concept of monodrama, as developed by Evreinov and his collaborators, fuses elements from psychoanalysis and traditional morality plays to achieve a satirical depiction of modern society.[55] *Theatre of the Soul* itself, the action of which 'takes place in the soul within the space of thirty seconds', was written as early as 1912, but remained in the repertory of the Crooked Mirror Theatre in St. Petersburg until 1931, by which time it had become well known to theatre-goers in western European capitals, especially after its author's self-imposed exile from Russia from the mid twenties. Evreinov's sardonically paradoxical harlequinade *A Merry Death,* in which, anticipating Lorca's 'leyenda del tiempo' the time progresses from six o'clock to twelve

[54] The description of the play given here is taken directly from Evreinov's own comments on the nature of the play and monodrama in general in a contemporary lecture, together with his comments on a similar early monodrama, *The Theatre of Love*. See *Life as Theatre: five modern plays by Nikolai Evreinov*, translated and edited by Christopher Collins (Ann Arbor: Ardis, 1973), pp. xiii-xiv. *Theatre of the Soul* is briefly mentioned in a footnote as a possible antecedent for Lorca's play in Knight, 'Federico García Lorca's *Así que pasen cinco años*', p. 46.

[55] It is worth noting that *Teatro de almas*, Lorca's youthful prototype for this style of experimental theatre, begins, like Evreinov's play, with a prologue explaining the meaning of the work delivered by one of the actors. See Ucelay (ed.), *Federico García Lorca: Así que pasen cinco años*, p. 53.

o'clock, at which hour the comic protagonist expires (although, unlike Lorca's El Joven, who dies just before the servant enters with a 'candelabro encendido', he first mockingly hands the lamp to Death), similarly enjoyed decades of popularity in progressive European theatrical circles.

There are other parallels between Lorca's play and influential pieces by Evreinov. One intriguing set of similarities concerns the Russian's play *The Main Thing*. Before looking at them in detail, it is worth pointing out that this work, written in 1921, and staged in Europe by Pirandello and other theatrical innovators, was popular with the émigré community in New York, and, as well with university theatre-groups, and was successfully staged there by the Theatre Guild some two years before Lorca's arrival in the city, in a production that was supervised by Evreinov himself. The manuscript of *Así que pasen cinco años* is dated August 1931, but it is almost certain that the main ideas of the play were worked out by Lorca during his nine-month stay in New York in 1929 and early 1930.[56] While there is little detailed information available as to the productions Lorca attended during his stay there, it is clear that he took a keen interest in the lively 'teatro de vanguardia' scene in New York. Significantly, perhaps, he also mentions, in a letter to his parents, a plan to attend a Chinese theatre performance with a group of Russian friends.[57] It is also worth noting that one of Evreinov's most influential theoretical works on the theatre, described by Oliver Sayler as 'the first adequate statement of the psychological foundations of the revolt against dramatic realism',[58] was published in New York in 1927. One passage in particular of this work highlights the fascination psychoanalytic theory held for avant-garde theatre writers and directors interested in exploiting to the full the expressive possibilities of meta-theatre. It certainly helps us understand why a play such as *Así que pasen cinco años* so

---

[56] See Ucelay (ed.), *Así que pasen cinco años*, pp. 17-18.
[57] See Christopher Maurer (ed.), *Federico García Lorca: Poet in New York*, translated by G. Simon and S. White (Harmondsworth: Penguin, 1990), p. 226.
[58] Foreword to Nikolai Evreinov, *The Theatre in Life* (London: Harrap, 1927), p. ix.

insistently links inner experiences and subjective perceptions with the form, devices and language of the theatre itself.

> [Freud] has given us a lucid and penetrating picture of the very essence of our subconscious self, and has proved that this self is pre-eminently dramatic and theatrical in its mysterious activity. Is this strange author of dreams, so masterfully described by him, not a real 'playwright' and 'stage-manager'? The dream is a drama of our own invention.[59]

At the same time, Evreinov gives a salutary warning against treating the theatre as a convenient space for the exposition of theories, psychoanalytical or otherwise. The presentation on stage of inner realities needs to be balanced against what is effective in the theatre in terms of the communicative relationship between spectacle and audience. For Evreinov, pure symbolism, just as much as pure realism, is irreconcilable with the true nature of the theatre, the former because 'to duplicate life [...] means to kill art' and the latter because it is 'hostile to the direct and straightforward enjoyment of visual perception'. He thus advocates 'conventional' or 'stage' realism, 'the free imaginative creation of stage images which command belief to the spectators' receptive minds'.[60]

In a way that is perhaps more overtly echoed in Lorca's other major experimental work, *El público,* but is nevertheless an important structural feature of *Así que pasen cinco años*, Evreinov's *The Main Thing* consistently exploits an action set in a theatrical milieu to achieve paradoxical transformations of settings and personae and interrogations of reality and identity, not only through the presentation of traditional stock figures, but also via properties and artefacts of the theatre such as optical devices, frames and curtains, costumes, masks and disguises.[61] The play brings into contact actors from a touring theatre company in a provincial city

---

[59] Evreinov, *The Theatre in Life*, p. 55.

[60] Evreinov, *The Theatre in Life*, p. 148.

[61] For a detailed discussion of the use these devices in Lorca's experimental theatre, see Millán, *El público*, pp. 53-55; for the heavily metatheatrical texture of *Así que pasen cinco años*, see Farris Anderson, 'The Theatrical Design of Lorca's *Así que pasen cinco años*', *Journal of Spanish Studies*: *Twentieth Century*, VII (1979), 249-278.

and non-thespian guests lodged in the same boarding house. An interesting point of comparison with Lorca's play is provided by the character of the Typist, since one of the most important figures in *Así que pasen cinco años* is that of the Mecanógrafa, the 'dangerous woman' who dejectedly leaves El Joven's house in the first act, but reappears in the last act as the new object of his erotic longings. Like Lorca's, Evreinov's typist is involved in striking reversals of role, attitude and appearance. Initially prone to burst into tears and claiming her life is intolerable because she is unloved, she longs for 'burning caresses, just the thought of which makes your head whirl and your heart pound, so hard and so painfully'.[62] Later, having found a lover, she paradoxically accepts with equanimity the revelation that he is already married and will soon abandon her.

It is instructive to compare speeches of the two characters in the third act of each play (in each case the topic of conversation is the gratifying postponement of erotic fulfilment):

> TYPIST *(having recovered from her embarrassment, in merry, coquettish tones*). Let's save a few sweets for next time.[63]

> MECANÓGRAFA. ¡Qué hermoso es esperar con seguridad el momento de ser amada! [...] De pequeña, yo guardaba los dulces para comerlos después.[64]

In fact, the words of Lorca's Mecanógrafa are an ironic echo of a remark made early in the first act by El Joven, a remark that sums up his confession of a temperamental preference from childhood onwards for deferring gratification of desire, an attitude that underlies his five-year postponement of marriage to a girl with whom he claims to be passionately in love:

> JOVEN. Yo guardaba los dulces para comerlos después
> VIEJO. Después, ¿verdad? Saben mejor. Yo también.[65]

---

[62] *Five Modern Plays*, p. 53.
[63] *Five Modern Plays*, p. 96.
[64] Ucelay (ed.), *Así que pasen cinco años*, p. 308.
[65] *Así que pasen cinco años*, p. 192.

It is shortly after this exchange, and an ensuing brief commentary on the advantages of being able to remember the future, 'recordar hacia mañana', that La Mecanógrafa first puts in an appearance:

> *(Un reloj da las seis. LA MECANÓGRAFA cruza la escena llorando en silencio.)*
> VIEJO. Las seis.
> JOVEN. Sí, las seis y con demasiado calor. *(Se levanta.)* Hay un cielo de tormenta.[66]

It is at this point that the principal topic of conversation between El Viejo and El Joven—the play's opening conversation had begun *in medias res*—is made clear to the audience, as the talk moves to matters connected with El Joven's engagement and his decision to put off marriage for five years. The final appearance of the La Mecanógrafa in this act, the moment of her rejection and departure from the house,

> MECANÓGRAFA. *(En la puerta.)* ¿Me necesitas?
> JOVEN. (Cerrando los ojos). No. No te necesito. *(La MECANÓGRAFA sale mirando con ansia y esperando la llamada.)*[67]

is linked, as is her first appearance, to a pointed disclosure that the time has mysteriously remained the same. The servant, Juan, answering El Joven's query 'con intención', informs him it is 'las seis en punto señor'.

When we next encounter La Mecanógrafa she is involved, dressed in a garish sporting costume and a cape, in the strange harlequinade that takes up most of the last act of *Así que pasen cinco años*. (Evreinov's *The Main Thing* similarly ends with a masquerade, in which the typist appears masked and in a different costume.) La Mecanógrafa is now in conversation with the equally garish figure of an older woman (La Máscara Amarilla), their exchanges enacting a parodic reversal both of El Joven's declarations to El Viejo about his feelings for La Novia and his indifference to La Mecanógrafa's

---

[66] *Así que pasen cinco años*, pp. 194-95.
[67] *Así que pasen cinco años*, p. 242.

own desperate appeals in the first act. El Joven now woos her with ardent declarations of passionate impatience, but, appropriately, since she has now adopted his strategy of deferment, she repeats his original stipulation of a five-year postponement: 'Me iré contigo. (*Tímida)* Así que pasen cinco años'.[68]

The principle of diametrical reversal at work here, it should be said at once, is a long-established device in narratives and drama, associated with terms such as 'poetic justice' or 'contrapasión', a neat closure that forcibly conveys the moral lessons to be derived from the spectacle of characters having done to them what they have, reprehensibly, done unto others. There is a more contemporary relevance of the reversal motif, however, one that is particularly associated with psychoanalytic theory. Before looking at this link in more detail, however, it is worth examining the way the motif of reversal is consistently embodied at the level of the play's language.

(iii) Meta-discursive Exchanges

One of the most striking features of the dialogue in *Así que pasen cinco años* is the incidence of repetition and parallelism. This is partly to be expected, of course, since, apart from the fact that key images and allusions are often repeated at a later stage in the play to point up reversals, a number of scenes contain extended verse passages (with the parallelistic patterns we have already commented on), and others make use of ritualized language games, such as the 'Mentira' / 'Verdad' alternations of Arlequín, La Muchacha and El Payaso in the last act, or the three-times repeated exchange in which La Novia mockingly mimics her maid's consternation, and which perfectly captures her newly acquired impatient scorn for conventional constraints.

> NOVIA. *(Autoritaria.)* Tíralas.
> *(La Criada arroja por el balcón unas flores [...].)*
> CRIADA. ¡Ay, señorita!
> NOVIA. *(Furiosa.)* ¿Qué señorita?

---

[68] *Así que pasen cinco años*, p. 328.

CRIADA. ¡Señorita!
NOVIA. ¡Quéeee! [69]

The frequent appearance of this dialogue device emphasises the way conversational interaction in the play tends to consist of competitive and even confrontational exchanges between characters whose opposed points of view and objectives often take the form of appropriating and adapting the content of each other's utterances. In effect, it is a case not of repetition for stylistic ends, but for rhetorical purposes, ranging from pointing up contradictions between different points of view to the use of meta-linguistic commentary, questioning or negation as the weapon of choice in verbal duels. Exchanges such as the following, where an assertion is explicitly contested, are the rule rather than the exception in many passages in the play:

VIEJO. *(Entusiasmado.)* Se hunden las casas.
AMIGO 1. *(Enérgico y en actitud de defensa.)* Las casas no se hunden.[70]

In its simplest form this tendency takes the form of one character picking up a conversational topic from another. The play's opening lines provide a good example of such topical repetition and of the type of low-level metalinguistic comment ('mention' as opposed to 'use' of language) that is standard fare in the play's dialogue as a whole:[71]

JOVEN, Recuerdo que...
VIEJO. (Ríe) Siempre recuerdo.
[...]
JOVEN. Y recuerdo que un día...
VIEJO. (*Interrumpiendo con vehemencia.)* Me gusta tanto la palabra recuerdo. Es una palabra verde, jugosa.[72]

---

[69] *Así que pasen cinco años*, p. 248.
[70] *Así que pasen cinco años*, p. 238.
[71] For a discussion of this distinction in linguistic philosophy, see Roy Harris, *The Language Connection* (Bristol: Thoemmes, 1996), pp. 6-10.
[72] *Así que pasen cinco años*, p. 108.

Meta-linguistic repetition is not used purely for thematic underpinning, but can also be associated with traits of character. For instance, El Viejo uses it to enhance the persuasiveness of his sophisms:

> JOVEN. Muy jovencita. Quince años.
> VIEJO. No me gusta esta manera de expresar. Quince años [...]. Pero, ¿por qué no decir que tiene quince nieves, quince aires, quince crepúsculos?[73]

Whereas in the mouth of El Joven this drawing of attention to choice of linguistic form seems more a symptom of his evasive, fantasizing propensities, which result (and it is a consequence of which El Viejo seems well aware) in words acquiring an influence greater than that of real states of affairs in determining the nature of perceptions and experiences.

> VIEJO. Diga usted: mi novia. Atrévase.
> JOVEN. No.
> VIEJO. ¿Pero por qué?
> JOVEN. Novia..., ya lo sabe usted; si diga novia la veo sin querer amortajada en un cielo sujeto por enormas trenzas de nieve. No, no es mi novia (*hace un gesto como si apartara la imagen que quiere captar*), es mi niña, mi muchachita.[74]

Where other characters are concerned, the meta-linguistic mode is manifested in ways which suggests an automatic reflex of conversational engagement rather than any reflective habit of mind, as in the highly extrovert First Friend's unthinking use of hail-fellow-well-met formulas, such as 'hombre solo, hombre serio' and the spontaneous repartee of:

> AMIGO. ¿La quieres conocer?
> JOVEN. No.
> AMIGO. (Levantándose) ¡Noo y rúbrica![75]

---

[73] *Así que pasen cinco años*, p. 209.
[74] *Así que pasen cinco años*, pp. 201-202.
[75] *Así que pasen cinco años*, p. 211.

In the case of the Mecanógrafa, metalinguistic questions similarly serve to emphasize an absence of reflection—indeed, in her case, what is made clear is that she is on a completely different wavelength where many of the assumptions underlying what is sometimes termed rational discourse are concerned. It is worth looking at two examples because they provide clues (which will be followed up shortly) as to the symbolic identity of this character:

> JOVEN. Te he dicho algunas veces que te esperas.
> MECANÓGRAFA. Pero yo no espero. ¿Qué es esto de esperar?
> [...]
> JOVEN. Puedes irte.
> MECANÓGRAFA. ¿Lo ha oído usted? Me arroja de su casa.[76]

The most telling instances of metalinguistic negation in the play are probably found in the scene in which El Joven is jilted by La Novia, much of which consists a series of systematic rejections, on the part of one speaker, of the expressions through which the other attempts to define situations and meanings. For instance, the strong presupposition (that La Novia has indeed cheated on her fiancé) carried by her father's question '¿por qué lo has enganado?' is challenged head-on by her reply:

> Yo no lo he engañado.[77]

Since her speech and behaviour up to this point have been marked by candour rather than concealment, the audience can only assume she intends something other than a straightforward denial of her relations with the Jugador de Rugby. The contrastive emphasis of the non-elided 'yo' with which she begins her assertion probably articulates her perception—hinted at earlier in her claim that 'antes no existía yo'—that her personality has been completely transformed, with the result that the confidently sensual 'I' that is the subject of her present utterances is totally different from the 'I' of the dreamy adolescent who had agreed to the five-year

---

[76] *Así que pasen cinco años*, pp. 207, 209.
[77] *Así que pasen cinco años*, p. 263.

engagement.[78] The effect is to make it plain that the dictates of authentic feeling take precedence over the constraints created by mere verbal undertakings, drawing attention yet again to El Joven's preference for words and the images they evoke, as against the direct translation of emotional needs into action. Her diagnosis of this fatal flaw in his character is strikingly summed up in the clinching pieces of metalinguistic negation in this scene:

> NOVIA. *(Desasiéndose.)* ¡Déjame! Todo lo podías haber dicho menos la palabra sueño. Aquí no se sueña. Yo no quiero soñar.
> JOVEN. ¡Pero se ama!
> NOVIA. Tampoco se ama. ¡Vete!
> JOVEN. ¿Qué dices? *(Aterrado.)*
> NOVIA. Que busques otra mujer a quien puedas hacerle trenzas.[79]

The accusation is clear. La Novia interprets his ability, in a situation such as this, to talk about love in an abstract, speculative way, rather than spontaneously experiencing and expressing it—to say 'se ama' rather than 'te amo' as it were—as revealing a personality incapable of genuine desire. El Joven's loquacity when engaged in sentimental fantasies of love corresponds to an inward silence of feeling.

(iv) Expressing the Unconscious

It will have begun to become apparent that the high incidence of conversational meta-language is not merely an echo of the thematic importance of reversals in the play's action, but in itself constantly raises the question of how truth and falsity are to be defined; indeed the use/mention distinction was originally introduced in linguistic philosophy to underpin the semantic conception of truth.[80] The embedding of reversals, opposites, contradictory contrasts and paradoxes in linguistic (and visual) symbols, it should be noted, is

---

[78] *Así que pasen cinco años*, p. 261.
[79] *Así que pasen cinco años*, p. 269.
[80] The standard example, originating with the Polish-born logician L. Tarski, is 'the sentence "Snow is white" is true if, and only if, snow is white'. See Harris, *The Language Connection*, p. 9.

also an important aspect of psychoanalytic theory, especially the question of 'compromise formations', the 'distortion toward coherence' of the images and expressions which, in Freudian theory represent the return of the repressed and are systematically the site of contradictory tendencies of emergence and suppression. Again, in a more general sense, the overall thrust of psychoanalytical theory is to challenge the principle of rationality itself in many aspects of human behaviour, and it is often in the form of unresolved paradoxes and arbitrary contradictions that the intromission into conscious thinking of mechanisms that belong to the primary processes tends to manifest itself.

By and large, there have been two broad lines of psychoanalytical approach to this play, one Jungian, the other Freudian. Both of them tend to treat images as disguised signs or as something to be 'read' for particular symbolic significance. The Jung-based approach, as evidenced by Rupert Allen, for example,[81] concentrates on symbolic representation of a fragmented psyche and an (unsuccessful) search for psychic wholeness and harmony. The Freudian approach tends to concentrate on the problematic influence exercised by the unconscious (especially its sexual dimension) on conscious perceptions and thoughts, with a particular interest in the content of dreams as an index to unconscious impulses. It seems legitimate for a discourse approach to concern itself with psychoanalytical interpretations because of the latter discipline's view of verbal expression as confessional talk which can be interpreted to reveal underlying psychic conflicts. Psychoanalytical literary criticism has thus always been predicated on the assumption that the mechanisms of the mental agencies are themselves mechanisms of language.[82] But it is also important to remember we are dealing here not with a neurotic patient's utterances but with verbal art. Indeed, in the writings that touch on aesthetics, Freud recognized an insoluble tension between analysis

---

[81] See Rupert Allen, *Psyche and Symbol in the Theatre of Federico García Lorca* (Austin: University of Texas Press, 1974).

[82] See Elizabeth Wright, *Psychoanalytic Criticism* (London: Routledge, 1984), p. 4.

and rhetoric, and was well aware of the way verbal artists exploit the symptomatic character of speech in general through their skill in the strategic use of language. He took equal cognizance, however, of the need, in what he termed 'psychopathological' drama, for dialogue and action to be attuned to 'non-neurotic' spectators, who would reject too blatant a therapeutic exposure of the conflict between conscious and repressed impulses. The dramatist's skill lies in securing the collusion of an audience in the playful creation of illusions than rather than in verifying analytical insights.[83]

In spite of Lorca's attested interest in Freud, it seems doubtful that Lorca would intend a play such as *Así que pasen cinco años* to serve as a technical illustration of specific areas of Freudian theory.[84] Even an educated audience of the time could not be expected, as a whole, to have more than a generalized awareness of principles such as the shaping effect of early experiences on adult life, of the way apparently rational conscious behaviour and beliefs could be determined by unconscious, especially erotic drives, and the nature of dreams as constructed images and narratives which represent unconscious forces in a disguised but interpretable form. The psychological 'character' of the central figure and the significance of his story seem intended, however, to be understandable along non-technical lines, and the play as a whole designed to provide insights into the nature of life and love in ways that are sufficiently generalized to be recognizable by the audience as relevant to their own experience.

It is for reasons of this sort that it seems perhaps wiser to avoid direct psychoanalytical interpretation of textual details which seem to have Freudian or Jungian symbolic antecedents; the question of the symbolic significance of steps is a revealing example. A

[83] See the summary of Freud's comments in 'Psychopathic Characters on Stage' (1905/6), 'Delusion and Dreams in Jensen's *Gradiva*' (1907), and 'Creative Writers and Daydreaming' (1908), in Wright, *Psychoanalytic Criticism*, pp. 26-36.

[84] As, for instance, with the psycho-dynamics of dreams, in the interpretation of the play proposed by Julio Huélamo, 'La influencia de Freud en el teatro de García Lorca', *Boletín de la Fundación Federico García Lorca,* 6 (diciembre de 1989), 59-83.

number of commentators have not hesitated to link the allusions to steps in *Así que pasen cinco años* (and, in the final act, the physical presence of them on stage) with the Freudian interpretation of climbing stairs as symbolizing 'el acto sexual'.[85] It should be kept in mind, however, that steps had become virtually a cliché in the European experimental theatre of the nineteen-twenties. The first expressionist stage use was in Sorge's *Der Bettler* and the device became extremely well known after the influential German director Jessner used it to impressive effect in his prestigious production of Shakespeare's *Richard III*. Awareness of the possibilities of using vertical stage space in this way to convey vividly a range of social, moral and psychological relationships and contrasts became so widespread that Jessner remarked to a journalist after a tour of provincial German theatres in the mid nineteen twenties that he had seen 'nothing but steps'.[86] The point is not that the Freudian interpretation is necessarily mistaken in itself, but to insist on it to the exclusion of other sorts of symbolism probably is. Certainly the flight of steps of the stage within-a-stage in *Así que pasen cinco años* can have more accessible meanings as a cognitive metaphor for a link between different—lower and higher—domains of experience or consciousness. Similarly, the association of the sound of the car-horn with El Jugador de Rugby's passionate embrace of La Novia is not necessarily to be interpreted along the lines of a classic Freudian example of unconscious autoeroticism.[87] It would be more to the point, perhaps, to keep in mind an epochal fascination with mechanized travel, and view it as a pointedly modern variant on traditional elopement motifs, the dynamic masculine capacity to 'carry away' symbolized by horse-power rather than an actual horse.

Where the 'exemplary' quality of the character and fate of the young man is concerned, one can only agree with Margarita Ucelay

---

[85] For instance, Ucelay (ed.), *Así que pasen cinco años*, pp. 138-39.

[86] Innes, *Avant Garde Theatre*, p. 93.

[87] Freud, in his comments on condensation in *The Interpretation of Dreams*, notes that the co-presence, in a patient's account, of a car and a kiss, matches the linking of the two parts of the term 'auto-eroticism'. (See Wright, *Psychoanalytical Criticism*, p. 20.)

that the end of the play depicts the defeat of a heart 'que no ha sabido amar'. El Joven, that is, is shown in the play as unwilling—or afraid—to commit himself, to abandon his self-control in love or desire for another person. Such a character-type is not in need of specialist psychoanalytical explanation, though some relatively late (1923) comments of Freud on the process of sexual overvaluation of the sort that 'regularly happens with a young man's sentimental passion' are, nevertheless, usefully apposite:

> If the sensual impulsions are more or less effectively repressed or set aside, the illusion is produced that the object has come to be sensually loved on account of its spiritual merits. [...] We love it on account of the perfections which we have striven to reach for our own ego, and which we should now like to procure in this roundabout way as a means of satisfying our narcissism.[88]

Some subsequent comments of Erich Fromm on a particular manifestation of his notion of alienation, the 'psychopathology of modern man', a 'sickness of the self' manifested in failure to experience one's identity, are also very suggestive where the action of *Así que pasen cinco años* is concerned.[89] For Fromm, alienation often takes the form of functions of feeling and thought being transferred to an outside object. One of the particular types he describes, manifested in instances of false 'great love' and feelings of utter loss (including the loss of his heart) on the part of the 'lover' when the increasingly doubting girl finally breaks with him, provides a useful insight into the rejection of El Joven by La Novia and the reaction it provokes.

> Losing her, so he feels, he has lost his one chance to love. [...] His predicament is one of alienation. He never was capable of loving actively, of leaving the magic circle of his own ego, and of reaching out to and becoming one with another human being. What he did was to transfer his

---

[88] Sigmund Freud, *Civilization, Society and Religion,* Pelican Freud Library, XII (Harmondsworth: Penguin, 1987), pp. 142-43.
[89] Erich Fromm, *Beyond the Chains of Illusion* (London: Abacus, 1980), p. 50.

> longings for love to the girl and to feel that being with her he experiences his 'loving' when he really experiences only the illusion of loving.[90]

As Fromm observes, the real meaning of the young man's loss is not losing the girl but losing himself as a potentially loving person. Again, it is worth insisting that his comments are offered here not as specialized description, but as useful and accessible explanation of emotions and relationships which are intuitively comprehensible and which, to judge by the reaction attributed by Lorca to his young man, were as apparent to an insightful writer as to a trained analyst. Lorca's El Joven, like Fromm's young man, reveals the essentially selfish—and consequently self-destructive—nature of his feelings:

> JOVEN. Y porque después no hay nada, porque después no puedo amar, porque después se ha acabado todo.
> NOVIA. ¡Suelta!
> JOVEN. No es tu engaño lo que me duele. Tú no eres nada. Tú no significas nada. Es mi tesoro perdido. Es mi amor sin objeto.[91]

The concept of alienation also provides a clue as to the interpretation of existential-temporal issues raised in the play and the link between failure of repetition and failure of reproduction symbolized in the frequent allusions to 'mi hijo' (an interpretation, moreover, that is of a broader human and artistic significance than the speculations based on Lorca's sexual orientation often inspired by this motif). Fromm quotes Freud's 'Men cannot remain children forever' to introduce a discussion of why it is that nothing can ever be authentically prolonged or repeated, that to 'guardar los dulces para comerlos después' may be innocently harmless in the child yet have dangerous consequences for the adult: 'What is normal at one stage is pathological at another stage. The adult who "repeats" an infantile stage at the same time does not and cannot repeat it, precisely because he is no longer a child.'[92] Following this line of thought, we could interpret the play as a commentary on individual

[90] Fromm, *Beyond the Chains of Illusion*, pp. 50-51.
[91] Ucelay (ed.), *Así que pasen cinco años*, pp. 271-272.
[92] Fromm, *Beyond the Chains of Illusion*, p. 58.

existential development, the need for every person to escape from self-perpetuating inhibitions and make responsibly free choices that assert his or her humanity rather than following patterns that confirm estrangement from it. This is a theme we will return to; for the moment, it is worth staying a little longer with the play's 'staging' of some basic Freudian concepts.

Apart from the use of lighting, costumes and other devices to suggest oneirically structured stage environments, perhaps the clearest example of the 'mind as theatre' effect mentioned by Evreinov is the presentation of spatial metaphors associated with basic psychoanalytic notions. The fact that the stage-within-a-stage in the third act shows steps apparently leading up to the library in El Joven's house in which the first act takes place suggests a conversion into stage terms of the spatial model of psychoanalytical theory. The first act is a place of rationalizations on the part of most of the characters (that is, false explanations motivated by an individual's personal need for self-deception, that have a plausible ring of rationality).[93] In the opening of the third act, set in a great wood where distant hunting horns can be heard, some bizarre new characters appear and speak in ways that suggest discursive disorganization and irrationality. Non-sequiturs, contradictions and clashes of meaning abound, but seemingly go unnoticed, in marked contrast to the frequent meta-discursive challenges found in the first two acts of the play. The overall impression given is of a zone of experience that bears more than a passing resemblance to the structure, from the psychoanalytical point of view, of unconscious thought-processes:

> In the unconscious there is no sort of organization or coordination: each separate impulse seeks satisfaction independently of all the rest, uninfluenced by one another; contradictions are completely inoperative and the most opposite impulses flourish side by side. Associations of

[93] See Paul Roazen, *Freud: Political and Social Thought* (New York: Vintage, 1968), p. 69.

> ideas proceed along lines without any regard to logic; similarities are treated as identities, negatives are equated with positives.[94]

In the opening sequences of Act 3 Arlequín first plays a game of switching a sleeping and a wakeful mask, then initiates a ritual alternation, in verse, of 'mentira' and 'verdad' with a Muchacha, and then a Payaso.

> ARLEQUIN. (*En voz alta y gracioso.*) Mentira.
> MUCHACHA. Verdad.
> Perdí mi corona,
> perdí mi dedal,
> y a la media vuelta
> los volví a encontrar.
> ARLEQUIN. Tu amante verás
> a la media vuelta
> del viento y el mar,
> MUCHACHA. *(Asustada.)* Mentira.
> ARLEQUIN. Verdad.
> Yo te lo daré.
> MUCHACHA. *(Inquieta.)* No me lo darás.
> No se llega nunca
> al fondo del mar.[95]

This rather sinister game played around the meaning of 'el fondo del mar' is then picked up by El Payaso, before La Mecanógrafa appears and 'recalls' a conversation which exactly reverses the sense and structure of the exchanges which preceded her departure from El Joven's house in the first act.

> Él me dijo: '¿Me habías llamado?'; a lo que yo contesté, cerrando los ojos: 'No.' Y luego en la puerta, me dijo: '¿Me necesitas?'; y yo le dije 'No, no te necesito'.[96]

This sort of equivocation is one of the oddest of the reversals in which the play abounds. The test of the audience's memory is not

---

[94] James Strachey, 'Sketch of Freud's Life and Ideas', in Freud, *Civilization, Society and Religion*, pp. 11-23 (at p. 20).
[95] Ucelay (ed.), *Así que pasen cinco años*, pp. 294-95.
[96] *Así que pasen cinco años*, p. 304.

as demanding as might seem, since the actress playing La Mecanógrafa presumably replicates El Joven's original gestures (mentioned in the stage directions), and, in any case, what is involved is not recognizing the exact repetition of a piece of dialogue, but rather noticing the overall reversal of roles, a change which, in its turn, alerts the audience to the way the original utterances of each character are now put in the mouth of the other. The effect is still, perhaps, one of mocking 'quotation'. The tables have been turned; in this place it is the formerly spurned who do the spurning. (Indeed, in a further pointed reversal, El Joven woos the now desirable Mecanógrafa with a directness and physical ardour very notably lacking in his courtship of La Novia.)

The pivotal role of La Mecanógrafa in the characteristic reversals of the play's action (she prefigures the jilting of El Joven by La Novia, then takes over as the object of El Joven's erotic aspirations, only to reject him, in turn, in a manner that duplicates the cause of the failure of his engagement) is clearly of central importance for any overall interpretation of its meaning. In La Mecanógrafa's interventions in the first act, one element of her 'character' particularly stands out: the irrational and peremptory force of desire. She cannot understand the meaning of the term 'waiting', and passionate love is envisaged as completely beyond the remit of reason, rather than simply being too powerful for rational control.

> JOVEN. Siempre acabas no dando razones.
> MECANÓGRAFA. ¿Qué razones voy a dar? No hay más de una razón y esa es...que te quiero. ¡No se asuste, señor! La de siempre.[97]

It is with reason—literally—that El Viejo warns that 'es peligrosa esta mujer', since she is the complete antithesis of his cautious nature and seeks to undermine his strategy of rational control of emotions through displacing them into the future. It is tempting to see La Mecanógrafa as embodying the sexual impulse, the strongest of the instinctual drives (it does not really matter whether we term it instinct, desire or libido). We know she has been a member of the

[97] *Así que pasen cinco años*, p. 208.

household since El Joven's childhood (she reminds him of what seems to have been an early, erotically-charged experience of seeing his own blood flow) and leaves only under extreme provocation. Even El Joven seems somehow aware that to cut himself off from her is to cut himself off from the natural gratification of desire: 'Yo quisiera quererla como quisiera tener sed delante de los fuentes' (a backsliding El Viejo immediately rules out of court: 'De ninguna manera. ¿Qué haría usted mañana?').[98] La Mecanógrafa leaves the house—the world of conscious management of feelings and actions—because, in her view, El Joven has effectively banished her ('me arroja de su casa').[99] By simply being able to say the words 'puedes irte', that is, he proves he has organized his life in such a way as to be able to dispense with primary, instinctual desire. Deprived of any role in day-to-day life, the impulses represented by the Mecanógrafa retreat to the world of primary processes, the unconscious. When El Joven realizes his fundamental mistake—he has alienated the essence of his emotional life—he seeks to be reunited with her. However, the repressed is vindictive in its return, and what has been pushed wholly into the unconscious cannot be restored by conscious decision, a paradox neatly summed up by the Mecanógrafa's imposed stipulation of five years' delay, a move that exacts full retribution for the injury of rejection.

(v) Expression and Life-Choices

Apart from youthful ventures by Lorca into the main topics and situations of *Así que pasen cinco años*, such as *Teatro de almas* and the closing section of *Suites,*[100] two antecedents have been proposed for the particular anecdotal framework of the play. One is 'Légende du beau Pécopin et de la belle Baldour', in Victor Hugo's *Le Rhin*; the other, with a more explicitly homoerotic relevance, is André

---

[98] Ucelay (ed.), *Así que pasen cinco años*, p. 209.
[99] *Así que pasen cinco años*, p. 209.
[100] See Ucelay (ed.), *Así que pasen cinco años*, pp. 53-62 for a discussion of a number of such youthful antecedents.

Gide's *Corydon.*[101] Hugo's tale, a favourite of the young Lorca according to his brother Francisco, concerns a young man who plans to marry his sweetheart after a journey which turns out to last five years. On the last night he is tricked by the Devil into joining an enchanted hunt that, in reality, lasts a hundred years, thus depriving him both of his young bride and his own youth. The young man in *Corydon*, on the other hand, is motivated more by his own doubts and inhibitions in imposing a delay which finally ends in the engagement being broken off. In suggesting yet another possible 'source', it seems better to follow Smith in merely reflecting on structural similarities of situation rather than attempting to prove a definite influence;[102] indeed, the intention is more to use the earlier work as a useful interpretative guide to the meanings of the later one. The antecedent in question is a well-known instance of literary biography, involving the problematic engagement of a young man who has intimate doubts, linked to childhood experiences, as to his erotic commitment, a journey abroad as a way of circumventing the dangerous force of desire, and a girl who, after five years' patient frustration, finds solace in the arms of another, leaving the original fiancé 'dead to all forms of erotic love'.[103]

The elements mentioned above are features of 'the love-story, so involved and so strange',[104] spanning five years of the early eighteen-forties, of the engagement of the young Søren Kierkegaard to Regine Olsen (Kierkegaard himself consistently preferred the Latin spelling, Regina).[105] Particularly intriguing, where parallels with *Así que pasen cinco años* are concerned, are the ambivalent 'off-on' progression of the affair and the reversals of situation in the

---

[101] See Smith, *The Theatre of Lorca*, pp. 84-91; and Ucelay (ed.), *Así que pasen cinco años*, pp. 33-34 and 49-50.

[102] Smith, *The Theatre of Lorca*, p. 85.

[103] Ronald Grimsley, *Kierkegaard: a biographical introduction* (London: Studio Vista, 1973), p. 26.

[104] Regis Jolivet, *Introduction to Kierkegaard* (London: Muller, 1950), p. 21.

[105] His account of the affair in the *Journal* for 1849 has a Virgilian epigraph 'infandum me jubes, Regina, renovare dolorem'—see Walter Lowrie, *A Short Life of Kierkegaard* (Princeton: Princeton University Press, 1942), p. 135.

relationship between the still youthful philosopher and a girl ten years younger than himself. Beset by doubts as to the nature of his feelings and his ability to sustain a relationship, it was Kierkegard who proposed calling off or at least postponing the engagement. However, after securing Regine's acquiescence and moving from Copenhagen to Berlin, he was beset by a sense of guilt and loss, and reacted to the girl's eventual (after five years) betrothal to Schlegel as if he had lost the great love of his life. What qualifies this affair as a possible literary antecedent of Lorca's play is not, of course, the biographical details in themselves, but the fact that Kierkegaard produced a number of fictionalized—if sometimes barely fictionalized—accounts of these events and the self-introspection and philosophical enquiry they inspired. Quite apart from thirty-eight entries in the *Journals*, the 'pitiful story' (as one of his biographers terms it)[106] and the mental agonizing that went with it is also transparently visible in many of the highly-influential works Kierkegaard published during the early eighteen-forties. Although the question of whether these works constitute literary sources in a conventional sense is not an issue here, it is worth mentioning that there is an obvious potential link between Kierkegaard and Lorca through Miguel de Unamuno. It is well attested that Unamuno, whom Lorca knew well (and whose existentialist drama *El otro* can be considered an antecedent of Lorca's experimental theatre)[107] adapted and reflected on Kierkegaardian lines of thought in many of his works.[108]

It would be tedious to list every one of the numerous coincidences between Kierkegaard's account of the problematic nature of his feelings for Regine and the attitude of Lorca's young man toward his feelings for La Novia. Two details might suffice to

---

[106] Lowrie, *A Short Life of Kierkegaard*, p. 136.

[107] See Millán, *El público*, pp. 53-54.

[108] The link has been extensively studied; perhaps the most convincing detail is the fact that Unamuno's library at the university of Salamanca includes the complete works of Kierkegaard, in the original Danish, with substantial marginal notes added by the Spanish philosopher. See Gemma Roberts, *Unamuno: afinidades y coincidencias kierkegaardianas* (Boulder, Colorado: Society of Spanish and Spanish-American Studies, 1986), p. 13.

give an initial idea of the intriguing similarities. Kierkegaard acknowledged at an early stage in his courtship that in his experience of love he was 'seized by a secret dread lest I may have confused an ideal with a reality. This dread makes me long to know the future, and yet fear it'.[109] Of the agreement to put the engagement on hold (as described in a *Journal* entry nine years later) Kierkegaard recalls that he kissed Regine, 'but without passion' ('Merciful God!', he adds).[110] In a letter to his fiancée of August 1841, in which he expresses his doubts and sense of inadequacy for marriage, he gloomily predicts his own emotional death, naming a symbolic object that receives a similarly fateful treatment both in the laments of Lorca's Maniquí and in the sinister games of the play's final act: 'to send a silk cord is in the Far East capital punishment for the receiver; to send a ring is here a sentence of death'.[111]

The details themselves are of relatively secondary concern. What is of more interest here is the way Kierkegaard developed his anxieties about the contradiction-fraught relationship into broader, universalized or fictionalized reflections on the nature of the human existential condition in general and on the individual's search for integrity and fulfilment. The scope of such reflections is not limited to the personal and moral plane, but also extends—and in a way that seems particularly relevant to what may well have been Lorca's estimation of his own personal and artistic development at the end of the nineteen-thirties—to the creative-aesthetic plane. As Gemma Roberts observes in her study of the affinities between the thought of Unamuno and Kierkegaard, it is in the writings of the

---

[109] Grimsley, *Kierkegaard*, p. 20.

[110] Lowrie, *A Short Life*, p. 142.

[111] Kierkegaard actually went so far as to reproduce the actual letter in his fictionalized account of the affair in *Guilty/Not Guilty* (1845). It is interesting to note (as evidence of memorability) that these details are invariably quoted in accounts of Kierkegaard's life and work; indeed, they constitute the only substantial original Kierkegaardian passages quoted in David Lodge's novel *Therapy* (Harmondsworth: Penguin, 1995), the protagonist of which seeks a solution to his own problems in the Danish philosopher's Regina-inspired writings.

eighteen-forties that the dialectical opposition of aesthetic and ethical concern is posed most consistently by the Danish philosopher.[112] Similarly, it is in the pseudonymous works of this period, *Either/Or*, *Repetition*, *Fear and Trembling* and *Guilty/Not Guilty*, revolving almost obsessively around themes connected with the Regine affair (and indeed, one work is cryptically dedicated to her) that the most suggestive parallels with Lorca's play are to be found.

Even a cursory reading of these writings throws up curious similarities with Lorca's play. *Either/Or*, for instance, has its 'brides of sorrow', a set of forsaken women of whom Lorca's Manequí and the Máscara Amarilla could easily be sisters, turning constantly in the circle of their memories; and there is the narcissistic figure of Johannes in 'The Seducer's Diary', who becomes, like Lorca's El Joven, so absorbed in the subtle imaginative and psychological implications of his relationship with his fiancée that he seems to lose sight of its physical basis, and gives the impression—as Kierkegaard himself notes—of needing to incorporate the woman's essence in himself in order to feel the reality of his own being.[113] Curiously, the fictional editor's preface with which this work begins pointedly introduces the motif of a five-year postponement:

> The point I have now reached, I had arrived at five years ago. I had arranged the papers as at present, had decided to publish them, but thought it best to postpone it for a time. Five years seemed long enough. The five years are now up, and I begin where I left off.[114]

Repetition contains some particularly suggestive parallels. The reflections of the pseudonymous author, Constantinus Constantius, on the work's central topic (that is, on repetition, in Kierkegaard's sense of the term, as an act of faith offering a way out of the twin

---

[112] Roberts, *Unamuno*, p. 16.

[113] See Grimsley, *Kierkegaard*, pp. 34-35.

[114] Søren Kierkegaard, *Either/Or. A Fragment of Life*. Translated by David Swenson and Lillian Marvin Swenson (Princeton: Princeton University Press, 1949), p. 10.

traps of hope and recollection) are clearly relevant to the treatment, in *Así que pasen cinco años*, of the theme of time and the trajectory of human life. Lorca's El Joven is similarly brought to mind when Constantius recounts his conversations with a young man who claims to have fallen deeply—and in a deeply melancholic way—in love. The young man constantly repeats lines from a poem of Poul Møller:

> Then, to my easy chair,
> Comes a dream from my youth,
> To my easy chair
> A heartfelt longing comes over me for you
> Thou sun of women.[115]

The novelist David Lodge, via a fictional character and apropos of a slightly different translation of these lines, interprets the young man's obsessive reciting of them in the following terms: 'instead of living in the present, enjoying his engagement, he remembers the future; that is to say, he imagines himself looking back on his youthful love from the vantage point of old age, like the speaker of the poem'.[116] Such an interpretation immediately reminds us of the collusion of Lorca's El Joven with El Viejo in 'recordar hacia mañana',[117] and indeed, Kierkegaard's Constantius goes further and specifically mentions, in the general observations that precede the young man's story, that the equally flawed counterpart to love as recollection is love as hope: 'he who will merely hope is cowardly, he who will merely recollect is voluptuous',[118] a judgement that helps us assess the outlook on life of Lorca's Amigo 2°, whose *lema* is 'quiero morirme siendo amanecer'.[119]

The whole question, in fact, of the way individual maturity is tested by the need to come to terms with the limitations of human existence is discussed at length by Kierkegaard's narrator. He

---

[115] Søren Kierkegaard, *Fear and Trembling and Repetition*, edited by H.V. Hong and E.H. Hong (Princeton: Princeton University Press, 1983), p. 135.
[116] Lodge, *Therapy*, pp. 123-124.
[117] See Ucelay (ed.), *Así que pasen cinco años*, p. 194.
[118] *Fear and Trembling and Repetition*, p. 132.
[119] *Así que pasen cinco años*, p. 237 ff.

observes sardonically that the young man, in falling in love, 'took such a tremendous step that he leapt over life', and tellingly notes that recollection is an attractive strategy precisely because it is safe: 'it begins with the loss; the reason it is safe and secure is that it has nothing to lose'.[120] The young man's experience of love was shaped from the start as recollection, so that 'in the very first moment he became an old man in regard to the whole relationship.' Both recollection and hope are characterized in Constantius's opening remarks as life-strategies—albeit self-defeating ones—associated with youth: 'it takes youthfulness to hope, youthfulness to recollect, but it takes courage to will repetition'. One should not treat one's life-experience either as 'a tablet on which time writes something new every instant' or 'a memorial volume of the past', but as repetition, that is 'the actuality and earnestness of existence'. Anyone who fails to grasp 'the beauty of life' in this way 'deserves nothing better than what will happen to him anyway—he will perish'.[121] Repetition is thus associated with a mature outlook that positively accepts existential constraints rather than trying to disguise (and therefore impoverish) their nature. Notions of this sort are clearly capable of providing insight into the self-protective 'I' and feigned commitment to the other of which different facets are represented by El Joven and his youthful or aged companions in *Así que pasen cinco años*.

One feature of Kierkegaard's treatment of this theme that particularly repays attention is the way existential-ethical aspects of the broken engagement motif shade into vocational and aesthetic concerns. For the young man of *Repetition*, just as for the somewhat passionless seducer of *Either/Or*, failure of erotic relationship is closely associated with a heightened consciousness of poetic vocation. Similarly, the young man, Quidam, of *Guilty/Not Guilty* is presented by the work's narrator as a thinker and a poet and for that very reason unable to marry the girl he loves.[122] Kierkegaard himself observed, apropos of the importance

---

[120] *Fear and Trembling and Repetition*, p. 136.
[121] *Fear and Trembling and Repetition*, pp. 132-33.
[122] See Grimsley, *Kierkegaard*, p. 48.

of the Regine episode in the development of his powers of imagination that 'women or ideas are what beckon men out into existence', adding that in his case 'a girl was used as a middle term against me in a very unusual way'. Again, it is to the central, Regine-inspired topics of *Repetition* and *Fear and Trembling* that he was referring when he claimed in 1854: 'I am a poet, but long before I became a poet I was intended for the life of religious individuality. And the event whereby I became a poet was an ethical break or a teleological suspension of the ethical'.[123] It is worth noting that the more confidence the young man of *Repetition* develops in his powers as a poet the more inhibited he feels as a lover, just as Kierkegard was coming to regard himself as better suited to literary than flesh-and-blood procreation. In a letter of 1943, describing his completion of the work, Kierkegaard mentions that 'ideas are cascading upon me: healthy, happy, merry, gay, blessed children, born with ease.'[124] One of the stories inserted in *Guilty/Not Guilty*, moreover, concerns a book-keeper obsessed with the idea he has fathered a child. The analogy is, again, a suggestive one for Lorca's play, with its insistent motif of a lost or trapped child (although, as has already been suggested, it is invariably risky to postulate a direct link between personal experience and artistic representation or, for that matter, between a particular sexual orientation and the deployment of symbolic motifs in creative writing).

In the view of many commentators the period around 1930 (when *Así que pasen cinco años* was germinating) represented a point of self-definition—if not a crisis—in Lorca's development as a man and as an artist. Kierkegaard, in the early eighteen-forties, was of the same sort of age and had similarly come to a crossroads in terms of personal and artistic life-choices. Much of his writing in this period is taken up precisely with the topic of defining his practice and outlook as an imaginative writer (his preferred term is poet), and with transcending potential contradictions between the

---

[123] All cited in H.V. Hong's 'Historical Introduction', in Kierkegaard, *Fear and Trembling and Repetition*, pp. xvi-xvii.
[124] Hong, 'Historical Introduction', p. xiv.

personal-ethical and the aesthetic orientations of his life. Whether or not Lorca was familiar with any of these works, we would expect, in any case, to encounter in his writings during this period preoccupations of a broadly similar kind to those expressed by Kierkegaard some ninety years earlier. In particular, Lorca may have felt, like Kierkegaard, an impulse toward transcendence of some kind, a need to base his existence on principles capable of subsuming a fragmented sense of self in some more authentic identity (for Kierkegaard, the religious impulse, for Lorca perhaps some other existential category).

Discussion of such matters is inevitably speculative, but the focus of attention in *Así que pasen cinco años* on the whole enterprise of finding adequate expression for emotions and perceptions as something fraught with contradictions and problems is itself revealing. The concept of expression, or self-expression, can be an ambivalent one. On the one hand the notion can be viewed in terms of agency, of making oneself present in the world; on the other, there is often a perception of a gulf between the sphere of active achievement and that of verbal signification, a sense in which talk is a substitute for action and utterance the form of the never-to-be. There are detectable hints in *Así que pasen cinco años* of a deep, complex and problematical link between self-expression and self-fulfilment that was to develop a few years later, in *Yerma*, into a fully-fledged tragic theme.

3.4 BY WAY OF CONCLUSION

The consideration of analogies between Lorca and Kierkegaard in the treatment of matters of emotional and artistic commitment has taken us what might seem a questionably long way from the sort of close attention to surface textual features that is normally considered to be the particular strength of discourse stylistics where the study of literature is concerned. While it is true that discourse analysis is sensitive to the functions of language at a detailed level, and can provide useful insights into the way grammatical choices, for instance, can contribute to the creation of aesthetic effects, its input to the study of literature is by no means restricted to or inherently biased toward the formal domain. The ultimate objective is to account for the complexities of the way formal and contextual features interact in the reception and interpretation of literary texts. It is precisely through the central importance accorded to context that discourse approaches to literature are particularly open-ended in the range of issues that can be engaged with. Having said this, however, it should be admitted that considerations of space often rule out any comprehensive attempt to explore the situational, historical and socio-cultural contexts that are relevant for the meanings assigned to literary texts. In the case of Lorca's *Así que pasen cinco años*, for instance, we would need to take into account a growing consciousness of modernity in Spain at large, not simply in terms of the trends and fashions of European (and North American) cultural production, but also at the broader level of awareness of a gradual emergence of the economic, technical and social institutions and values associated with modernization. Certainly, where political institutions are concerned, it was becoming clear to many in Spain at the end of the nineteen-twenties and the start of the nineteen-thirties that the old system had finally exhausted its strategies for self-preservation and that radical change was imminent. The nature of the links in this epoch between constructions of the self and personal identity and emergent concepts of individual civic responsibility—including the social role of artists and the potential contribution of cultural activity to progressive social engineering—are certainly matters that an examination of contextual factors relevant to Lorca's play could profitably address. The practical requirements of such a project, however, in terms of charting the cross-currents and complexities of the contemporary 'climate of opinion' are daunting, to say the least, and certainly beyond the scope of the present work (which has aimed, in any case, to draw eclectically from a variety of areas within discourse studies, rather than concentrating on a particular line of approach).

There are clear practical advantages, then, in focusing, in the first instance, on conveniently specific issues and relatively small-scale passages of text. Indeed, a good proportion of the analysis in the present study has been directed to elucidating the functional principles underlying particular lexical and morpho-syntactical choices in individual poems or in passages of dialogue in theatrical texts. Consequently, matters of context on a broad socio-cultural scale have, for the most part, been outlined or briefly alluded to rather than examined in depth. The crucial importance of context has been reflected, however, at the intermediate level of speech situation, through a consistent attention to the status and relationship of participants and their assumptions as to the type of communicative activity that is taking place. What has consistently been kept in view is the way available contextual information is drawn on in interpretation in order to identify the force of speech acts or the nature of the inferences that should be drawn from foregrounding and other deviations from discursive norms. In particular, whether considering the situation of address embodied in a poem of Machado, or the communicative structure of theatre dialogue in general and Valle-Inclán's or Lorca's exploitation of it in particular, the present work has followed the trend of discourse studies in general in allotting a more active and central role in the communicative process to the audience or reader than is the case with more conventional approaches to literature. Analysis has proceeded on the basis that meanings are collaboratively created and negotiated rather than simply produced and received. The fact that discourse studies as a discipline is concerned with a very wide variety of texts acts as an effective antidote to the notion, encouraged by the specialized model of literary texts, of readers as passive consumers of predetermined pieces of communication, or of reading as a site of interaction controlled by the writer.[125] Indeed, from a pragmatics perspective, Jacob Mey argues that readers and audiences provide not just cooperation, but innovation, so that, to all effects, they are engaged in a process of co-production with the author.[126]

---

[125] See Michael Hoey, *Textual Interaction* (Routledge: London, 2001), pp. 13-14.
[126] See J. L. Mey, 'Literary Pragmatics', in D. Schiffrin, D. Tannen and H.E. Hamilton (eds), *The Handbook of Discourse Analysis* (Oxford: Blackwell, 2001), pp. 787-97. Mey quotes with approval (at p. 788) the observation of the novelist A.S Byatt to the effect that fiction 'is made in the head and has to be remade in the head by whoever reads it, who will always remake it differently'.

It is this dynamic and egalitarian view of the process of reading (as opposed to the traditional source-based concept) that underlies the basic approach to literary texts that has been adopted here. This is because, in the first place, the method of building on intuitions—such as the parallels proposed between Lorca and Kierkegaard—is inherently more suited to such a perspective. Regardless of Lorca's degree of familiarity with Kierkegaard's writings, that is, it seems reasonable to assume that many among present-day audiences might well treat what is probably the most widely-known episode of the Danish philosopher's life as relevant contextual information for interpreting the significance both of the title of Lorca's play and of the nuptial moratorium to which it refers. A more important underlying objective, however, has been to illustrate the advantages of an open-ended approach to the analysis of the effects achieved in literary texts, one that, rather than insisting on the validity of particular readings, proposes instead methods for gaining a firmer analytical purchase on the meanings intuitively assigned by the reader. This methodology is particularly important when the envisaged readership includes university students engaging with texts that have a canonical status in the culture of a second language. For such students, contact with works of literature is often regarded both a means of promoting certain intellectual disciplines and as a source of insight into the linguistic culture concerned. In such circumstances it seems preferable to avoid the inhibiting effect of powerfully-asserted exegesis and to stress instead that texts can have many of levels of meaning and are susceptible to multiple interpretations. This view, of course, is far from saying that texts can mean anything we like. What it highlights, rather, is the importance of readers being equipped to reflect, through sound analytical awareness of linguistic choices made by writers, on their own processes of interpretation.

Again, the distinctive aesthetic qualities of literary writing as a product of the capacity of creative verbal invention to establish important new relationships between people, their words and their world is something that benefits more from being concretely demonstrated than from being more or less impressionistically asserted. For this reason, discourse approaches, while well capable of producing the sort of insights that lead to new readings, can also make useful further contributions to established lines of interpretation. The texts studied in the present work were produced by arguably the three most highly-regarded writers of the last century in Spain. Although their output has been analyzed on a selective basis rather than systematically, it is hoped that their prestigious status has been practically justified through demonstrating the ability of each of them to combine a rare gift for exploiting the resources of the Spanish language with exceptional skill and imagination in the deployment of communicative strategies—in short, their powers of utterance.

BIBLIOGRAPHY

Aguilera Sastre, Juan, 'La versión escénica de *Divinas palabras* en el estreno de 1933', in Manuel Aznar and Juan Rodríguez (eds), *Valle-Inclán y su obra* (Barcelona: Associació d'Idees, 1995), pp. 553-62.

Alberti, Rafael, *Fermín Galán*, in R. Alberti, *El poeta en la calle* (Madrid: Aguilar, 1978), pp. 631-746.

Alberti, Rafael, *Poesías completas* (Buenos Aires: Losada, 1961).

Allen, Rupert, *Psyche and Symbol in the Theatre of Federico García Lorca* (Austin: University of Texas Press, 1974).

Anderson, Andrew A., 'The Strategy of García Lorca's Dramatic Composition 1930-1936', *Romance Quarterly,* XXXIII (1986), 211-229.

Anderson, Andrew A., 'Bewitched, Bothered and Bewildered: Spanish dramatists and surrealism, 1924-1936', in C. Brian Morris (ed.), *The Surrealist Adventure in Spain* (Ottowa: Dovehouse, 1991), pp. 240-81.

Anderson, Andrew A., '*El público, Así que pasen cinco años y El sueño de la vida:* tres dramas expresionistas de Lorca', in Dougherty and Vilches, *El teatro en España*, pp. 215-26.

Anderson, Farris, 'The Theatrical Design of Lorca's *Así que pasen cinco años*', *Journal of Spanish Studies*: *Twentieth Century*, VII (1979), 249-78.

Austin, J. L., *How To Do Things With Words*, 2nd ed., edited by J.O. Urmson and M. Sbisà (Oxford: Clarendon Press, 1975).

Azar, Inés, 'Self, Responsibility, Discourse: an introduction to speech act theory', in Elias Rivers (ed.), *Things Done With Words: speech acts in Hispanic drama* (Newark: Delaware: Juan de la Cuesta, 1984), pp. 1-13.

Azevedo, Andrés de, *El lugar de la metáfora* (Montevideo: Universidad de Montevideo, 1998).

Aznar, Manuel, 1995: 'Esperpento e historia en *¿Para cuándo son las reclamaciones diplomáticas?*', in Manuel Aznar and Juan Rodríguez (eds), *Valle-Inclán y su obra* (Barcelona: Associació d'Idees, 1995), pp. 565-78.

Bakhtin, M., *The Dialogic Imagination*, edited by Michael Holquist, translated by Caryl Emerson and Michael Holquist (Austin: University of Texas Press, 1981).

Bakhtin, M., *Speech Genres and Other Late Essays*, edited by Michael Holquist and Caryl Emerson, translated by Vern McGee (Austin: University of Texas Press, 1986).

Bell, Allan, *The Language of News Media* (Oxford: Blackwell, 1991).

Blakemore, Diane, *Understanding Utterances* (Oxford: Blackwell, 1992).

Brooks, Peter, *The Melodramatic Imagination* (New Haven: Yale University Press, 1976).

Brown, Gillian and George Yule, *Discourse Analysis* (Cambridge: Cambridge University Press, 1983).

Brown, Gillian, *Speakers, Listeners and Communication* (Cambridge: Cambridge University Press, 1997).

Buero Vallejo, Antonio, *Tres maestros ante el público* (Madrid: Alianza, 1973).

Carter, Ronald and Paul Simpson, *Language, Discourse and Literature: an introductory reader in discourse stylistics* (London: Routledge, 1995).

Cornish, Francis, *Anaphora, Discourse and Understanding* (Oxford: Clarendon, 1992).

Coulthard, Malcolm, 'Forensic Discourse Analysis', in M. Coulthard (ed.), *Advances in Spoken Discourse Analysis* (London: Routledge, 1992), pp. 242-58.

Crystal, David, *An Encyclopedic Dictionary of Language and Languages* (Harmondsworth: Penguin, 1994).

Culpepper, Jonathan, Mick Short and Peter Verdonk (eds), *Exploring the Language of Drama* (London: Routledge, 1998).

Davies, Eirian C., 'Questions: a significance generating device for building in context', in E. Steiner and R. Veltman (eds), *Pragmatics, Discourse and Text: some systemically-inspired approaches* (London: Pinter, 1988), pp. 29-45.

Davis, Steven (ed.), *Pragmatics: a reader* (Oxford: Oxford University Press, 1991).

Del Caño, Amelia, 'Los géneros orales informativos', in Santiago Alcoba (ed.), *La oralización* (Barcelona: Ariel, 1999), pp. 109-68.

Dijk, Teun van (ed.), *Discourse Studies: a multidisciplinary introduction. Vol. I, Discourse as Structure and Process* (London: Sage, 1997).

Dougherty, Dru, *Un Valle-Inclán olvidado: entrevistas y conferencias* (Madrid: Fundamentos, 1983).

Dougherty, Dru and M. Francisca Vilches (eds), *El teatro en España entre tradición y vanguardia* (Madrid: C.S I.C., 1992).

Drew, Paul and Andrew Wootton (eds), *Erving Goffman: exploring the interaction order* (Cambridge: Polity, 1988).

Evreinov, Nikolai, *The Theatre in Life* (London: Harrap, 1927).

Evreinov, Nikolai, *Life as Theatre: five modern plays*, translated and edited by Christopher Collins (Ann Arbor: Ardis, 1973).

Fabb, Nigel, *Linguistics and Literature: language in the verbal arts of the world* (Oxford: Blackwell, 1997).

Fairclough, Norman, *Critical Discourse Analysis. The Critical Study of Language* (London: Longman, 1995).

Ferrara, A, 'Condiciones de adecuación para secuencias enteras de actos de habla', in Julio and Muñoz (eds), *Textos clásicos de pragmática*, pp. 41-65.

Foley, William, *Anthropological Linguistics: an introduction* (Oxford: Blackwell, 1997).

Fowler, Roger, *Linguistic Criticism* (Oxford: Oxford University Press, 1986).

Fowler, Roger, *Language in the News* (London: Routledge, 1991).

Freud, Sigmund, *Civilization, Society and Religion*, Pelican Freud Library, XII (Harmondsworth: Penguin, 1987).

Fromm, Erich, *Beyond the Chains of Illusion* (London: Abacus, 1980).

García Lorca, Federico, *Bodas de sangre*; *Yerma* (Madrid: Espasa-Calpe, 1971).

García Lorca, Federico, *La casa de Bernarda Alba*, edited by Herbert Ramsden (Manchester: University of Manchester Press, 1983).

García Lorca, Federico, *Primer romancero gitano; Llanto por Ignacio Sánchez Mejías*, edited by Miguel García-Posada (Madrid: Clásicos Castalia, 1988).

García Lorca, Federico, *La casa de Bernarda Alba*, edited by Allen Josephs and Juan Caballero (Madrid: Cátedra, 1989).

García Lorca, Federico, *Obras completas*, ed. Arturo del Hoyo (Madrid: Aguilar, 1989).

García Lorca, Federico, *Poet in New York*, edited by Christopher Maurer, translated by Greg Simon and Steven White (Harmondsworth: Penguin, 1990).

García Lorca, Federico, *El público,* edited by María Clementa Millán (Madrid: Cátedra, 1991).

García Lorca, Federico, *Romancero gitano*, edited by Derek Harris (London: Grant & Cutler, 1991).

García Lorca, Federico, *Yerma,* edited by Robin Warner (Manchester: Manchester University Press, 1994).

García Lorca, Federico, *Así que pasen cinco años,* edited by Margarita Ucelay (Madrid: Cátedra, 1995).

García Lorca, Federico, *Four major plays*, translated by John Edmunds, introduction by Nicholas Round (Oxford: Oxford University Press, 1997).

Georgakopolou, Alexandra and Goutsos Dionysis, *Discourse Analysis: an introduction* (Edinburgh: Edinburgh University Press, 1997).

Gibson, Ian, *Federico García Lorca*, 2 vols (Barcelona: Grijalbo, 1987).

Giglioli, P.P. (ed.), *Language and Social Context* (Harmondsworth: Penguin, 1982).

Givón, Talmy, *Syntax: a functional typological introduction* (Amsterdam: Benjamin, 1990).

Givón, Talmy, *Functionalism and Grammar* (Amsterdam: Benjamin, 1995).

Green, Georgia, *Pragmatics and Natural Language Understanding* (Hillsdale, N.J.: Lawrence Erlbaum, 1989).

Grice, J.P., *Studies in the Way of Words* (Cambridge, Mass.: Harvard University Press, 1991).

Grimsley, Ronald, *Kierkegaard: a biographical introduction* (London: Studio Vista, 1973).

Grundy, Peter, *Doing Pragmatics* (London: Arnold, 1995).

Guillén, Claudio, *Literature as System: essays toward the theory of literary history* (Princeton: Princeton University Press, 1971).

Guillén, Claudio, 'Proceso y orden inminente en *Campos de Castilla*', in J. Ángeles (ed.), *Estudios sobre Antonio Machado* (Barcelona: Ariel, 1976), pp. 195-216.

Gumperz, John, 'Contextualization and Understanding', in A. Duranti and C. Goodwin (eds), *Rethinking Context* (Oxford: Oxford University Press, 1993), pp. 229-51.

Habermas, Jürgen, *The Theory of Communicative Action*, I, translated by Thomas McCarthy (London: Heinemann, 1984).

Habermas, Jürgen, *The Theory of Communicative Action*, II, translated by Thomas McCarthy (Cambridge: Polity Press, 1989).

Habermas, Jürgen, *Moral Consciousness and Communicative Action* (Cambridge: Polity Press, 1990).

Habermas, Jürgen, *Between Facts and Norms*, translated by W. Rehg (Cambridge: Polity Press, 1996).

Habermas, Jürgen, *On the Pragmatics of Communication*, edited by Maeve Cook (Cambridge, Mass.: MIT Press, 1998).

Halliday, Michael A.K., *An Introduction to Functional Grammar*, second edition (London: Arnold, 1994).

Harris, Roy, *The Language Connection* (Bristol: Thoemmes, 1996).

Heaney, Seamus, *Opened Ground, Poems 1966-1996* (London: Faber and Faber, 1998).

Hess-Lüttich, E. 'How Does the Writer of a Dramatic Text Interact With His Audience?', in R. Sell (ed.), *Literary Pragmatics* (London: Routledge, 1991), pp. 225-51.

Hickey, Leo, *Curso de pragmaestilística* (Madrid: Coloquio, 1987).

Hodge, Robert and Gunther Kress, *Social Semiotics* (Cambridge: Polity Press, 1988).

Hoey, Michael, *Textual Interaction* (Routledge: London, 2001).
Hong, Howard V., 'Historical Introduction', in S. Kierkegaard, *Fear and Trembling and Repetition*, pp. iv-xxiv.
Huélamo, Julio, 'La influencia de Freud en el teatro de García Lorca', *Boletín de la Fundación Federico•García Lorca*, VI (diciembre de 1989), 59-83.
Innes, Christopher, *Avant Garde Theatre* (London: Routledge, 1993).
Jefferson, Ann and David Robey, *Modern Literary Theory*, second edition (London: Batsford, 1986).
Jolivet, Regis, *An Introduction to Kierkegaard* (London: Muller, 1950).
Joyce, James, *Dubliners* (London: Cape, 1967).
Julio, María-Teresa and Ricardo Muñoz (eds), *Textos clásicos de pragmática* (Madrid: Arco, 1998).
Kierkegaard, Søren, *Either/Or. A Fragment of Life*, translated by D. Swenson and L.M. Swenson (Princeton: Princeton University Press, 1949).
Kierkegaard, Søren, *Fear and Trembling and Repetition*, edited and translated by Howard V. Hong and Edna H. Hong (Princeton: Princeton University Press, 1983).
Klein-Andreu, Flora, 'Grammar in Style: Spanish adjective placement', in F. Klein-Andreu (ed.), *Perspectives in Syntax* (New York: Academic Press, 1983), pp. 143-79.
Knight, R.G., 'Federico García Lorca's *Así que pasen cinco años*', *Bulletin of Hispanic Studies*, XLIII (1966), 32-46.
Labov, William. 'Rules for Ritual Insults', in D. Sudnow (ed.), *Studies in Social Interaction* (New York: Free Press, 1972), pp. 120-69.
Labov, William, 'The Study of Language in its Social Context', in P.P. Giglioli (ed.), *Language and Social Context* (Harmondsworth: Penguin, 1982), pp. 283-307.
Lakoff, George and Mark Johnson, *Metaphors We Live By* (Chicago: University of Chicago Press, 1980).
Lakoff, George and Mark Turner, *More Than Cool Reason: a field guide to poetic metaphor* (Chicago: University of Chicago Press, 1989).

Leith, Dick and George Myerson, *The Power of Address: explorations in rhetoric* (London: Routledge, 1989).

Levinson, Stephen, *Pragmatics* (Cambridge: Cambridge University Press, 1983).

Levinson, Stephen, 'Putting Linguistics on a Proper Footing', in Drew and Wootton (eds), *Erving Goffman: exploring the interaction order*, pp. 161-227.

Levinson, Stephen, *Presumptive meanings: the theory of generalized conversational implicature* (Cambridge, Mass: MIT Press, 2000).

Lodge, David, *Therapy* (Harmondsworth: Penguin, 1996).

Loureiro, Ángel (ed.), *Estelas, laberintos, nuevas sendas: Unamuno, Valle-Inclán, García Lorca* (Barcelona: Anthropos, 1991).

Lowrie, Walter, *A Short Life of Kierkegaard* (Princeton: Princeton University Press, 1942).

Lyon, John, *The Theatre of Valle-Inclán* (Cambridge: Cambridge University Press, 1983).

Lyons, John, *Language and Linguistics* (Cambridge: Cambridge University Press, 1981).

McCarthy, Michael and Ronald Carter, *Language as Discourse: perspectives for language teaching* (Harlow: Longman, 1994).

Machado, Antonio, *Campos de Castilla*, edited by Geoffrey Ribbans (Madrid: Cátedra, 1989).

Machado, Antonio, *Obras: poesía y prosa*, edited by Aurora de Albornoz and Guillermo de Torre (Buenos Aires: Losada, 1973).

Mainer, J. C., *La edad de plata* (Madrid: Cátedra, 1981).

Martínez de Velasco, Luis, 'De la lírica temporal a la acción comunicativa', in J.L. de la Iglesia *et al.* (eds), *Antonio Machado y la filosofía* (Madrid: Orígenes, 1989), pp. 97-125.

Mason, Ian, 'Discourse Connectives, Ellipsis and Markedness', in Leo Hickey (ed.), *The Pragmatics of Translation* (Clevedon: Multilingual Matters, 1998), pp. 170-84.

Mey, Jacob L., *Pragmatics: an introduction* (Oxford: Blackwell, 1993).

Mey, Jacob L., 'Literary Pragmatics', in D. Schiffrin, D. Tannen and H.E. Hamilton (eds), *The Handbook of Discourse Analysis* (Oxford: Blackwell, 2001), pp. 787-97.

Montolío Durán, Estrella, *Gramática de la caracterización en Valle-Inclán* (Barcelona: PPU, 1992).

Nash, Walter, *Language in Popular Fiction* (London: Routledge, 1990).

Neruda, Pablo, 'Explico algunas cosas', in Pablo Neruda, *Obras completas* (Buenos Aires: Losada, 1967), pp. 275-77.

Nunan, David, *Introducing Discourse Analysis* (Harmondsworth: Penguin, 1993).

O'Connor, Frank, *The Mirror and the Roadway: a study of the modern novel* (London: Hamish Hamilton, 1957).

Ozimek-Maier, Janis 'Power Plays in La casa de Bernarda Alba', in Elias Rivers (ed.), *Things Done With Words: speech acts in Hispanic drama*, pp. 73-84.

Page, Norman, *Speech in the English Novel*, second edition (London: Macmillan, 1988).

Patterson, Michael, *The Revolution in German Theatre* (London: Routledge, 1981).

Petrey, Sandy, *Speech Acts and Literary Theory* (London: Routledge, 1990).

Portillo, Rafael and Jesús Casado, *Abecedario del teatro* (Madrid: Centro de Documentación Teatral, 1988).

Potter, Jonathan and Margaret Wetherell, *Discourse and Social Psychology* (London: Sage, 1987).

Reyes, Graciela, *La pragmática linguística* (Barcelona: Montesinos, 1990).

Ribbans, Geoffrey, 'Antonio Machado, ¿poeta provinciano o poeta universal?', in A. Vilanova y Adolfo Sotelo Vasco (eds), *La crisis española de fin de siglo y la generación del '98* (Barcelona: Universidad de Barcelona, 1998), pp. 241-53.

Ricoeur, Paul, *Freud and Philosophy* (New Haven: Yale University Press, 1970).

Rivers, Elias (ed.), *Things Done With Words: speech acts in Hispanic drama* (Newark: Delaware: Juan de la Cuesta, 1984).

Roazen, Paul, *Freud: Political and Social Thought* (New York: Vintage, 1970).

Roberts, Gemma, *Unamuno: afinidades y coincidencias kierkegaardianas* (Boulder, Colorado: Society of Spanish and Spanish-American Studies, 1986).

Round, Nicholas G., 'The Three Caballeros: Don Guido and his relations', in D. Gareth Walters (ed.), *Estelas en la mar: essays on the poetry of Antonio Machado* (Glasgow: University of Glasgow, 1992), pp. 83-99.

Schiffrin, Deborah, *Approaches to Discourse* (Oxford: Blackwell, 1994).

Searle, John, *Expression and Meaning: studies in the theory of speech acts* (Cambridge: Cambridge University Press, 1979).

Sell, Roger D. (ed.), *Literary Pragmatics* (London: Routledge, 1991).

Short, Mick, *Exploring the Language of Poems, Plays and Prose* (London: Longman, 1996).

Short, Mick, 'Discourse Analysis and the Analysis of Drama', in Carter and Simpson, *Language, Discourse and Literature*, pp. 139-70.

Simpson, Paul, *Language, Ideology and Point of View* (London: Routledge, 1993).

Smith, Paul Julian, *The Body Politic: gender and sexuality in Spanish and Spanish-American literature* (Oxford: Clarendon, 1989).

Smith, Paul Julian, *The Theatre of García Lorca: text, performance, psychoanalysis* (Cambridge: Cambridge University Press, 1998).

Sperber, Dan and Deirdre Wilson, 'Irony and the Use-Mention Distinction', in Davis, *Pragmatics*, pp. 550-63.

Sperber, Dan and Deirdre Wilson, *Relevance: communication and cognition*, second edition (Oxford: Blackwell, 1995).

Strachey, James, 'Sketch of Freud's Life and Ideas', in Freud, *Civilization, Society and Religion*, pp. 11-23.

Tannen, Deborah, (ed.), *Coherence in Spoken and Written Discourse* (Norwood, N.J.: Ablex, 1984).

Tannen, Deborah, *Talking Voices: repetition, dialogue and imagery in conversational discourse* (Cambridge: Cambridge University Press, 1989).

Terry, Arthur, *Antonio Machado: Campos de Castilla* (London: Tamesis, 1973).

Torres Sánchez, M.A., *Aproximación pragmática a la ironía verbal* (Cádiz: Universidad de Cádiz, 1999).

Torres Sánchez, M.A., *Estudio pragmático del humor verbal* (Cádiz: Universidad de Cádiz, 1999).

Tsui, Amy, 'Sequencing Rules and Coherence in Discourse', *Journal of Pragmatics*, XV (1991), 11-29.

Tsui, Amy, 'A Functional Description of Questions', in M. Coulthard (ed.), *Advances in Spoken Discourse Analysis* (London: Routledge, 1992), pp. 89-110.

Unamuno, Miguel de, *San Manuel Bueno, mártir* (Madrid: Espasa-Calpe, 1933).

Ungerer, F. and H.J. Schmid, *An Introduction to Cognitive Linguistics* (London: Longman, 1996).

Valle-Inclán, Ramón del, *Obras completas* (Madrid: Plenitud, 1954).

Valle-Inclán, Ramón del, *¿Para cuándo son las reclamaciones diplomáticas?*, in R. del Valle-Inclán, *Martes de Carnaval*, 4th edition (Madrid: Espasa-Calpe, 1977), pp. 233-43.

Valle-Inclán, Ramón del, *Martes de carnaval*, edited by Ricardo Senabre (Madrid: Espasa-Calpe, 1990).

Valle-Inclán, Ramón del, *Divinas palabras*, edited by Luis Iglesias Feijoo (Madrid: Espasa-Calpe, 1991).

Valle-Inclán, Ramón del, *Cara de Plata,* edited by Antonio Risco (Madrid: Espasa-Calpe, 1992).

Valle-Inclán, Ramón del, *Luces de Bohemia*, edited by A. Zamora Vicente (Madrid: Espasa-Calpe, 1993).

Volosinov, V.N., *Marxism and the Philosophy of Language* (New York: Seminar Press, 1973).

Warner, Robin, 'Critical Reports: ideology and expression in Machado's *Campos de Castilla*', *Neophilologus*, LXXIII (1989), 230-42.

Warner, Robin, 'Questioning the Rules: concepts of deviance and conformism in *Campos de Castilla*', in D. Gareth Walters (ed.), *Estelas en la mar: essays on the poetry of Antonio Machado* (Glasgow: University of Glasgow, 1992), pp. 52-63.

Warner, Robin, 'Making Things Clear: contextualization cues and coherence in parallel versions of a popular song', *Bulletin of Hispanic Studies* [Glasgow], LXXV (1998), 109-22.

Warner, Robin, 'Words of Power: dialogue and dominance in Valle-Inclán's *Divinas palabras*', *Modern Language Review*, LXXXVIII (1993), 343-53.

Warner, Robin, 'Co-operative Contests: dialogue modes in the late novels and plays of Ramón del Valle-Inclán', in D. Cruikshank (ed.), *A Lifetime's Reading* (Dublin: University College Dublin Press, 1999), pp. 203-13.

Williams, William Carlos, 'The Jasmine Lightness of the Moon', in Lakoff and Turner, *More Than Cool Reason*, pp. 140-41.

Wright, Elizabeth, *Psychoanalytic Criticism* (London: Routledge, 1984).

York, R.A., *The Poem as Utterance* (London: Methuen, 1986).